NO SAFE HAVEN

MALE VIOLENCE AGAINST WOMEN AT HOME, AT WORK, AND IN THE COMMUNITY

NO SAFE HAVEN

MALE VIOLENCE AGAINST WOMEN AT HOME, AT WORK, AND IN THE COMMUNITY

MARY P. KOSS
LISA A. GOODMAN
ANGELA BROWNE
LOUISE F. FITZGERALD
GWENDOLYN PURYEAR KEITA
NANCY FELIPE RUSSO

American Psychological Association
Washington, DC

Published by the
American Psychological Association
750 First Street, NE
Washington, DC 20002

Copies may be ordered from
APA Order Department
P.O. Box 2710
Hyattsville, MD 20784

Typeset in Minion by Techna Type, Inc., York, PA

Printer: Braun-Brumfield, Inc., Ann Arbor, MI
Cover Designer: Michael David Brown, Inc., Rockville, MD
Technical/Production Editor: Miria Liliana Riahi

Library of Congress Cataloging-in-Publication Data

No safe haven : male violence against women at home, at work, and in the community / by
    Mary Koss . . . [et al.].
        p.   cm.
    Includes bibliographical references and index.
    ISBN 1-55798-237-6 (hardbound).—ISBN 1-55798-244-9 (pbk.)
    1. Women—Crimes against—United States.   2. Abused women—United States.
3. Abusive men—United States.   4. Conjugal violence—United States.   5. Sexual
harassment of women—United States.   6. Rape—United States.   I. Koss, Mary P.
HV6626.2.N62   1994
364.1'5553'0973—dc20   94-15637
                                                                                CIP

British Library Cataloguing-in-Publication Data
A CIP record is available from the British Library

Printed in the United States of America
First edition

Contents

CONTENTS

Authors

Angela Brown, The Better Home Foundation, Newton Centre, MA
Louise F. Fitzgerald, University of Illinois, Urbana–Champaign
Lisa A. Goodman, University of Maryland, College Park
Gwendolyn Puryear Keita, American Psychological Association,
Washington, DC
Mary P. Koss, University of Arizona
Nancy Felipe Russo, Arizona State University

Preface

Male-perpetrated violence is a major cause of fear, distress, injury, and even death for women in this country. Such violence crosses the lines of ethnicity, economic status, sexual orientation, and age (Coley & Beckett, 1988; Goodman, Koss, & Russo, 1993a; Koss, 1988b; Straus, Gelles, & Steinmetz, 1980).

During the past two decades, scholarly, public, and policy attention to this social problem has increased dramatically, and a number of important national policy reports have identified violence against women as a critical economic (Bureau of Justice Statistics, 1992; Coles, 1986), criminal justice (see, e.g., Family Violence Project, 1990), and public health issue (see, e.g., Eichler & Parron, 1987; Goodman, Koss, Fitzgerald, Keita, & Russo, 1993; President's Task Force on Victims of Crime, 1982; Public Health Service, 1985). Despite this increased recognition, the health community's response has been limited. Only in the last few years have health-care providers begun to address the problem of violence against women in a systematic fashion, for example, by establishing guidelines for health-care providers and making recommendations to researchers and public-policy makers (see, e.g., Council on Scientific Affairs, 1992; Koss, 1990a; National Women's Health Resource Center, 1991).

In the fall of 1991, the American Psychological Association's (APA) Committee on Women in Psychology joined these efforts by establishing APA's first Task Force on Male Violence Against Women. The Committee directed the Task Force to review current psychological research on the prevalence, causes, and effects of different forms of violence against women and to describe existing and recommended interventions, legal changes, and policy initiatives to address the problem. This report represents the final product of the Task Force's efforts.

Acknowledgments

To keep the material current, this report was written on a tight deadline. As a result, there were multiple occasions when we had to ask for assistance with less than a comfortable amount of time to get the task accomplished. Yet, time after time individuals came through and made time. Clearly, the production of this report was possible only because so many who work on the topic of male violence against women have a dedication to their work that supercedes personal motives and convenience. In spite of the tight schedule, the material was subjected to review at several points during the preparation of this book. The reviewers were members of the Advisory Board, and we express our deepest appreciation for their timely, thoughtful, and constructive input to the final product.

We would like to thank the many individuals whose contributions helped make this report possible. First and foremost, we want to thank the staff of the APA Women's Programs Office for their support, particularly Wanda Robinson for her assistance in the compilation of the report, and to Lynn Letourneau for her devotion to accuracy in resolving the editorial queries. We also want to thank Dr. Janet O'Keefee of the APA Public Policy Office for her assistance in formulating policy options and Dr. Laura Brown for pitching in to write a few sections at the last minute.

Some sections of the material drew on previously published work. Portions of the material on sexual harassment first appeared as part of a science seminar presented by Louise F. Fitzgerald under the sponsorship of the Federation of Behavioral, Psychological, and Cognitive Sciences of the Library of Congress; and in the *American Psychologist*. The material on rape is based in part on papers that appeared previously in *Applied and Preventive Psychology*, *Archives of Family Medicine*, *Journal of Interpersonal Violence*, *Journal of Women's Health*, and *Violence Update*.

We are indebted to Arizona State University students Amy Dabul, Rebecca Huey, and Lucy Pope for their suggestions and assistance, and to Jody Horn, who provided assistance on the partner violence section; University of Arizona Research Technician Melinda Tharan and Rose Gurdy for their research and technical support; and Howard University students and Women's Programs Office Interns, Jennifer Tucker and Tanya Burrwell for their assistance.

Finally, we would like to acknowledge the organizations who provided support to the task force members during preparation of the report. Lisa A. Goodman's work was supported through the James Marshall Public Policy Research Fellowship given by the Society for the Psychological Study of Social Issues. Mary Koss gratefully acknowledges the support received from a Research Scientist Development Award from the Antisocial and Traumatic Stress Studies Branch of the National Institute of Mental Health and a supplement under the Women's Health Program provided by the Office of Research on Women's Health of the National Institutes of Health.

In addition to the people named here, there were others behind the scenes who carried out their specific task to contribute to the achievement of the final report. We are very grateful to each and every person for the opportunity to work collaboratively and to produce a book that may play a part in stopping violence.

Introduction

Violence against women takes many forms, ranging from forced prostitution to involuntary pregnancy, infanticide, and genital mutilation (see, e.g., Bunch, 1991). In developing a manageable and conceptually meaningful scope for this book, we chose to focus on *male-perpetrated* violence against women, despite the burgeoning literature on lesbian violence (see, e.g., Kanuha, 1990; Levy, 1991; Renzetti, 1992), for two reasons: (a) such a focus permits the broad examination of the confluence of individual, social, cultural, and institutional factors that shape relationships between men and women and contribute to the problem of violence; and (b) the substantial multidisciplinary literature on male-perpetrated violence, accumulated over the last two decades, places the psychological research in context and can be brought to bear on the development of solutions. Within the broad arena of male violence against women, we have chosen to focus on three common types of abuse, each of which affects the lives of millions of women in this country: (a) physical assault against women by male partners, (b) sexual harassment in work and educational settings, and (c) rape and other forms of sexual violence. Given our mandate to focus on adult women, we have not reviewed literature on violence against girls as children or adolescents (for a thorough review of this topic, see APA's recently published report on violence and youth) nor have we discussed the psychological effect on adult women of sexual abuse in childhood. Although we have highlighted what little literature we could find on male violence against ethnic minority and low-income women, we have not focused separately on other groups—such as elderly and disabled women—who may, nevertheless, experience especially high levels of male violence.

DEFINING OUR TERMS

One of the many important feminist contributions to understanding male violence against women has been the development of a vocabulary to describe and analyze women's experience of violence. Feminists have sought to "name" violent acts in ways that give voice to women's subjective experiences rather than using labels that obscure or even distort women's experiences (McHugh, Frieze, & Browne, 1993). Terms such as battered women, marital rape, and date rape, which have been created over the last two decades, have helped to reframe discussions of the nature of violence against women and have empowered women to talk about their own experiences with greater clarity and legitimacy (McHugh et al., 1993).

However, the study of violence continues to be plagued by terminological and, consequently, conceptual difficulties that influence our understanding of women's experiences as well as our research approaches.

Labels and definitions imposed on acts or sets of acts can affect research results ranging from reported incidence rates, to models of causal dynamics, to assessment of effects. For example, Straus et al. (1980) concluded that husbands and wives are "equally" violent in partner relationships. However, by using terms such as *domestic violence* and *spousal violence*, these researchers failed to distinguish acts attempted in self-defense from acts aimed at domination and control. Furthermore, they asked respondents questions about physical aggression initiated to settle disputes, but did not inquire about attacks "out of the blue," and they failed to distinguish between slapping a face and breaking a rib.

Even researchers who wish to name and define violence in a way that conveys that women are the targets and men are the perpetrators have difficulty formulating terms. The term *wife abuse*, for example, leads to a research focus on marital violence and ignores dating violence, despite the obvious conceptual link between the two. Also, use of the phrase *violence against women* rather than *male violence against women* to describe male-to-female violence implicitly renders invisible intimate violence in lesbian couples.

The way in which we have used various terms in this book to organize information on violence against women further distorts the nature of women's subjective experiences. For example, because this report is a review of the literature, we have followed the research convention of separately labeling, defining, and describing discrete forms of violence. Analyzing the nature and effect of diverse forms of violence separately from one another, however, obscures women's subjective experiences. Survey data clearly reveal that separating acts such as rape, battering, and harassment into discrete analytic categories imposes distinctions that are more convenient than real. Many women who are raped are also viciously physically assaulted (Caputi, 1989; Zillman, 1984); battered women are frequently sexually assaulted and raped by their male partners (Browne, 1987; Frieze, 1983; Shields & Hanneke, 1983); and victims of sexual harassment are not only insulted, propositioned, and coerced (Fitzgerald, 1993c) but also physically threatened, brutally assaulted, and raped (MacKinnon, 1979; Meritor v. Vinson, 1961). In reality, then, various forms of violence frequently cooccur, succeed one another, and blend together to form a pervasive culture of violence within which women must conduct their daily lives.

There seems to be no "best" language for all circumstances. Therefore, at the very least, we as psychologists must be self-conscious at every stage of our work, particularly as we frame our questions and define our terms, and we must recognize and respect diverse perspectives on violence. We must carefully choose and define both the labels we use and the rationales we develop to explain various concepts; we must be aware of unintended connotations and recognize how our names and definitions exclude as well as include.

Although there are many ways to conceptualize and define violence, our Task Force sought a definition that would illuminate the diverse forms of violence against women while simultaneously recognizing the commonalities among these forms and emphasizing the importance of women's subjective experiences. Furthermore, we sought to bring the traditional physical dimension of violence *and* the psychological dimension of violence together under one definitional umbrella. Thus, our working definition of male violence toward women encompasses *physical, visual, verbal, or sexual acts that are experienced by a woman or girl as a threat, invasion, or assault and that have the effect of hurting her or degrading her and/or taking away her ability to control contact (intimate and otherwise) with another individual* (adapted from Kelly, 1988, p. 41).

Finally, the Task Force struggled with the question of how to label women who have experienced male-perpetrated violence. Although the term *victim of violence* implies that an individual has been wrongfully harmed by another (appropriately placing responsibility for violence on the perpetrator), it also implies that the individual is passively, centrally, and forever damaged by violence. The term *survivor of violence* is a preferred alternative; but this term implies that the violence itself, as well as its consequences, are over—past history. It, therefore, fails to reflect either the chronicity of violence or its potential to inflict permanent physical injury and irreparable psychological harm. Furthermore, the term does not entirely preserve a sense of purposeful interpersonal harm; one "survives" a drought. For some, *survival* denotes biological more than psychological endurance and, therefore, does not do justice to the significance of psychological recovery. Given the complexities of this issue, we have chosen to use the two terms, victim and survivor, interchangeably to highlight the dual nature of the experience.

AN OVERVIEW OF WHAT IS TO COME

The first section of this book discusses the causes and correlates of male violence against women. Literature on causes at the familial, institutional, and sociocultural levels is reviewed in chapter 1. This analysis continues in chapter 2, but at the level of the individual. The next three sections of the book, which encompasses chapters 3 through 11, focus on partner-perpetrated violence, sexual harassment, and rape, respectively. In these sections, we review the literature on the prevalence of each form of violence as well as its physical and psychological effects. We also review the literature on prevention and treatment.

A set of common themes emerges from these chapters: Most salient of all is the important role that gender plays in directing acts of violence. The vast majority of acts of violence against women are perpetrated by men who have some sort of relationship with their victims, be it an initimate relationship, a working relationship, or an acquaintance relationship. In addition, the prevalence of each of these forms of violence is extraordinarily high; far from being unusual events, acts of violence against women are commonplace.

The victim-focused or even victim-blaming emphases that run through the theory, research, and system repsonses are also common. Theories that attempt to explain why a particular woman is battered, harassed, or raped frequently point to "women's masochism" (she liked it) or behavior (she asked for it), despite contradictory research that documents women's attempts to prevent and avoid such actions.

Additionally, the responses of others, including family members, friends, co-workers, and the criminal justice system have often compounded, rather than ameliorated, the damaging consequences of male violence, be it rape, battery, or sexual harassment. And finally, gender-related norms, roles, and cultural myths have been shown to sanction battery, sexual assault, and sexual harassment of women by failing to hold men accountable for their actions, trivializing the consequences of the violence, and closing off strategies that women might use to protect themselves.

These themes, particularly the high prevalence of violence against women and the critical role that gender plays in directing such violence, suggest that acts of violence against women cannot be understood solely through common psychological approaches that emphasize individual psychopathology or troubled communication patterns (Goodman, Koss, et al., 1993). Thus, chapter 12, the final chapter, offers a broad multidimensional set of recommendations for psychologists—in their roles as researchers, educators, clinicians, and advocates—as well as for policy makers.

We hope that this book will inspire psychologists and other health professionals to use their knowledge and skills to address the crisis of violence against women. We also hope that the information presented here provides new insight into a problem that cannot be fully understood, let alone solved, by focusing exclusively on individual psychology. Only by simultaneously changing the social and cultural institutions that have given rise to the problem can a lasting solution be achieved.

PART 1

An Overview of the Problem

1

The Culture and Context of Male Violence Against Women

Why are men violent toward women? There is no simple answer to that question. What is known is that violence against women is so pervasive and tenacious that it cannot be explained as solely the product of individual psychopathology or faulty communication. We also know that violence against women takes many forms, including, but certainly not limited to, battering, sexual harassment, and rape. We also know that this violence has devastating consequences for the woman, the family, and society.

When discussing violence against women, it is important to understand that, even though each act of violence is perpetrated by an individual, violent behavior takes place in a sociocultural context. It is increasingly recognized that multiple levels of coinfluences—from societal to individual—determine the expression of violence. Therefore, before one can begin to understand and address the phenomenon of violence against women—in all its various forms—one must understand the context in which that phenomenon is allowed to occur. This chapter examines sociocultural determinants of male violence and the role such determinants play in initiating and perpetuating violence against women.

THE SOCIOCULTURAL CONTEXT OF MALE VIOLENCE

At the societal level, male violence against women is seen as a manifestation of gender inequality and as a mechanism for the subordination of women. The critical roles that gender and gender relations play in directing male violence against women force the conclusion that male violence against women has deep roots in sociocultural constructions of gender and heterosexuality. To understand violence against women, one must understand why men believe they are entitled to control women, and why they feel they may use intimidation, coercion, threats, and force to do so. We cannot expect either prevention or intervention efforts to be successful unless the gendered nature of violence is understood and directly addressed. Thus, understanding and preventing violence requires integrative biopsychosocial models that consider sociocultural as well as psychological determinants of violent acts (see, for example, Barbaree & Marshall, 1991; Berkowitz, 1992; Craig, 1990; Ellis, 1989, 1991; Frieze & Browne, 1989; Hall, 1990; Hall & Hirschman, 1991; Malamuth & Dean, 1991; Pagelow, 1984; Prentky & Knight, 1991; Quinsey, 1984; Shotland, 1992; Sugarman & Hotaling, 1989; White & Koss, 1993).

Although many researchers have focused on the influence of cultural myths and gender roles on male violence against women, it is important to recognize that the sociocultural determinants of such violence go beyond myths and roles. Culture is the "all-encompassing" whole that includes the concepts, habits, skills, instruments, arts, morals, laws, customs, institutions, and any other capabilities acquired by human beings as members of a society (Kottak, 1991). Throughout history, gender has been a central organizing feature of human cultures (Lerner, 1986; Shepard, 1987). Consequently, gender—like race and class—is an integral part of our social structures and institutions. Gendered social structures, which include family, peer groups, school, sports, military, and religious institutions, directly impinge on the daily lives of men and women.

The concept of gender is multifaceted, encompassing complex psycho-

4

logical, social, economic, and political relations between women and men in society. The many ways in which our culture is gendered—from the gendered design of our tools and instruments to our social institutions—have yet to be fully recognized and studied. Basic research and theory development that integrates historical, anthropological, sociological, economic, political, and psychological perspectives is needed before we can fully comprehend the cultural and structural aspects of gender and their influences on the behaviors of women and men.

Meanwhile, there are many obvious reminders that we live in a gendered sociocultural context: A woman's conflict between work and home is viewed as an individual problem rather than as a problem of the design of home and work environments that make it difficult to integrate activities in these two spheres; gender differences in accident rates on the job are still looked at in terms of "mistakes" rather than in terms of problems created by equipment that has been designed to fit male bodies, and many delivery services are designed based on the assumption someone will be home to receive things during normal working hours. These are just a few of the countless reminders, both obvious and subtle, of the all-pervasive influence of gender. The important thing for psychologists to recognize, however, is that gender is a *social construct*, and not a personal attribute or particular behavior. The particular personal attributes that become linked to gender depend on the sociocultural context and the definition of gender as a social category. They also vary depending on intersections with other social categories such as ethnicity and sexual orientation.

Although psychology has much to contribute to the understanding of violence, the building of a useful psychological knowledge base depends on recognizing that individual behaviors and cognitive processes are embedded in gendered social structures that define and direct the gendered meaning of sexual and violent behaviors. Because gender pervades our social structures, its relationship to violence must be conceptualized and addressed at institutional and individual levels (Anderson, 1993).

Sexual Inequalities and the Propagation of Violence

Understanding male violence against women requires examining the power inequalities between men and women, including—but not limited to—legal, economic, and physical power inequalities. Such inequalities pervade the social constructions of gender and sexuality and profoundly affect the intimate relationships between men and women (Brush, 1990; Burt, 1980; Costin, 1985; Darke, 1990; Dobash & Dobash, 1979; Grauerholz & Koralewski, 1991; Hall, Howard & Boezio, 1986; Kelly, 1988; Walker, 1989).

A variety of scholars have suggested that violence functions as a mechanism of social control of women and serves to reproduce and maintain the status quo of male dominance and female subordination (e.g., Dutton, 1988a; McHugh, Frieze, & Browne, 1993). Indeed, psychologists have documented the powerful and ubiquitous effects that the fear of rape and of other violent acts has on women's lives (Gordon & Riger, 1989). This fear serves to control women's freedom of action at home, at work, and in the community, and often requires them to seek protection from others (the majority of the time, male others).

Other researchers have found cultural links between violence, gender inequality, and social disorganization. Male-dominant societies, which are characterized by a general acceptance of violence, support the highest levels of rape. Significantly greater frequencies of rape and a high degree of interpersonal violence are seen in preliterate societies characterized by patrilocality and an ideology of male toughness (Otterbein, 1979; Sanday, 1981). Rape is also prevalent under conditions of marked social inequity such as slavery (Quinsey, 1984). In the United States, rape rates in individual states are correlated with societal-level indicators of social disorganization and inequality. For example, higher rape rates are associated with a state's lack of vigilance in controlling gun ownership and hunting, greater urbanization and poverty, and larger numbers of citizens who subscribe to pornographic magazines and are divorced (Baron & Strauss, 1989; Jaffee & Strauss, 1987).

Cultural Norms and Expectations

Cultural norms and expectations play critical roles in promoting and shaping male violence against women, minimizing or covering up its harmful effects, and preventing the development of effective policies and programs designed to prevent such violence. Norms and expectations prescribe and proscribe the rights and responsibilities (i.e., the roles) of all persons in a particular social status or social category, including those social roles assigned by gender. It is through gender-related roles that specific cultural norms related to gender and violence are patterned, learned, and transmitted from generation to generation. Sociocultural norms and role expectations that support female subordination and perpetuate male violence are transmitted in the home (Bowker, 1986; Dobash & Dobash, 1979; Pagelow, 1984; Russell, 1982a, 1982b; Stanko, 1985; Yllö & Boggard, 1988), in the peer group (Ageton, 1983; Ehrhart & Sandler, 1985; Martin & Hummer, 1989; Sanday, 1990), at the workplace (Fitzgerald, 1992; Fitzgerald & Ormerod, 1993), and in the military (Russell, 1989). These norms and expectations pervade our legal system, our literary works, and our everyday discourse (see, e.g., Straus, 1976).

Cultural Myths

Cultural norms and expectations about behaviors of women and men lead to myths that perpetuate violence and deny assistance to its victims. As Leidig (1981) observed, the "linkage among all ... acts of violence is the commonality of the numerous myths attached to them" (p. 199). Cultural beliefs that support rape also support sexual harassment, battering, sexual murder, and other forms of violence against women (Fitzgerald, 1990; Kelly, 1988). These are summarized in Table 1.

Such myths help explain why research and intervention efforts have been victim-focused and often victim-blaming, and why the responses of others, including family members, friends, co-workers, health-care workers, and the criminal justice system have often compounded, rather than ameliorated, the damaging consequences of male violence. For example, medical personnel in emergency rooms have been found to define battered women as "social" rather than true "medical" cases (Kurz, 1987). The acceptance of beliefs that foster rape has been found among a variety of groups in the United States, including average citizens, police officers, and judges (Burt, 1980; Field, 1978; Mahoney, Shively, & Traw, 1986). Further, inade-

7

Table 1

Common myths and stereotypes about male violence against women

Myth	Rape	Battering	Harassment
Victim masochism			
They enjoy/want it.	It wasn't rape, only "rough sex." Women say no when they mean yes. Some women enjoy rape.	Some women are masochistic, seeking out violent men. Women don't leave so it can't be that bad.	It wasn't harassment, only teasing. Women invite it and feel flattered by the attention.
Victim precipitation			
They ask for/deserve it.	Women provoke by the way they dress, by "leading men on." They take risks by going out alone, accepting lifts.	Women provoke men by nagging, not fulfilling household "duties," refusing sex.	Women invite it by flirting or the way they dress, by working late or traveling on business trips.
It only happens to certain types of women/in certain kinds of families.	Women who live in poor areas; women who are sexually active; women who take risks; women who have previously been abused.	Working-class women; women who are "bad" housewives; women who saw or experienced violence as children.	Paranoid women; women with an ax to grind; women who behave inappropriately in the workplace.
Victim fabrication			
They tell lies/exaggerate.	Women make false reports for revenge, to protect their "reputation."	It wasn't violence, only a fight. Women exaggerate to get a quick divorce.	Disgruntled workers or women who are scorned file harassment charges.
Men are justified in their behavior or not responsible for unintentional effects.	He paid for her date; he had to release his sexual "tension"; he didn't mean it.	He was punishing her for unwifely behavior; he had a bad day at the office; he didn't mean it.	He's just expressing his interest in her, she should be flattered; he's just trying to be nice to her; he didn't mean it.

(continues)

Table 1			
(Continued)			
Myth	Rape	Battering	Harassment
The acts are not really harmful.	She wasn't a virgin; there are no bruises.	She didn't break any bones; she'll heal.	He didn't hurt her; she didn't lose her job or promotion.
The acts are very unusual or deviant.	He was drinking and not himself; he must be sick or under stress and needs help and understanding.	He was drinking and not himself; he must be sick or under stress and needs help and understanding.	He was drinking and not himself; he's under a lot of stress and needs help.

NOTE: Adapted from Fitzgerald, 1993a; and Kelly, 1988.

quacies in police response to domestic violence have been linked to institutionalized beliefs that wife abuse is a private matter and that intervention undermines preservation of the family (Brown, 1984). Thus, understanding and preventing violence (as well as ameliorating its effects) requires countering the gender-related cultural norms, roles, and myths that eroticize and sanction male violence, fail to hold men accountable for their actions, trivialize its consequences, and ultimately close off strategies (such as taking children across state lines) that women might use to protect themselves and their children.

Sexual Scripts

The theater has been a source of concepts that describe human interactions, including the concepts of social scripts and roles. Among the threads that weave together different manifestations of gendered violence are the sexual scripts created by sociocultural expectations and norms; these scripts assign different roles and behaviors to men and women and guide their interactions (particularly their dyadic interactions) over time in various settings. As Bem (1993) and others have so clearly articulated, the basic heterosexual script in our culture reflects an androcentric heterosexuality that eroticizes sexual inequality and supports male dominance as normal and natural. Supports for gender inequality are woven into sexual scripts through cultural expectations that women will have relationships with men who are bigger, taller, stronger, older, smarter, more educated, higher in status, more experienced, more talented, more confident, and more highly paid than themselves. When heterosexual encounters do not go according to script, with males playing less dominant or assertive roles, such encounters are considered emasculating for men and defeminizing for women. Heterosexual scripts are also characterized by a male-centered objectification of women that emphasizes their physical attractiveness and ability to stimulate and satisfy men's desires (Bem, 1993).

Variations of this culturally transmitted heterosexual sexual script are seen in adolescent dating rituals and shape young people's dating expectations. Such scripts support violence when they encourage the male to be a sexual stalker and the female his prey, deprive the female of her right to say "no" to further sexual advances, and hold the female responsible for the extent of sexual involvement that occurs (White & Koss, 1993).

Parents socialize daughters to resist sexual advances and sons to initiate sexual activity (Ross, V. M., 1977). By adolescence, scripts about sexual interaction and romantic love that justify rape and violence have already been established. For example, a study of 1,700 middle school children, conducted by the Rhode Island Rape Crisis Center, found that 65% of the boys and 57% of the girls believed it is acceptable for a man to force a woman to have sex if they have been dating for more than 6 months (Teens express themselves, 1988). Approximately 25% of the boys said that it was acceptable for a man to force sex on a woman if he had spent money on her. These findings have been widely replicated among both high school and college students (Goodchilds & Zellman, 1984; Goodchilds, Zellman, Johnson, & Giarrusso, 1988; Muehlenhard, Friedman, & Thomas, 1985). Beliefs and myths that justify rape and violence are particularly disturbing given that both rapists and nonrapists are sexually aroused by rape stimuli (Hall, 1990; Malamuth, Check, & Briere, 1986; Quinsey & Chaplin, 1984). Briere & Malamuth (1983) reported that even nonrapists said they would be more likely to commit rape if they could be assured they would not be caught.

Other research has suggested that high school students and college students may define possessiveness, jealousy, and other abuse as "a contemporary, accepted version of love and war" (Henton, Cate, Koval, Lloyd, &

Christopher, 1983, p. 16). As Pagelow (1984) observed, reduction of family violence requires that "male/female roles and attitudes about love and intimacy need to be restructured in ways that develop less emphasis on possession and domination, and more on empathy, respect, and consideration for their own and others' rights" (p. 298).

Gender-related scripts have been linked to violence in research that indicates men who function with traditional dating scripts—initiating the date, paying all expenses, and driving the car—are more likely to be sexually aggressive than other men (Muehlenhard & Linton, 1987). Although little is known about the psychological characteristics of harassers, Pryor (1987) suggested that so-called "masculinity" may play an important role in their behavior as well.

The current rates of violence among cohabiting or dating college students on some campuses are similar to that of married couples (Center for Disease Control, 1989). This phenomenon appears to be increasing (Browne & Williams, 1990). Studies of dating violence suggest that the primary purpose of such violence for males is to coerce females into doing something (typically, to have sex; Sugarman & Hotaling, 1989). This phenomenon might be explained as a reflection of anticipatory socialization into the roles of husband and wife on the part of sexually intimate or cohabiting couples. It could also reflect the increasing disinhibition of violence toward women that occurs as college men are exposed to college institutions and participate in such activities as fraternities and athletics, which promote alcohol use, male entitlement, devaluation of women, and the victimizing sexual scripts that consider coercion and force legitimate strategies for getting one's way in a relationship (Koss & Gaines, 1993; Martin & Hummer, 1989; Sanday, 1990). Although the concept of sexual scripts is primarily found in rape literature, it may prove useful in research that attempts to integrate psychological and social levels of analysis across all forms of violence and to answer the question of why particular forms of violence occur in particular settings.

The behavior deemed appropriate in sexual scripts changes over time in a relationship. Violence has been found to occur in casual dating (e.g., Henton et al., 1983; Levy, 1991). Nonetheless, the degree of acquaintanceship between a young man and his potential victim appears to determine in part the likelihood and severity of interpersonal violence or sexual assault. Some studies suggest that the risk for dating violence increases after a relationship becomes intimate (Cate, Henton, Koval, Christopher, & Lloyd, 1982), and that violence is more likely to happen in more involved rather than in less involved relationships (Laner & Thompson, 1982).

Prior intimacy between partners may increase a man's belief that he is entitled to sex any time he desires and that a forced sexual encounter is harmless to the woman because she has already had intercourse with him (Johnson & Jackson, 1988). Although some researchers have suggested that the earliest stages of acquaintanceship pose the highest risks of rape (Muehlenhard & Linton, 1987), others have implicated longer-term relationships (Kirkpatrick & Kanin, 1957; Russell, 1984, 1990). Completed rape is more likely to occur among couples who know each other well than among persons who are acquaintances (Belnap, 1989). Assault by an acquaintance, as opposed to rape by a stranger, is more likely to occur indoors, to involve drinking by both parties, and to involve less violence and more verbal threats (Bownes, O'Gorman, & Sayers, 1991). The acquaintance rapist is also more likely to kiss the victim, verbally abuse her throughout the assault, commit rape repeatedly, and demand secrecy after the attack (Bownes et al., 1991). The degree of the relationship also affects perceptions of the assault. The greater the intimacy, the less likely people are to judge an instance of forced sexual intercourse as rape, to tell anyone about the assault, or to seek help (Goodchilds et al., 1988; Koss, Dinero, Siebel, & Cox, 1988).

Sexual scripts contain an intrinsic tension between men and women and create the opportunity for miscommunication that can lead to sexual coercion, rape, and battering. Among the factors that contribute to the risk of acquaintance rape is the fact that many people feel uncomfortable discussing sexual intentions and desires. As a result, they attempt to infer sexual intent from indirect and nonverbal cues, a strategy that is bound to produce frequent errors (Abbey, 1991). Some men may interpret a woman's friendly behavior in a more sexual way than she intends (Abbey, 1991), may not take a woman's objections to sexual contact seriously (Check & Malamuth, 1983), and may perceive refusal as a threat to their manhood

(Beneke, 1982). More than 66% of the students in one survey believed that on various occasions their friendliness had been misperceived as a sexual invitation (Abbey, 1987a, 1987b). Some young women and men believe that a woman should pretend to say "no," even when she intends to consent (Muehlenhard & Hollabaugh, 1988). This is contrary to recent evidence that suggests women rarely say "no" when they mean "yes." Instead, they say "no" as a shorthand for more extended excuses like not feeling well, not being attracted to the person, or not being ready. It is important that sexual scripts and the male-female communication associated with them not be analyzed in a vacuum, however. They must be studied with recognition of the power differential between men and women in a male-dominated society and the constraints such a power differential places upon women's potential to be heard (Pinneau, 1987).

Gender and Gender-Related Social Roles

Psychologists have important roles to play in reconceptualizing gender so that its sociocultural origins are appropriately recognized and it is not merely viewed as a personal attribute. For example, Russo and Green (1993) suggested that it may be useful to conceptualize all gender-related behaviors as gender-*role* related, rather than *trait*-related. From this point of view, the cluster of traits associated with masculinity are recognized as external impositions that are dependent on what is considered masculine in the larger sociocultural context, rather than something intrinsically located inside males. These researchers argued that psychologists should stop talking about masculinity and femininity as if they are located inside a person, that is, as traits, and start talking about masculine and feminine gender roles that may conflict or be congruent with other gender-related social roles assigned to women and men such as wife, husband, mother, father, daughter, son, and so forth.

This perspective recognizes that cultural expectations associated with the masculine and feminine gender roles apply to all persons assigned to the social category of male and female in society, although the specific content of the roles may vary with ethnicity, class, and other cross-cutting social statuses or categories. The traditional masculine gender role ascribes higher status and more power to men than women. With this higher status comes the prerogatives of male privilege, including the privilege of dominating women and exploiting them sexually. In the masculine gender role, power, sexuality, and violence against women become intertwined.

In this context, it is of particular concern that in today's sociocultural context, males young and old are increasingly bombarded with images that confound sex and violence and equate physical and psychological domination and abuse of women with sexual pleasure. Television shows, films, magazines, and music are increasingly riddled with such images. In effect, men who have doubts about sexual adequacy are taught to seek reassurance through power and domination over women, and their sexuality becomes the vehicle to express both power and anger towards women (Groth & Birnbaum, 1979; Sonkin, Martin, & Walker, 1985). Rape and sexual harassment can be viewed as expressions of defense of the masculine gender role as well as the need to control and dominate women. Hate crimes against lesbians can also be understood in this context. From this perspective, preventing violence against women requires directly focusing interventions on cultural conceptions of the masculine gender role.

Other socioculturally defined expectations for gender-related social roles such as wife, husband, son, and daughter, can have additional, different, and sometimes conflicting expectations that may affect the dynamics of violence. This is seen particularly in the research on intimate violence (including marital rape) between husbands and wives. The culturally mandated (often legally mandated) rights and privileges of the husband role have historically legitimized a man's power and domination over his wife, promoted her economic dependence on him, and warranted his use of violence and threats of violence to control her. Men are more accepting of marital violence than are women, in general, and it is the most traditional men who are the most accepting of marital violence (Greenblatt, 1985). As discussed previously, the clinically based literature suggests that a common characteristic of batterers is the need to control or dominate. This need is combined with a perception that female autonomy implies male loss of control (Dutton, 1988). Interviews with batterers have revealed that such men justify their use of violence by pointing to their wives' "unwifely" behaviors (Adams, 1988; Dobash & Dobash, 1979; Ptacek, 1988).

Husband–wife role definitions have also granted men unlimited sexual access to their wives to the point that marital rape and sexual abuse have not been recognized as possible. Even in the 1990s, there is resistance to conceptualizing forced sex in marriage as rape or sexual coercion. In the words of a recent defendant who was acquitted of marital rape in South Carolina despite the fact that he had videotaped his acts, which included tying up his wife and putting duct tape on her eyes and mouth, "How can you rape your own wife?" (*Washington Post*, 1992, p. A2).

Our discussion so far has focused on male violence against women and the way in which cultural expectations and norms shape that violence and target it against women. Some theorists have suggested that the occurrence of partner violence in lesbian relationships is inconsistent with theories linking male violence towards women to gender and societal roles. Little is known about the frequency and severity of violence in lesbian relationships, although, it clearly does occur (Bologna, Waterman, & Dawson, 1987; Hart, 1986; Kahuna, 1990). However, as Saakvitne and Pearlman (1993) pointed out, lesbians are subjected to both cultural misogyny and homophobia that may shape and interfere with lesbian relationships in destructive ways. Both heterosexual and lesbian women share the feelings of stigma and the belief that no one will understand that contribute to silence about their abuse (Lobel, 1986; McHugh et al., 1993; Renzetti, 1992). But lesbian batterers do not have the context of male privilege and support for their violence, and comparisons between these two situations break down rapidly when their contexts are examined. Research on lesbian relationships needs to be done for a variety of reasons, not the least of which is the desire of lesbians to know more about their contexts and relationships. But in addition, research on lesbian relationships—violent and nonviolent—can reveal some of the possibilities for human interaction that are not encumbered by heterosexual gender role mandates, privileges, and obligations, and may help us imagine a wider range of positive alternatives to current norms and circumstances for heterosexual women.

Alcohol Use

Recognition of a link between violence against women and alcohol is not new. In fact, many women supported the temperance movement in the

United States during the nineteenth century because they believed excessive drinking contributed to wife abuse (Rendall, 1985). Today, alcohol clearly continues to be a risk factor for multiple forms of violence (Pagelow, 1984).

Cultural expectations and norms associated with alcohol (e.g., "he's not responsible, he was drinking;" or "she should have known better than to get drunk") may contribute to risk for rape at parties (Lisak & Roth, 1988; Muehlenhard & Linton, 1987; Richardson & Hammock, 1991). One- to two-thirds of college student rapists and approximately half of victims had consumed alcohol prior to the rape (Koss, 1988; Muehlenhard & Linton, 1987; Wilson & Durrenberger, 1982; Wolfe & Baker, 1984). The effect of alcohol on sexual aggression is not a direct physiological effect; with actual ingestion of alcohol penile responses to pornographic stimuli decrease. Instead, alcohol is thought to influence sexual aggression through men's expectations of what its effects will be; studies have found that penile responses to pornography increased with the belief that alcohol had been consumed, when in fact the drinks contained no alcohol (for reviews, see Abbey, 1991; Abbey & Thomson, 1992; Quinsey, 1984; Richardson & Hammock, 1991).

Alcohol may serve multiple functions in physical and sexual aggression: as a disinhibitor for the man; as an excuse for his behavior after the fact; and as a strategy to reduce victim resistance (George & Marlatt, 1986; Ptacek, 1988; Richardson & Hammock, 1991). Furthermore, in cases of rape, alcohol may function as a cue; men may perceive women who drink as "loose" or more interested in sex. Many men believe that rape is justifiable if the woman is drunk or "stoned" (Goodchilds et al., 1988). Prevention and intervention strategies aimed at male violence against women must address issues of alcohol norms and expectations and their relationship to violence if they are to be maximally effective.

CONCLUSION

In summary, male violence against women takes place in a sociocultural context: therefore, understanding that violence requires an understanding of how multiple levels of influences—from societal to individual—deter-

mine its expression. Such violence has deep roots in sociocultural constructions of gender and heterosexuality, constructions that promote male entitlement and social and political inequality for women. Cultural norms and
myths, sexual scripts and social roles link various forms of violence and deny
assistance to its victims. Neither prevention nor intervention efforts can be
expected to be successful unless the gendered nature of violence in various
contexts is understood and directly addressed.

2

Understanding the Perpetrator and the Victim: Who Abuses and Who Is Abused?

Psychology's contributions to understanding violence have yet to be fully developed. At the psychological level, the focus has been on behaviors and cognitive processes that promote and maintain violence and that shape individual responses to it. Although psychologists recognize that behavior reflects the interaction of the person and the situation (which includes one's position in the social structure), psychologists have tended to focus unidimensionally on the personal characteristics of perpetrators or victims and how individuals become socialized to be violent.

PERPETRATOR ATTRIBUTES

The most salient characteristic of perpetrators of violence against women—whether they are rapists, batterers, harassers, or some combination—is that the vast majority of such perpetrators are male. Research that has focused on the characteristics of perpetrators of different kinds of violence suggests that perpetrators are a heterogeneous group. This is true even when only one form of violence, rape, for example, has been considered (Prentky & Knight, 1990; Quinsey, 1984). A number of different types of rapists have been empirically derived. Each type has somewhat different determinants

(Bard et al., 1987; Prentky & Knight, 1991). Similarly, there is no single "type" of batterer (Dutton, 1988a; Gondolf, 1988; McHugh, Frieze, & Browne, 1993; Sonkin & Dutton, 1988) or sexual harasser (Pryor, 1987, 1992). For instance, in Hamberger and Hastings' (1986) study of personality and demographic differences among three groups of men (alcoholic abusers, nonalcoholic abusers, and nonabusers), factor analyses identified three major personality types among abusers: narcissistic/antisocial, schizoidal/borderline, and passive dependent/compulsive.

Researchers continue to try to identify personality traits that distinguish men who perpetrate physical and sexual aggression against their intimates from those who do not. An array of men's personality characteristics has been linked with sexual aggression. These include hostility toward women (Malamuth, 1986; Malamuth et al., 1991), low socialization and responsibility (Rapaport & Burkhart, 1984), hypermasculinity, self-reported drug use, aggressive behavior, dangerous driving, and delinquent behavior (Mosher & Anderson, 1986; Mosher & Sirkin, 1984).

In an inquiry using the California Psychological Inventory, Barnett and Hamberger (1992) assessed the responses of three groups of men drawn from treatment groups and from the community: (a) maritally violent men ($n = 87$), (b) maritally nonviolent but maritally discordant men ($n = 42$), and (c) maritally nonviolent and maritally satisfied men ($n = 48$). Their findings generally indicated that maritally violent men exhibited different personality characteristics than did the other two groups in the areas of intimacy, impulsivity, and problem-solving. Compared with both groups of nonviolent men, men who physically assaulted their wives were more rigid and stereotyped, and they demonstrated greater difficulty developing intimate relationships based on mutuality and trust.

Murphy, Meyer, and O'Leary (1991) used the Millon Clinical Multiaxial Inventory–II to compare men who were attending a program for batterers with a sample of maritally discordant but nonviolent men. These authors reported that physically abusive men in the program evidenced more autonomous and expressive personality disturbances than the nonabusive men did. Affective dysregulation and antisocial/narcissistic tendencies were especially prominent among the abusers.

Studies of husbands who are violent toward their wives have suggested three risk factors that distinguish them from husbands who are not violent toward their partners: (a) witnessing parental violence while growing up, (b) sexual aggression toward the wife, and (c) the perpetration of violence toward children (Caesar, 1988; Fagan & Browne, in press; Hamberger & Hastings, 1991; Hotaling & Sugarman, 1986). Case control studies have consistently found a higher incidence of *antisocial behaviors* in abusive men (e.g., they were more likely to abuse alcohol, to use sexual force against their wives, to use violence against their children, to use violence against nonfamily members, and to have criminal arrest records). Such studies have not consistently found a pattern of psychopathology in men who assault female intimates (Fagan & Browne, in press; Hotaling & Sugarman, 1986).

Gondolf (1988) used the self-reports of abused women from 50 shelters in his attempt to develop a typology of abusers, some of whom were also rapists. Although based on secondary reports from a special population, cluster analyses suggested three general categories that appear to reflect the bulk of the literature on abusers to date: (a) abusers with antisocial personality characteristics who tend to perpetrate extreme physical and sexual violence (5%–8% of his sample), (b) abusers with antisocial personality characteristics who tend to perpetrate extreme physical and verbal, but not sexual, abuse (30%–40% of the sample), and (c) abusers without severely pathological profiles, who perpetrate both physical and verbal abuse but at less severe levels than the other two groups (52%–65% of the sample).

Hall and Hirschman (1991) suggested that a more complex psychological model is needed to account for the heterogeneity of sexual aggressors. They developed a model with four components: (a) physiological sexual arousal, (b) cognitions that justify sexual aggression, (c) affective dyscontrol, and (d) personality problems. They considered these components to function as motivational precursors that contribute to the likelihood of sexually aggressive behavior. Differences in the prominence of these precursors define major subtypes of sexual aggressors. The usefulness of this "quadripartite model" (p. 662) for understanding sexual aggression and other forms of male violence against women requires additional study. Although it is presented as a comprehensive model, it does not sufficiently elaborate gender-related variables, such as individual mental representations of the cultural scripts discussed above.

Advances in understanding the psychology of perpetrators of violence against women will indeed require more sophistication in theory and method. Dutton (1988a) reminds us that differing "profiles" of abusive men may in fact reflect variations in research strategies rather than substantive differences in types of abusers. To date, efforts to construct typologies of assaultive men have divided them on personality factors (Caesar, 1988; Elbow, 1977; Hamberger & Hastings, 1986), their involvement in violence toward strangers and intimates (Fagan et al., 1983; Saunders, 1992; Shields, McCall, & Hannecke, 1988), co-occurrence of assaultive and other behaviors such as alcohol use (Gondolf, 1988) or sex-role stereotyping (Saunders, 1987). These efforts at times have confounded dependent and explanatory variables (Fagan & Browne, in press; O'Leary & Jacobson, 1992; and Sonkin & Dutton, 1988, review this literature).

Moreover, existing studies of personality characteristics in men who assault female partners have been limited to small samples of repeatedly assaultive participants in treatment programs, voluntary or self-selected respondents, or assailants identified by the criminal justice system (Fagan & Browne, 1993; Sonkin & Dutton, 1988). Findings based on these samples cannot be considered representative of the characteristics of abusers in the general population, the vast majority of whom are *not* involved in either community or criminal justice interventions.

In particular, men engaged in court processes or mental health interventions are clearly not representative of abusers or harassers in the general population and may represent the extremes of the spectrum; that is, a minority of the most blatant or severe cases may be netted into the courts or grievance systems, whereas men who volunteer for treatment or rehabilitation are less violent and more positively motivated than violent men who remain unseen.

Underreporting of male violence against women and the use of selective samples (e.g., volunteer court samples, prisoners, treatment groups, and other specialized settings) in research studies is a problem in rape research as well. For example, only a small proportion of reported rapes (an estimated 16%) leads to conviction (Dietz, 1978). This small subsample of rapists is clearly not representative of rapists at large. The probability of reporting, arrest, and conviction is related to social status and race (LaFree, 1989). The image of a rapist derived from crime statistics is a young black urban male, often of lower-class status. However, this image says more about who gets convicted than it says about who rapes. Several large surveys have found either no significant differences or very small effects for race, social class, or place of residence in who admits to perpetrating sexually aggressive acts (Ageton, 1983; Hall & Flannery, 1984; Koss et al., 1987; Rouse, 1988). Additional problems in the literature include deceptive self-reporting of controversial and stigmatizing behaviors, a tendency to make causal conclusions from correlational data, and overreliance on univariate approaches to complex, clearly multivariate problems (see Hall, 1990, for a more detailed critique of the sexual aggression literature).

Socialization for Violence

The family plays a key role in transmitting and perpetuating the behaviors and cognitive processes that promote violence against women. A significant relationship between sexual victimization of boys and subsequent sexual aggression as young men has been observed in a series of longitudinal investigations (Friedrich, Beilke, & Urquiza, 1988). Both boys and girls, but particularly boys, are at increased risk to abuse an intimate partner in later adult relationships if they were abused as children or adolescents (e.g., Kalmuss, 1984; Straus et al., 1980).

Witnessing or experiencing family violence is predictive of sexually aggressive behavior among college men (Koss & Dinero, 1989a; Malamuth, Sockloskie, Koss, & Tanaka, 1991). Boys are also at greatly increased risk to abuse female partners in adult relationships if they witnessed abuse between parental figures in their childhood homes. Girls, on the other hand, are at somewhat increased risk to be abused by an intimate male in adulthood if they witnessed abuse between parental figures in childhood (Kalmuss, 1984; Straus et al., 1980). In Hotaling and Sugarman's (1986) review of case comparison studies, 88% of studies found a significant relationship between witnessing parental violence and later abusing a partner for men; 69% of the

studies found being the victim of child abuse was later associated with partner abuse. In their national probability sample, Straus and his colleagues
(1980) found that men who had witnessed violence between their parents
were nearly three times as likely to hit their wives as were men whose parents had not been violent. The sons of the most violent parents had a rate of
wife abuse 1,000 times greater than the sons of nonviolent parents. Data
from national probability samples also indicate that children who have both
experienced child or adolescent abuse and witnessed abuse between parental
figures have a higher risk of becoming involved in an abusive relationship as
adults than do individuals without these dual experiences (e.g., Kalmuss,
1984).

Although their study was not based on a random sample, Fagan,
Stewart, and Hanson (1983) found a correlation between exposure to violence in childhood and the severity of violence perpetrated against a wife.
These researchers, who interviewed 270 abused women identified in domestic violence projects, found that men's exposure to violence in childhood (as
known to their wives) was a predictor of the severity of physical injuries sustained by wives during assaultive incidents. It was also the strongest predictor of the occurrence of wife abuse.

It is estimated that about one third of children who are abused or
exposed to violence as children become violent themselves in later life
(Widom, 1989). Later involvement in violence is only one of many potential
outcomes of growing up in a violent home. Clearly, not all men who are
abused or exposed to violence as children later perpetuate violence against
their intimates, just as only a minority of women exposed to violence
between parental figures later become involved in relationships with violent
men (Widom, 1989). Similarly, not all men who physically or sexually
assault their wives come from homes in which they had experiences with
interpersonal victimization. Nonetheless, being assaulted by or witnessing
assaults among family members in childhood or adolescence appears across
empirical studies as a primary risk factor for later involvement in abusive
relationships for both women and men.

The exact mechanisms leading to later involvement with violence are
unclear. Early sexual experiences, especially abusive ones, may alter a young

man's notions of what normal sex is and may lower his self-esteem. Early initiation into sexual activity also increases the opportunity for sexual assault to occur simply by increasing a young man's potential number of contacts. Patriarchal family attitudes toward sexuality and traditional male—female roles also contribute to socialization for physical and sexual aggression. Sexually assaultive behavior in young men may be encouraged by their fathers' attitudes towards sexual aggression (Kanin, 1985).

It is likely that violence and abuse in the family "socializes for violence" in multiple ways. Those homes in which a pattern of physical violence or sexual aggression exists among family members are never otherwise "normal" homes (van der Kolk, 1987). Such behaviors involve a marked violation of personal boundaries and choice as well as an extreme lack of empathy and protection of loved ones. Bessel van der Kolk (1987), in his discussion of trauma in the family, contended that despite many differences, child abuse, incest, and battering cause all members of the family—the victims, the perpetrators, and others—to rely heavily on denial, avoidance, and the reinterpretation of events. Victims or witnesses learn to sacrifice themselves or other family members to maintain the family structure or the family secret, adopt attributions of victim blame, accept the justification or inevitability of violence, and respond with a variety of behaviors, from passivity and withdrawal to paranoia and rage. In her discussion of trauma and recovery, Judith Herman (1992) noted:

> The child trapped in an abusive environment is faced with formidable tasks of adaptation. She must find a way to preserve a sense of trust in people who are untrustworthy, safety in a situation that is unsafe, control in a situation that is terrifyingly unpredictable, power in a situation of helplessness. (p. 97)

A discussion of the effects of child abuse and of witnessing abuse between parental figures on children and adolescents is beyond the scope of this report. The point here is that these experiences provide a socialization context that teaches inappropriate, victim-blaming, perpetrator-justifying responses to victims of violence—lessons that perpetrators, victims, and observers learn and in turn transmit.

Peer-group socialization is also a powerful influence on sexually assaultive behavior (Ageton, 1983). Headlines about sexual harassment and rape in conjunction with athletic teams and fraternities provide numerous examples of the destructive effects of peer-group influence at both the high school and college level. Several indices of school-related functioning also predict sexual aggression, including lower academic aspirations, poorer current school success, and school normlessness (Ageton, 1983). Organized religion, another important socialization agent, has been found to teach and write about rape in ways that have not always supported the legitimacy of the rape victim (Fortune, 1983). The recent Tailhook scandal is but a recent, highly publicized example of a long history of U.S. military contributions to male violence against women (Russell, 1989).

The media is a potent socializing agent as well. Psychologists have articulated the powerful effect of observational learning in gender role socialization, and have documented the harmful effects of cultural images purveyed in the media that increasingly merge violence and male sexuality (Linz, Wilson, & Donnerstein, 1992). For example, Court (1976) found that rates of attempted and completed rape have increased in Denmark, England, Sweden, the United States, Australia, and New Zealand following the ready availability of sadistic pornography (although lesser sexual crimes decreased).

Exposure to depictions of sexual violence under laboratory conditions has been found to increase aggression toward women, particularly when they have affronted, insulted, or provoked the man (see Linz, Wilson, & Donnerstein, 1992). Sexual arousal as a result of viewing pornography is characteristic of sexual offenders (see Hall, 1990). However, males who have not been sexually aggressive may also be aroused by rape depictions that involve adult women, especially if the woman is portrayed as enjoying the experience. A serious deficit in the data is that no research of this type has involved adolescent boys, who have the highest rates of sexual aggression. Rapists in prison admit to less experience with erotica (sexual material that does not contain violent themes or acts) compared with nonincarcerated men (see Quinsey, 1984), whereas sexually aggressive college men have been differentiated from other men in part by their greater use of pornography

(Koss & Dinero, 1989a). Many experts, including the U. S. Attorney General's Commission on Pornography, have concluded that exposure to media depictions of violence against women promotes rape (Ellis, 1989; Linz et al., 1992; Quinsey, 1984).

Sex and Power Motives

How best to conceptualize the motivation of men who harass, assault, injure, rape, or kill women continues to be debated. For example, men differ greatly in the extent to which they are aroused by sexual aggression and the possibility that they would rape a woman if guaranteed not to be caught or punished (Malamuth, 1989a, 1989b; Malamuth & Dean, 1991). Many scholars have also argued that violence at an individual level serves as a mechanism for the personal control of men over women and is a response to female autonomy (e.g., Dobash & Dobash, 1979; Martin, 1976; McHugh, Frieze, & Browne, 1993; Walker, 1979). Earlier work that focused on risk markers for partner violence did not conceptualize and measure power and control issues in systematic ways. In addition, traditional sex role expectations permeated the early literature. For a time, evidence on marital power issues was considered inconclusive. In fact, Hotaling and Sugarman (1986), speculated that male-dominant expectations were so pervasive in our society that it was not possible to differentiate violent from nonviolent men on this dimension alone.

More recently, clinically based literature on partner-precipitated violence has strongly supported the idea that men's power and control issues underlie the expression and direction of violence towards women (Browne & Dutton, 1990; Novaco, 1976; Sonkin, Martin, & Walker, 1985). Common forms of abuse associated with male violence against female intimates include the use of intimidation and threats to obtain desired outcomes, demeaning comments, sexual coercion, and continual attempts to monitor and determine the partner's activities and associations (Browne, 1987; Follingstad et al., 1991; Pagelow, 1984; Sonkin, Martin, & Walker, 1985). As Dutton (1988a, 1988b) has observed, a common theme underlying aggressive reactions is "the need to control or dominate the female, feelings of powerlessness vis-a-vis the female, and descriptions of female independence as male loss of control" (Dutton, 1988a, p. 16; see also Goldsmith, 1990; Sonkin & Dutton, 1987).

Men in these studies experienced anger most readily in circumstances in which they perceived an impending loss of control over either intimacy or distance (Browning & Dutton, 1988). Clinical research on abuser attributions (Ptacek, 1988) has suggested that men often attribute their abuse to their partner not fulfilling their obligations to be good wives (i.e., by being silent, knowing when to talk, being sexually responsive, or being a good cook).

In a review of empirical studies of dating violence, Sugarman and Hotaling (1989) found that male respondents were most likely to report that the primary purpose of their violence was to "intimidate," "frighten," or "force the other person to do something" (p. 13). Men also reported that when they were denied sexual access to women, they used force to obtain it. In contrast, women most frequently gave self-defense or retaliation as the motivation for their aggression. Thus, as Sonkin & Dunphy (1982) observed, many men batter because it works: It "puts a quick stop to an emotional argument or a situation that is getting out of control" and also acts as a relatively safe outlet for frustration, whether that frustration arises from inside or outside the home (p. 3). Gratification from establishing control through violence also may reinforce many abusers. Gratification from the use of violence against wives or girlfriends may thus come from (a) the release of anger in response to perceived violation of entitlements or power deficits, (b) the temporary neutralization of concerns about dependency or vulnerability, (c) maintenance of dominance over the partner or situation, and (d) the attainment of positive social status that such domination affords (Fagan & Browne, in press).

The theme of male control—or the perceived loss of control via female independence, "disobedience," or attempts at autonomy—resurfaces in in-depth studies of partner homicide. Although based on a small sample, the findings of Barnard et al. (1982) are interesting in this regard. In a clinical study of both male and female perpetrators, the reason most often given by men for the killing of their mates was their "inability to accept what they perceived to be a rejection of them or their role of dominance over their eventual victim" (Barnard et al., 1982, p. 278). The men in this study reported that a walk-out or threat of separation was especially provoking, representing an "intolerable desertion, rejection, or abandonment." In killing their women partners, men in this study believed they were reacting to a previous offense against them (i.e., leaving) on the part of their wives. Interestingly, 57% of the men in this study who had killed their wives were living apart from them at the time of the murder. Homicide case histories suggest that attempting to terminate a relationship with a violent partner, or even discussing the possibility of termination, can lead to severe aggression or reprisal (e.g., Browne, 1987; Sonkin, Martin, & Walker, 1985). Yet far more attention has been focused on why abused women might not leave a violent partner than on what interventions with violent men would prevent women from being severely harmed, or killed, when they do leave.

Whether the crime of rape is best described as a sexual act motivated by sexual drives or a violent act motivated by drives to humiliate, dominate, or control women has been a particular source of contention in the literature. Attempts to resolve this debate have focused on patterns of sexual arousal to depictions of pure violence, pure consensual sex, and nonconsensual sex that includes violence. As previously mentioned, this research has shown consistently that some men with no known history of sexual aggression may be aroused by rape stimuli involving adults (Hall, 1990).

Sexually aggressive males do appear to be generally more sexually aroused by both consenting and rape stimuli, however (Rapaport & Posey, 1991). Sexually aggressive men openly admit that they harbor aggressive and sadistic sexual fantasies (Greendlinger & Byrne, 1987; Quinsey, 1984). Measurement of sexual and aggressive motives in nonincarcerated sexually aggressive men have suggested that other motives are stronger than sex, including power and anger (Lisak & Roth, 1988).

Date rapists have been found to have more sexual partners than their nonsexually aggressive peers do, a finding that challenges assumptions that their behavior is motivated by greater-than-average sexual frustration. However, it may be that sexually aggressive men have higher sexual expectations that lead them to feel deprived, even though, objectively, they are obtaining more sexual opportunities than other men (Kanin, 1985; Koss &

Dinero, 1989a; Malamuth, 1986; Malamuth et al., 1991). The greater the number of sexual partners a man has had, the greater the likelihood that he will have been sexually assaultive at least once (Kanin, 1967; Koss & Dinero, 1989a; Mahoney et al., 1986; Malamuth, 1986; Malamuth et al., 1991). Contemporary thought is that rape will be best defined as an integration of both components, and the field will be advanced by attempts to understand how sexual and aggressive elements interact (Barbaree & Marshall, 1991).

In the meantime, the persistence of rape and severe and lethal violence by men against women underscores the need for more effective psychological inquiries and interventions with men who perpetrate and model such violence.

Gender Schemas

At the individual level, mental representations of gender-related cultural myths, gender scripts and roles, and male entitlements are conceptualized as gender schemas. Gender schemas serve as expectancies that selectively organize and even bias perceptions of the world. The link between gender schemas and violent behavior toward women is suggested by psychological studies in which sexually aggressive men have described themselves in more traditional terms than other men (Koss & Dinero, 1989). Also abusive men have demonstrated a strong need to control and dominate, which are the quintessential aspects of the traditional masculine role (Dutton 1988b; Senkin & Dutton, 1988).

Men who lack characteristics traditionally incorporated into the feminine gender schema are deficient in the social skills associated with the feminine gender role. These skills include concern for and the ability to empathize with others (Dietz, Blackwell, Daley, & Bentley, 1982; Quackenbush, 1989). These men rely on social myths to negotiate social interactions. Once they develop a schema about women, these men are also likely to interpret ambiguous evidence as confirmation of their beliefs (Abbey, 1991). Men who lack feminine attributes in their gender schema are more sexually aggressive than those who have them (Quackenbush, 1989). The traditional male gender schema is also associated with antihomosexual attitudes and greater tendencies toward violence against lesbians and gays (Herek, 1986).

Sexually aggressive men endorse more strongly than nonaggressive men a set of attitudes that are supportive of rape, including myths about rape and the use of interpersonal violence as a strategy for resolving conflict (Koss & Dinero, 1989a; Koss, Leonard, Beezley, & Oros, 1985; Malamuth, 1986, 1988; Malamuth & Ceniti, 1986; Malamuth et al., 1991; Mosher & Anderson, 1986; Rapaport & Burkhart, 1984). Sexually aggressive men have more resistance than other men to perceiving forced sexual relations on a date as rape; they are also more likely to perceive a rape victim as a seductress who desired sexual relations (Jenkins & Dambrot, 1987; Muehlenhard et al., 1985; Muehlenhard & Linton, 1987). Even incarcerated rapists often rationalize that their behavior was wanted or deserved by the victim (Scully & Marolla, 1984). These beliefs allow some men to convince themselves that a forced sexual act would be enjoyable for the victim (Hall & Hirschman, 1991).

Other Cognitive–Behavioral Factors

Expectations of male entitlement reflect a combination of male internalization of the cultural norms of the rights and privileges of both the masculine gender role, which says that men should be strong and dominant over women, and the husband role, which grants men control over their wives. Thus, as would be predicted by the cognitive-motivational-relational theory of emotions (Lazarus, 1991b), men often respond with anger, outrage, and noncompliance when civil authorities and others use punishment in an attempt to stop them from raping, beating, or harassing their wives or intimate partners.

Aggression is not an inevitable response to pain and adversity. People differ in the amount of anger they feel in response to various conditions. Further, reinforcing people to take positive, nonaggressive actions to adversity while at the same time punishing aggressive responses can change the likelihood of aggression based on anger. Teaching people to deal with feelings of anger is thus an essential component of programs designed to modify the behavior of aggressive individuals.

In dealing with aggressive men, however, it is important to recognize that the expression of aggressive behavior reduces feelings of anger and is consequently self-reinforcing. Irritated people report that they feel "good"

31

after being aggressive (Bramel, Taub, & Blum, 1968). Although the physiological mechanisms involved in such "good feelings" have not been fully defined, researchers have found that being verbally or physically aggressive toward a source of anger can reduce blood pressure in angry subjects (Hokanson & Burgess, 1962a, 1962b; Hokanson, Burgess & Cohen, 1963). These and other findings suggest that unless specific measures are taken to prevent violence against women, it will persist and be difficult to eradicate.

As would be expected based on psychological knowledge about the effects of punishment, when authorities resist involvement in disputes until the violence disturbs the neighbors, or judges give initial offenders mild "slaps on the wrist," the interventions are often not sufficient to suppress the violence. In addition, the effectiveness of a punishment is influenced by the *meaning* of the punishment. If a violent man views punishment as a challenge to his manhood and as an illegitimate intrusion into his rightful role as family head (culturally defined entitlements that become psychological variables when they are internalized), punishment may only serve to make him angry, not inhibit his behavior.

Such interventions as orders of protection and battered women's shelters are important and needed. But this reconceptualization suggests that helping violent men to understand that such interventions are legitimate will require helping them to change conceptions of both (a) their masculine gender role and (b) their husband role. Without such changes in cognition, such orders may be ignored, and shelters will only be able to provide temporary refuge from continuing danger. Depending on the background and context of the person, different authorities (police, family members, counselors, church leaders) may be seen as the appropriate "authorities" for changing male conceptions of entitlement with regard to their social roles.

A social–psychological analysis that conceptually separates the masculine gender role from other roles such as husband also helps to clarify the link among diverse forms of violence. Sexual harassment can be viewed as an assertion of a masculine gender role. Through legal mandates, some male privileges (including access to women's bodies) are now prohibited from being linked to employer roles (although, as evidenced by the pervasiveness of sexual harassment, many men clearly have yet to get this message).

Nonetheless, as studies of sexual harassment in nontraditional occupations have documented (e.g., Swerdlow, 1989), even when men recognize women as competent co-workers and accept their right to be in the workplace, they continue to sexually harass them to enforce masculine gender role norms of male supremacy. Thus, the development of programs to re-educate men about the limits of male rights and privileges in the masculine gender role as well as in employer and work roles is needed if sexual harassment is to be eliminated in workplace.

Biological Factors

Biological factors clearly contribute to the expression and form of violence toward women. The fact that men, on the average, are larger and physically stronger than women means that the same acts (e.g., slapping or shoving) have very different meanings, levels of threat, and physical consequences for victims. Aggression is self-reinforcing, and boys who are physically larger than other children may be more likely to learn to use aggressive acts to achieve their ends. Physiological mechanisms are involved in the development and expression of anger, as well as in the reinforcement properties of violence in response to feelings of anger. Without early and effective intervention, the aggressive acts of boys may ultimately become shaped and directed towards women, who are often viewed as legitimate targets in our culture.

Some researchers have even attempted to apply sociobiological approaches to violent acts, arguing that historically such acts (particularly rape) may have yielded reproductive advantages for violent men (see Ellis, 1989). We have not attempted to review such theorizing here, because it cannot be proven one way or another. Nor do we believe that it would shed light on the mechanisms that promote and maintain violent acts against women. Further, given the integral part that cognitive processes play in the development and expression of human emotions, work based on other species that have not developed the higher brain centers that govern conscious behavior in human beings is of limited usefulness.

The variability in prevalence, incidence, and forms of violence toward women across cultures, the premeditation that is clearly part of many violent acts, and the obvious control that violent men often use to manage their violence (for example, many violent men avoid beating a woman's face so that she can go to work, and, in most instances, they stop short of hurting her so badly that she is killed or needs to be hospitalized) demonstrate the role that cognitions and behavioral contingencies play in the expression and perpetration of violence. Whatever its historical or evolutionary origins, male violence toward women is clearly a learned behavior (Lore & Schultz, 1993) and it is most likely that prevention and intervention approaches that are both effective and ethical will be based on cognitive social-learning theory, not evolutionary theory.

VICTIM ATTRIBUTES

Some investigators have focused on characteristics of the victim, asserting that certain women are more likely to be raped, battered, or harassed than others. Early work on rape and violence between adult partners focused primarily on women who had sought special services. Presenting characteristics or symptomatology of these women *posttrauma* were proposed by some theoreticians as the cause of the violence against them (e.g., Kleckner, 1978; Schultz, 1960; Shaniness, 1977; Snell, Rosenwald & Roby, 1964; cf. Symonds, 1979; Walker, 1979).

Unfortunately, such research all too often failed to recognize the interaction of the person with the situation and confused correlation with causation, as empirical investigations over a wide range of samples have shown. In particular, psychological theories that attempted to explain why a particular woman is raped, battered, or harassed, by pointing to personal attributes such as motivation ("she asked for it") or masochism ("she liked it") have been discredited by research that documents women's attempts to prevent and avoid these acts.

Using comparisons of rape victims to "resistors" (i.e., victims of attempted rape) and to nonvictims, researchers have suggested that women who are raped are less assertive, less socially poised, and more self-identified with traditional notions of femininity than those who successfully thwarted a rape (Myers, Templar, & Brown, 1984; Selkin, 1978). However, these conclusions have been challenged on methodological grounds (Wieder, 1985). For example, Myers et al. (1984) employed recruitment techniques for their rape victims and nonvictimized women that may have biased the samples in exactly the direction of the differences that were found. In contrast, research that used the same procedure for selecting victims as well as non-victims found no differences in personality characteristics among these groups (Koss, 1985). The relative predictive powers of three groups of vic-tim risk factors for rape were compared in a national sample of college women by Koss and Dinero (1989b). The results offered no support for assertions that some women are uniquely vulnerable to rape by virtue of their personality characteristics, assertiveness, or degree of identification with feminine stereotyped behavior. A risk profile did emerge, but it applied to only 10% of the women. However, among this group the chances of being raped were twice as high as among women without the profile. Risk factors associated with elevated rape rates included a background of childhood sex-ual abuse, liberal sexual attitudes, and higher-than-average alcohol use and number of sexual partners. In interpreting these results, it is important to recognize that the latter three risk factors are considered traumatic after-effects of sexual abuse.

Victim characteristics have also been examined in studies of "rape avoidance." This work compares the resistance strategies of women who were raped with those used by women who experienced an attempted rape that was aborted before penetration took place. Studies of this type have consistently reported that active strategies such as screaming, fleeing, or physically struggling are associated with higher rates of rape avoidance (Bart, 1981; Javorek, 1979; Levine-MacCombie & Koss, 1986; Quinsey & Upfold, 1985; Siegel, Sorenson, Golding, Burnam, & Stein, 1989; Ullman & Knight, 1992). However, these researchers have all cautioned that it is the offender's behavior that largely determines the outcome of a sexual assault, not the victim's resistance (indeed, whether a woman uses the strategies of screaming and running may be based on the characteristics of the offender). Some studies have suggested that victims are more likely to be injured if they resist (Prentky, Burgess, & Carter, 1986; Ruback & Ivie, 1988). Critics charge that these studies have confounded the temporal sequence of events.

Most often the injuries preceded the victim's resistance rather than followed it (Quinsey & Upfold, 1985).

The concept of women's masochism, which has been used most often to explain women's responses to battering, continues to persist despite extensive critique (McHugh, Frieze, & Browne, 1993; Wardell, Gillespie & Leffler, 1983; Yllö & Bograd, 1988). The fact that many battered women express love for their husbands has been taken as evidence of their masochism (Walker, 1983). But examination of the development of relationships between battered women and their intimates discredits this explanation. Using masochistic personality to explain the behavior of battered women does not recognize the context of abuse for battered women and confuses the causes and consequences of abuse.

In fact, the attachment of battered women to their husbands typically reflects bonds that were well-established before their husbands became violent (Browne, 1987). Research suggests that more than three out of four women in long-term battering relationships were not battered until *after* they made a major commitment to or married their partners (Bowker, 1983; Dobash & Dobash, 1978; Mason & Blankenship, 1987; Pagelow, 1981). It is after such a commitment that their loved ones' expressions of interest and affection become more possessive and controlling, and the women become more socially isolated. The first act of violence is an "evolution" of these idealized romantic interactions, occurring when the women are committed and cut off from alternative sources of support (Browne, 1987; McHugh, Frieze, & Browne, 1993; Pagelow, 1984; Walker, 1979, 1984).

Labeling battered women as masochistic appears to be a prime example of what social psychologists call "fundamental attribution error" (Ross, L., 1977). That is, battered women's behaviors are inappropriately attributed to their intrapersonal characteristics rather than to situational causes. To attribute the cause of women's behavior to women's personality is to ignore strong gender-role norms to "stand by your man," live up to marital role obligations, and sacrifice one's needs for others. Women remain in abusive relationships for many situational reasons, including lack of alternatives, fear of disapproval from family or friends, concern about losing their children, and fear of retaliation by the violent partner (Browne, 1987; Frieze & Browne, 1989; Gelles, 1976; McHugh, Frieze, & Browne, 1993).

Some psychiatrists and psychologists have promoted a distorted view of the behavior of battered women by characterizing women in abusive relationships as having disordered personalities (Gellman, Koffman, Jones, & Stone, 1984; Palau, 1981). The proposed diagnosis of "self-defeating personality disorder" (initially termed "masochistic personality disorder"), which had originally been slated for inclusion in the revision of the American Psychiatric Association's *Diagnostic and Statistical Manual of Mental Disorders*, would likely have perpetuated this uninformed conceptualization of battered women (Rosewater, 1988). Protest to this effect was probably a key factor in the exclusion of the Self-defeating Personality Disorder from the *DSM-IV*.

A focus on ascertaining victim characteristics that might predict violence has persisted despite the lack of usefulness of the approach. For example, in their comprehensive review of 52 studies that included appropriate comparison groups conducted over a 15-year period, Hotaling and Sugarman (1986) found that only one of 97 potential risk markers for husband to wife violence—that of witnessing parental violence as a child or adolescent—was consistently associated with being the victim of physical aggression by a male partner. (This was also the one factor that characterized both abused women and their assailants.) Variables not found to be consistently related to being assaulted by a male partner included income or education level, being a full-time housewife, passivity, hostility, personality integration, self-esteem, alcohol use, or the use of violence toward children. As Hotaling and Sugarman noted, there is no empirical evidence "that the statuses a woman occupies, the roles she performs, the behavior she engages in, her demographic profile or her personality characteristics consistently influence her chances of intimate victimization" (p. 118). Characteristics of the man with whom the woman was involved are better predictors of a woman's risk of becoming a victim of partner abuse than are the characteristics of the woman herself. Hotaling and Sugarman concluded that "the most influential victim precipitant is being female. The victimization of women may be better understood as the outcome of male behavior" (p. 118).

In clinical studies, having a background of child sexual molestation typically does not distinguish victims of partner abuse from women who have not been abused by their partners, possibly because the overall level of childhood sexual abuse in clinical populations is so high. Community-based studies, however, suggest that being sexually abused as a child is associated with increased risk for revictimization by a range of assailants, including intimate partners, later in life (Browne & Finkelhor, 1986; Wyatt, Guthrie, & Notgrass, 1992). For example, in Russell's (1986) rigorous random-sample study, 33% to 68% of child sexual molestation survivors later experienced a rape (the proportion depending on the seriousness of the childhood abuse they suffered), compared with 17% of women who were not child victims. Victims of child sexual abuse are also more likely to be physically abused by husbands or other adult partners than are women without these childhood experiences (Briere, 1989; Russell, 1986). Clinicians speculate that this may be due to the lack of opportunity to develop adequate protective mechanisms (or the concept that the body *can* be protected), combined with other posttrauma effects such as difficulty screening situations or people for danger, fatalism related to depression or hopelessness, and traumatized responses to the threat of danger, ranging from denial and psychic numbing to dissociation (Leibowitz, Harvey, & Herman, 1993; Herman, 1992).

CONCLUSION

In summary, understanding behaviors and cognitive processes that promote and maintain violence and shape individual responses to it requires sophistication in theory and method. If psychological knowledge about violence is to advance, psychologists must go beyond studies that catalogue personal attributes of perpetrators and victims and develop more complex approaches that seek to understand the individual's interaction with his or her environments. The key role of socialization agents, including the family, peers, and the media in transmitting and perpetuating violence against women, suggests that violent behaviors are learned from multiple sources in our culture, and thus may be difficult to change. However, it also suggests that multiple points of intervention exist for breaking the cycle of violence.

PART 2

Violence At Home

3

The Prevalence
of Intimate Violence

Violent victimization historically has been thought about in terms of assaults occurring between nonromantic acquaintances and strangers. Yet *women's greatest risk of assault is from their intimates, particularly male partners.* In nationally representative surveys conducted a decade apart, more than 25% of the couples studied reported at least one incident of physical aggression occurring during the course of their relationships (Straus & Gelles, 1990; Straus, Gelles, & Steinmetz, 1980). We now know that women are more likely to be attacked, raped, injured, or killed by current or former male partners than by any other type of assailant (Browne & Williams, 1989, 1993; Finkelhor & Yllö, 1985; Langan & Innes, 1986; Lentzner & DeBerry, 1980; Russell, 1982a).

The repetition and severity of this aggression is facilitated by the fact that intimates are readily available, the amount of time at risk is high, and assaults can be carried out in private. Aggravated assault against a wife or girlfriend is also a relatively low-risk behavior for a perpetrator in terms of identification or sanctions (Gillespie, 1989). Estimates based on probability samples suggest that a minimum of 2 million women are severely assaulted by male partners each year in the United States (Straus & Gelles, 1990; Straus et al., 1980) and that between 21% and 34% of all women will be physically assaulted by an intimate male during adulthood (Frieze, Knoble, Washburn, & Zomnir, 1980; Russell, 1982a).

Early writings on violence in marital or dating relationships focused primarily on women victims of assault who sought special services (Kleckner, 1978; Schultz, 1960; Shainess, 1977; Snell, Rosenwald, & Robey, 1964). Interpreted without regard to the general pervasiveness of male violence toward women, information about the alleged characteristics of battered women quickly became biased toward the small proportion of victims who sought psychological or other help. Although pioneering work in the late 1970s and early 1980s explicated the broader context of male violence against female intimates (e.g., Martin, 1976; Russell, 1982a; Walker, 1979), psychologists continue to risk pathologizing victims and failing to identify potential danger when we neglect to integrate what is known about assaults by intimate partners with the rich literature on human responses to trauma.

Aggressive acts reported by women in epidemiologic studies range from being slapped, punched, kicked, or thrown, to being scalded, cut, choked, smothered, or bitten. In relationships in which ongoing violence exists, assaultive episodes often involve a *combination* of assaultive acts, verbal abuse, sexual aggression, and threats (Browne, 1987; Pagelow, 1984; Walker, 1984). Based on studies of both dating and marital aggression, the onset of ongoing violence often does not occur until the point of major commitment to the partner. For example, retrospective studies on patterns of physical assaults in marital relationships found that, *for 73% to 85% of abused wives,* the onset of violence did not occur until after they had married the abuser (Bowker, 1983; Dobash & Dobash, 1978; Pagelow, 1981; Rosenbaum & O'Leary, 1981; see Cate, Henton, Koval, Christopher, & Lloyd, 1982; Henton, Cate, Koval, Lloyd, & Christopher, 1983; Laner & Thompson, 1982; and Makepeace, 1981 for findings on dating violence). Once assaultive behavior occurs in a relationship, it often becomes chronic (Cascardi & O'Leary, 1992; Straus et al., 1980; Walker, 1984). On the basis of a study of more than 6,000 randomly selected households, Straus (1990b) noted, "when an assault by a husband occurs, it is not usually an isolated instance. In fact, it tends to be a recurrent feature of the relationship" (p. 9).

PREVALENCE OF PHYSICAL AGGRESSION

National Samples

The National Family Violence Survey and the National Crime Survey are the major sources of national estimates on family violence in the United States. The first National Family Violence Survey, conducted in the summer of 1975, involved hour-long, face-to-face interviews with married couples from more than 2,000 randomly selected homes about methods of resolving conflicts among family members (Straus et al., 1980). The survey included questions about behaviors that ranged from positive resolution strategies (e.g., discussed the issue calmly) to severe levels of aggression (e.g., beat up, threatened with or used a knife or gun). Of those interviewed, 28% reported at least one instance of physical assault during their current relationship; 16% reported at least one aggressive incident in the year before the survey. In a follow-up survey conducted in the summer of 1985, using 30-minute telephone interviews with more than 6,000 randomly selected households, Straus and Gelles (1990) reported that *nearly one out of every eight husbands* had carried out one or more acts of physical aggression against their wives during the survey year. More than three out of every 100, or 1.8 million women, were severely assaulted during the 12 months that preceded the survey. That is to say they were punched, kicked, choked, hit with an object, beaten up, threatened with a knife or a gun, or had a knife or gun used on them. In a nationwide study of courtship violence, which questioned 2,602 college women at 32 colleges and universities, it was reported that 32% had experienced physical aggression from a date or other intimate partner (White & Koss, 1991).

City Samples

More intensive interviewing strategies (e.g., in-person interviews with detailed and comprehensive protocols) were used by researchers in city studies during the late 1970s to investigate the lifetime prevalence of violence against women in intimate relationships. In a rigorous empirical inquiry that laid the foundation for much of the subsequent research on marital rape, Russell (1982a) interviewed a random sample of 930 women in San Francisco about their lifetime experiences with physical and sexual violence. Of that sample, 21% who had been or were currently married reported at least one occasion of physical violence against them by male partners (Russell, 1982b). In a study based in Pittsburgh, Frieze et al. (1980) interviewed a nonrandom sample of 137 women who had experienced physical assault from a male partner. Their subjects were drawn from battered women's shelters, lists of women filing legal actions against their husbands, and volunteers who responded to advertisements. In attempting to match the abused sample with a comparison group of women living in the same neighborhoods, Frieze and her colleagues found that 34% of the control group had also been assaulted by an intimate partner.

Based on the last 17 years of empirical inquiry, experts now estimate that as many as *4 million women experience severe or life-threatening assault from a male partner in an average 12-month period in the United States;* and that *one in every three women* will experience at least one physical assault by an intimate partner during adulthood. Therefore, to facilitate the physical and psychological well-being of women, social and mental health policies *must* respond to the realities of this aggression in more direct and effective ways.

Sexual Aggression within Marital Relationships

Marital Rape

Like physical assault, most sexual assault of women is perpetrated by male intimates. This finding is based on empirical studies during the last 15 years that have compared incidences of sexual aggression toward women by intimate partners with that by acquaintances or strangers (Finkelhor & Yllö, 1985; National Victims Center, 1992; Russell, 1982a). In her rigorous random sample study of 930 women 18 years and older, Russell (1982a), who used a conservative definition of rape, reported that 14% of ever-married women had been raped by a husband or ex-husband at least once—more than twice as many as were sexually assaulted by acquaintances or strangers. Russell noted that even this figure represents a significant underestimate. Interviewers did not ask about forced oral, anal, or digital sex unless respondents interpreted sexual assault in this way; however, such behaviors are now included in the reformed rape statutes in many states, and forced anal sex is one of the most commonly reported types of sexual attack in violent marriages (Koss & Harvey, 1991; Walker, 1984). Similarly, in a representative sample of 326 women in Boston, Finkelhor, and Yllö (1985) found that 10% of women cohabiting with a spouse or other intimate male partner reported at least one sexual assault occurring in that relationship; half of those respondents had been sexually assaulted at least 20 times by that partner. Again, more than twice as many women reported being raped by husbands as by strangers.

In an attempt to facilitate disclosure, researchers studying marital rape have typically avoided the term "rape" and instead asked respondents if they were ever sexually assaulted by their spouse or partner (Fagan, Friedman, Wexler, & Lewis, 1984), or if they were "forced to have sex" with their partner (Walker, 1984). Some studies ask about any "unwanted sexual experiences or having sex in response to force or the threat of force or violence" (Finkelhor & Yllö, 1983). Pagelow (1984) defined rape as "unwanted sexual contact accomplished by force, intimidation, or coercion that results in vaginal, anal, or oral sexual intercourse or penetration" (p. 419). Russell's (1982a) more conservative definition of rape included forced oral and anal sex only if this information was volunteered by the respondent, but excluded sexual fondling. Such diversity in item construction must be kept in mind when reviewing study results.

Patterns of Sexual Aggression

Sexually abusive acts reported in in-depth studies of violent relationships include the insertion of objects into the woman's vagina, forced anal or oral sex, bondage, other forms of severe physical violence during sex (such as biting, choking, pinching, smothering, or head-banging), and forced sex with others (Walker, 1984). Such reports are supported by other research findings that indicated (again, contrary to the usual assumption that violence perpetrated by strangers is more serious than violence occurring at home) that the *closer* the relationship between rapist and victim, the greater the level of violence in sexual assaults (Pagelow, 1984). Research on aggression by male partners indicates that the most violent episodes often include sexual as well as physical attack, and that battered women who are sexually assaulted by their partners typically experience more severe nonsexual attacks than other abused women (Bowker, 1983; Browne, 1987; Frieze, 1983; Shields & Hanneke, 1983; Walker, 1984). In severely abusive relationships, violent, forcible sexual assault may occur as often as several times a month (Browne, 1987).

Although marital rape is a neglected topic in discussions of both family violence and violence against women, it is an integral part of the patterns of partner abuse (Browne, 1987; Fagan et al., 1984; Frieze, 1983; Pagelow, 1984; Russell, 1982a, 1990; Walker, 1984). Marital rape has been reported in relationships in which no other forms of physical assault occur. However, women whose husbands are physically assaultive in other ways are particularly likely to become the victims of marital rape (Frieze, 1983; Russell, 1982a, 1990). In empirical studies that used detailed questions and face-to-face interviews, *sexual assault has been reported by 34% to 59% of women who have also been nonsexually assaulted by their partners*: 34% of women victims in Frieze et al.'s (1980) volunteer community sample, 37% in Pagelow's (1981) volunteer sample of abused women from shelters and the community, 46% in Shields and Hanneke's (1983) sample of the wives of violent men obtained through agency referrals, and 59% in Walker's (1984) volunteer sample of women responding to public service advertisements and referred from area medical and mental health facilities.

Sexual abuse is an extremely serious form of marital violence, one that can inflict an intense level of physical pain over a long period of time. Sexual abuse can cause a wide range of injuries, from superficial bruises and tearing to serious internal injuries and scarring (Koss & Heslet, 1992). Victims of rape by intimates suffer many of the same posttrauma reactions as other rape victims and are likely to exhibit particularly severe aftereffects, both emotional and physical, including very severe depression and suicidality (Browne, 1987; Pagelow, 1984; Walker, 1984). Repeated and forcible sexual assault also frequently forms a part of the abuse history preceding homicide incidents in which women kill their abusive mates (Browne, 1987; Walker, 1984). As the review on general reactions to trauma indicates, both nonsexual physical assault and sexual attacks have predictable and negative psychological aftereffects. For women who experience *both* of these forms of violence in an intimate relationship, and especially for those who experience them repeatedly, the risk of serious psychological harm is great (Dutton, 1992a; Herman, 1992; Russell, 1982a).

Moreover, except for child sexual molestation, this type of violence is least likely to be reported by women victims because of humiliation, fear that they will not be believed or will be devalued for having participated in such sexual activity, and belief that forcible sexual relations are the right of a husband or other male partner. Even if sexual assault does become known, societal sanctions—especially against husbands—are almost unknown, despite marital rape laws in more than 35 states. The effect that violent sexual assault by an intimate has on a woman's perception of self, of alternatives, of entrapment, and of danger cannot be overestimated. As one woman noted in describing her husband's sexual attacks, "It was as though he wanted to annihilate me. More than the slapping, or the kicks...as though he wanted to tear me apart from the inside out and simply leave nothing there" (Browne, 1987, p. 103).

Violence in Nonmarital Relationships

The prevalence of physical violence within marital relationships has led some researchers to call the marriage license a hitting license (e.g., Straus et al., 1980). Yet some studies have suggested that dating or cohabiting couples may have even *higher* prevalence rates of physical assault than couples who are married (Ellis, 1989). For example, Yllö and Straus (1981), who used nationally representative data from the 1975 Family Violence Survey, found higher rates of partner aggression among cohabiting couples than among married couples. Similarly, Stets and Straus (1989), using data from the 1985 Family Violence Survey as well as responses from a probability sample of 526 students at a midwestern university, reported a higher level of assault between cohabitants and dating couples than between individuals who were married. A 1983 study based on a national probability sample of young adults aged 18 to 24 ($n = 1,725$) that used similar measures to the Family Violence Surveys found rates nearly three times higher than those found by

Straus and his colleagues (Elliott, Huizinga, & Morse, 1986). Empirical studies also consistently find more *severely violent* physical aggression by men
toward their *estranged* partners (separated or divorced) than in intact marital or cohabitant relationships (Ellis, 1989; Lentzner & DeBerry, 1980).

Findings of violence between unmarried intimates are only now
becoming established in the social science literature (e.g., Pirog-Good &
Stets, 1989), although interpreting these findings can be problematic.
Studies of violence between nonmarried couples are limited almost exclusively to students in high school and college. Thus, almost nothing is known
about persons between the ages of 14 to 22 who are not attending school, or
who are past college age and are dating or living with intimate partners.
Moreover, most college and high school samples are convenience samples
and, thus, their representativeness of those populations or of the general
population is unknown. Further, as noted by Sugarman and Hotaling
(1989), many studies of courtship violence fail to disaggregate their data into
victim/offender or gender-based categories or to incorporate questions on
sexual and forcible sexual assault, making meaningful interpretations even
more difficult (cf. Miller & Simpson, 1991).

Homicide Trends

Reported levels of both nonsexual and sexual physical violence against
women by nonmarital intimate partners have dramatically increased during
the past 15 years (Koss, Gidycz, & Wisniewski, 1987; Koss & Harvey, 1991).
Although some of this increase is undoubtedly due to a greater sensitivity to
the issue, *severe and lethal* violence against nonmarried women partners
does seem to have actually increased. For example, whereas the rate of
homicides by unmarried women against their male partners varied nonsys-
tematically during the 12 years from 1976 through 1987, the rate of unmarried women being killed by their male partners increased quite sharply
(Browne & Williams, 1993). Indeed, an increase in the total rates of men
who killed female partners during this 12-year period was due to this sharp
rise in men killing their current or past girlfriends, and the trend continues.

At first glance, dating or cohabiting situations may appear to be more
open than marital relationships (i.e., they are easier to leave), and thus it

may seem as though partners are less likely to be trapped in abusive or dangerous situations than those in more committed relationships. Women in these relationships may perceive greater latitude in staying or leaving and not experience as heightened a sense of entrapment as women in more formal relationships or women who share family responsibilities with a partner. However, this very openness may threaten the perceived power of men in such relationships. In discussing the high prevalence of violence by men against dating partners, Browne and Williams (1993) speculated that—although unmarried relationships may be more open than marital ones—this very "openess" may simultaneously intensify the motivation for men to use violence with their female partners to prevent or retaliate against abandonment.

A lack of interventions targeted at dating and cohabiting couples also may contribute to the greater risk of severe and lethal violence. Violence in dating relationships traditionally has been considered relatively nonserious, with few services or remedies designed specifically to address it. For example, in practice, domestic violence legislation is focused primarily on addressing problems of safety and access for those who are married or in common-law relationships. Only a few states extend orders of protection and other provisions to women in dating relationships. Moreover, services that are available for nonmarried couples exist primarily on high school and college campuses. As such, this structure fails to reach a significant proportion of couples who are not married and disproportionately excludes the poor. Thus, it is possible that the relationship types with the highest risk for violence—and lethal violence—are the ones least served by current societal interventions.

NEGLECTED ISSUES: PREGNANCY AND ETHNICITY

Nationally randomized samples now document the diverse ethnic, socioeconomic, and psychosocial backgrounds of women who experience partner violence (Cazenave & Straus, 1990). Although consistent evidence in probability samples and community surveys shows that younger women and women living in poverty are more at risk for both nonmarital and marital violence (Pagelow, 1984; Russell, 1982a), relationships among risk variables are complex. The following discussion will focus primarily on partner violence against pregnant women and ethnic minority women—groups that have been almost completely neglected in the study of assaults by male intimates.

Minority women and women living in poverty, as a group, are at especially high risk for all types of violence—particularly severe and life-threatening assaults (Belle, 1990; Merry, 1981; Steele et al., 1982). For example, for the years of 1976 through 1984, the homicide victimization rate for African-American women exceeded not only that for Caucasian women but for Caucasian *men* as well (O'Carroll & Mercy, 1986). For women, a lack of economic resources can be devastating to their ability to alter their environments or live in safety. In many areas, women living in poverty reside in communities in which the levels of assault across all relationship categories are quite high. In all situations of poverty, opportunities for improving living conditions or escaping threatening situations may be severely limited by financial and other resources. Further, the level of protective or supportive services is typically low.

Pregnant Women

It is not clear whether the incidence of marital violence increases during an abused wife's pregnancy; however, we know that it does not cease. In the 1985 National Family Violence Survey of a representative sample, *154 of every 1,000 pregnant women* were assaulted by their mates during the first four months of pregnancy, and *170 per 1,000 women* were assaulted during the fifth through the ninth month (Gelles, 1988). Similarly, in a clinical study of 691 pregnant women, 17% of the sample reported physical and sexual abuse during pregnancy (McFarlane, Parker, Soeken, & Bullock, 1992). Estimates are much higher in retrospective studies of women who have been physically assaulted by their partners. For example, in Walker's (1984) study of 432 abused women, 59% had been physically assaulted during their first pregnancy. Of those becoming pregnant a second time, 63% were assaulted during that pregnancy. Of those becoming pregnant a third time, 55% were assaulted (Walker, 1984). Medical sources suggest that up to 37% of obstetric patients across class, race, and educational lines are physically attacked by a male intimate sometime during the three trimesters (e.g., Helton, McFarlane, & Anderson, 1987a).

Women who are pregnant and involved with a violent partner face the risk of especially severe outcomes. Pregnancy is a particularly high-risk time for injury for a woman (Saltzman, 1990). Advanced stages of pregnancy leave a woman less able to avoid blows or escape attacks and more at risk for secondary injuries to herself as well as to the fetus as a result of assault (Helton, McFarlane, & Anderson, 1987a, 1987b; McFarlane et al., 1992). Moreover, clinical reports indicate that assaults by male partners during pregnancy are frequently related to jealousy or anxiety about the upcoming birth, and that physically assaultive actions such as blows or kicks are often directed toward the abdomen (McFarlane et al., 1992). Such assaults can result in placental separation, hemorrhage, bruising, fetal fractures, rupture of the uterus, liver, or spleen, preterm labor, miscarriages, and stillbirths (Saltzman, 1990; see also Koss & Heslet, 1992).

Although few specific studies have been done on the birth outcomes of women who were abused while pregnant, physical violence during pregnancy has been linked to low birth weight in newborns and to failure to thrive (e.g., Bullock & McFarlane, 1989). Secondary causes of poor birth outcomes for women who are the victims of violence at home include social isolation, diminished personal and social support, inadequate access to prenatal care and other services, inadequate maternal nutrition, and concentration of injury on the reproductive organ systems (Helton et al., 1987a, 1987b; Newberger, Lieberman, Yllö, Gary, & Schechter, 1990; Sorenson, Stein, Siegel, Golding, & Burnam, 1987).

African–American Women

Little research is available on domestic violence in ethnic minority populations. Research has tended to look at African–American women or Hispanic women as they compare to Caucasian women. There has been even less information available on Asian–American or Native American women. Methodological problems have made it difficult to discern clear difference among racial groups. These methodological problems include the use of clinical samples, data from official police and agency reports, and the failure to control for social class (Lockhart, 1985). Few studies have attempted to examine violence between intimate partners within different cultures to understand the phenomenon better in a particular group or to understand the factors that may differentially impact that specific ethnic group.

In general, research based on nationally representative samples indicates that *race alone does not distinguish violent and nonviolent couples* (Coley & Beckett, 1988). Findings from national probability samples that compare African Americans with Caucasians have been inconsistent: They show either more abuse, equal rates of, or less abuse. However, widely held beliefs, that ethnic minority women, especially African–American women, are disproportionately victims or aggressors continues. Much of this "confusion" follows from results of one of the first nationally representative studies on wife abuse conducted in 1972 by Straus, Gelles, and Steinmetz (1980). They reported that rates of partner assault were higher among African–American than Caucasian couples. Lockhart (1980) noted that because the Straus, Gelles, and Steinmetz (1980) study was, for a long time, considered to contain the most current and representative data available, the results were often cited as an established fact. Subsequent analyses of those same data (Cazenave & Straus, 1979), that controlled for race and other factors such as family income and husband's occupation, revealed that, of the four family income groups examined, African Americans had *lower* rates of physical assaults between partners than Caucasians in three of the four categories (the two highest income groups and the lowest income group). Only in the $6,000–$12,000 income range was a higher incidence of assault against wives found among African–American than Caucasian couples.

Even these results have been questioned, however, because more than 40% of the sample's African–American couples were in that income range. This overrepresentation of African–American couples with family incomes between $6,000 and $12,000 raises the question of whether the two racial groups were comparable across class backgrounds, even with social class controlled. Another nationally representative study, the National Crime Survey of U.S. Households—which severely underestimates violence between adult parners—found no significant differences in the incidence of partner assault among African Americans and Caucasians (Gaquin, 1977–1978).

Close involvement with family and friends has been found to have a mediating effect on assaults against women in African–American families. In analyzing data from the National Family Violence Survey, Cazaneve and Straus (1979) found less assault of women among African–American couples when the couple was part of a strong network of family and friends. Although the same relationship was not found for Caucasians, the length of time the couple lived in the neighborhood and the presence of extended family members in the home were associated with substantially lower levels of wife assault in African–American couples.

In one of the few within-group studies to be conducted, Lockhart and White (1989) interviewed 155 African–American women from a range of social classes who were legally married to or cohabiting with their partners. Of this sample, 35% reported physical assaults occurring in their relationships. Social class was an important risk factor: A significantly smaller proportion of upper-class African–American women reported assaults (18%) than did middle-class or lower-class African–American women (46% and 44%, respectively). However, upper-class women who were physically attacked reported a higher median number of occurrences per year (5.8) than did middle-class (2.5) or lower-class (3.8) women who were assaulted. As with Caucasian populations, effects of witnessing violence in childhood appeared to increase African–American women's risk of experiencing violence by adult male partners. Lockhart and White (1989) reported that women whose fathers assaulted their mothers were more likely to report victimization themselves than respondents whose own marriages were discordant but whose parents' marriages were free from violence.

Although there seems to be little difference between African–American and Caucasian women in terms of the incidence of partner violence, levels of lethal violence are much higher in African–American couple relationships (Stark, 1990). Speculations about the high levels of severe and lethal violence include secondary effects of oppression by the dominant society, the lack of resources or other alternatives available to assaulted and threatened African–American women, and the lack of compelling reasons to refrain from violence for men for whom few opportunities or rewards for more constructive behaviors are available (e.g., Harvey, 1986; Hawkins,

1986). Beliefs that African Americans are "just violent people" seriously affect the responsiveness of formal help sources, including (a) how victims and perpetrators are treated by the police, (b) how seriously partner assaults are viewed, (c) how victims are counseled, (d) how medical and social service personnel treat and refer victims and perpetrators, and (e) the proportion of early interventions and other resources devoted to addressing violence within African–American communities. As Hawkins (1987) noted, the risk of homicide increases proportionately with the denial of protection against assault. Thus, the *expectation* that African Americans will be more violent than the Caucasian majority often becomes self-fulfilling.

In discussing the effects of poverty on minority women's risk of violence, Harvey (1986) observed that poor African–American women may be "virtually imprisoned in settings where they are most likely to be victimized and where the personal and institutional safeguards that they would be privy to in other places may not exist" (p. 168). He further suggested that, for some women, the increased risk of violence may be in part a "scapegoat effect, in which the black female becomes the repository of the anger and frustration of the black male" in American society (p. 167; see also Coley & Beckett, 1988). Similarly, Hawkins (1986) linked what Rose (1978) called the "geography of despair"—the sense of helplessness and unjust entrapment, coupled with a lack of alternatives to lives constricted by poverty and danger—to the high likelihood of violence in some minority communities.

Hispanic Women

Little research has been conducted specifically on physical violence between adult partners in Hispanic–American populations. Again, within-group analyses are critically needed. As Torres (1991) pointed out, Hispanics in the United States originate from at least 32 countries and—although they often share common traditions, religious beliefs, and language—there are significant cultural differences. In one of the few comparative analyses based on Epidemiological Catchment Area survey data for Los Angeles, Sorenson and Telles (1991) found no significant differences in physical violence toward a spouse or other intimate adult partner between Mexican–American and Caucasian couples. However, Mexican-*born* Mexican Americans had significantly *lower* rates of partner violence than either Caucasians or U.S.-born Mexican Americans.

In secondary data analyses based on information from 5,708 residents in shelters for abused women, Gondolf, Fisher, and McFerron (1988) found no differences in the frequency with which Hispanic, African–American, and Caucasian women were assaulted by their abusive mates. Of the total sample, 42% had been physically assaulted at least once a week. Differences were found in threats or actual use of weapons by the abusive partners, with 48% of African–American women reporting having had a weapon used against them, compared with 39% of Hispanic and Caucasian women. However, Hispanic women reported the longest *duration* of abuse: 32% had been abused for more than five years, compared with 21% of African–American and Caucasian women who reported abuse over that period of time. Hispanic women tended to marry at a younger age, have larger families, and stay in their relationships. Maybe in part because of this, they tended to be poorer and to have obtained less education than the other two groups. This, and their larger families, significantly inhibited their ability to establish a life apart from the abuser.

These findings have been supported by the work of Torres (1991), who interviewed 25 Mexican–American and 25 Caucasian women 18 years and older who had been physically assaulted by their husbands at least twice and who had resided in shelters for abused women. Whereas 56% of the Mexican–American women had been in their present relationships for seven or more years, only 16% of the Caucasian women had been in their relationships for that long. Mexican–American women exhibited a more tolerant attitude toward wife abuse than did the Caucasian women. They also perceived physically assaultive incidents committed either once or on a regular basis as less serious than Caucasian respondents did. Using the Survey of Family Violence Scale (Teske & Parker, 1982), Torres found that Caucasian women considered such actions as being constrained against their will, being slapped, having things thrown at them, and being pushed, shoved, or grabbed as physical abuse. Mexican–American women, on the contrary, did not consider such actions abusive.

Torres (1987) noted that Catholicism—the predominant religious affiliation of Hispanics—considers the maintenance of the family unit to be of primary importance, often more important than women's personal well-being, and this has an effect on many Hispanic women's responses to violence by husbands. Immigrant status and little knowledge of the English language also play an important part in the reactions of some Hispanic–American women (as well as other minority group) facing partner violence at home (Sorenson & Telles, 1991). Women residing in the country without legal documents are particularly inhibited from seeking help, as identification could lead to arrest and deportation. Immigrant women also may be in the country without friends or family who might otherwise provide important sources of protection and psychological or financial support.

Native American Women

Information on male violence against Native American women comes primarily from anecdotal data and descriptions of tribal reactions and mores. Allen (1990) warned that physical violence against women is at frightening levels throughout Native American populations. However, with few exceptions, tribal councils and official agencies are unwilling to discuss or document the extent of the problem. Allen contended that abuse of Native American women and children by Native American men was almost unknown until the introduction of alcohol and of patriarchal beliefs that sanction subservience of women to men. Before the influence of Westernization, Native Americans feared violations against women because respect for women was tied to their beliefs about women's powers over life and death. Men who assaulted women within the tribe were considered to be mad or "in the power of evil spirits" (p. 14). Duran, Guillory, and Tingley (unpublished) stressed the relationship among the extreme subjugation of Native Americans within U.S. society, internalized hatred, and violence by Native Americans against other Native Americans as a critical variable affecting the high levels of violence within Native American populations.

Asian–American Women

Few systematic studies have been conducted on family violence or on male violence against women in Asian–American populations. Ho's (1990) preliminary analysis of domestic violence in Asian–American communities, which was based on a series of focus groups, is one of the first. Most of the information presented here is based on that study. Ho noted that domestic violence within Asian–American communities has generally been ignored because it rarely comes to the attention of authorities. It is unclear whether this low-reported frequency reflects an actual lower rate of domestic violence among Asian Americans or a lack of use of public assistance. It could also be the result of inadequate mental health services directed toward Asian Americans or other factors. She noted that Asian Americans, like Hispanics, are a diverse group who differ from each other not only in their country of origin, language, history and religions, but also in assimilation and acculturation to Western culture. Their reasons for immigration and experiences of acceptance in the United States also differ. Despite these differences, Ho noted certain commonalities, such as traditional views toward the family, marriage, and sex roles, which affect domestic violence.

Ho (1990) stated that the problem of domestic violence is rooted in the oppression of women in Asian cultures, including the traditions of suffering and perservering, accepting fate, and the traditional hierarchical position of the male as the authority in the family. She noted that the family is viewed as more important than the individual and that the needs of the family take precedence over the individual's. Each member of the family is expected to adhere to the hierarchical roles and comply with familial and social authority to the point of sacrificing her or his own desires and ambitions. Self-restraint and "loss of face" are important issues. Ho found that the extent and acceptance of wife abuse seemed to vary among the different ethnic groups. However, because of pressure to prevent loss of face, Asian Americans tend to hide it within the family and avoid outside intervention. Many Asian Americans consider marital problems to be highly private matters that must remain within the family. An Asian–American woman who does bring her husband's violence to public or official attention often faces complete ostracism and isolation. Divorce is also uncommon among Asian–American families, and separation is not typically considered to be an option by women victims. Ho (1990) noted that the problem of wife abuse among refugees and immigrants is more complex than among second- and third-generation Asian Americans. For example, immigrants speak little or no English, lack traditional resources, and are unfamiliar or unable to use resources in the United States. Second- and third-generation Asian Americans tend to face culturally insensitive and inappropriate intervention and racism. In addition, many Asian Americans continue to hold some traditional values that discourage them from seeking outside help. Language and citizenship barriers may be especially difficult for Asian Americans. Although most police forces, hospital settings, and social service agencies have Spanish-speaking staff, interpreters for other languages are not readily available in most locales. For Asian–American women unable to converse in English who are married to English-speaking partners, their dependence on their husbands—and thus their isolation with abuse and violence—may be virtually complete. Changes in the social and family structure of Asian–American refugees also alter traditional resources available to cope with family problems, including violence. Traditionally, elders and other extended family members intervened in wife abuse. However, separation from the extended family removes one resource for traditional intervention (Ho, 1990).

THE UNDERREPORTING OF INTIMATE VIOLENCE

As the foregoing illustrates, there are many critical gaps in our knowledge base on women's experiences with violence by male intimates. Even those studies that purport to be "representative" of a community or of the nation as a whole leave out data on many groups who potentially experience some of the highest incidence and prevalence rates.

Estimates Based on Probability Samples

In particular, figures based on national surveys of partner violence represent marked underestimates of the problem. This is due, in part, to the faulty construction of survey questions. For example, in the National Crime Surveys, respondents are asked about experiences with criminal victimization, although many individuals do not think of assaults by family members as criminal activities. As a result, such surveys yield much lower estimates than more detailed inquiries would (Fagan & Browne, in press).

All national estimates of the incidence and prevalence of marital violence are derived from self-reports of assaultive behavior or victimization.

These reports are obtained through telephone surveys or in-person interviews with general probability samples of couples at home at the time interviewers call, who are willing to answer the telephone or come to the door for strangers, and who are able and willing to discuss the topic. National surveys typically do not include the very poor, those who do not speak English fluently, those whose lives are especially chaotic, military families who live on base, or individuals who are hospitalized, homeless, institutionalized, or incarcerated in a prison or jail at the time the survey is conducted. Further, estimates are based only on those respondents who are willing to report to an unknown interviewer, even anonymously, acts of violence that they have experienced or perpetrated in their intimate relationships. Respondents may not be alone at the time questions are asked, contributing to further underreporting of aggression, particularly of sexual or severely violent acts.

Single mothers, divorced and separated women, and women in same-sex relationships are also not well-represented in national or regional probability samples. For some women, assaults in couple relationships are perpetrated by female intimates (Kanuha, 1990; Levy, 1991; Lobel, 1986; Renzetti, 1992). Much less is known about the frequency or severity of this type of violence. As noted earlier, theorists disagree as to whether the occurrence of partner violence in same-sex relationships negates theories linking male violence toward female partners with gender and societal roles. Saakvitne and Pearlman (1993) contended that because lesbians are subjected not only to cultural misogyny but also to cultural homophobia, they may internalize this misogyny and project their self-hatred or frustration and discontent onto their partners. Feelings of stigma and the sense that no one will understand are especially severe for women experiencing physical assault in lesbian relationships, contributing to an additional silence shrouding their abuse (Levy, 1991; Lobel, 1986; Renzetti, 1992).

Moreover, omission of vital areas of inquiry from studies of aggression in couple relationships produces partial and often misleading results. Information on sexual assault in intimate relationships is especially difficult to obtain and must be done deliberately and with reference to measures used successfully in previous investigations. Many women do not define even forceful sexual advances as sexual assault when these actions are perpetrated by husbands or other male intimates. For example, some respondents in

Pagelow's (1984) sample reported physical aggression during sexual activity so severe that they were injured or lost consciousness, yet they did not define these as "sexual" assaults. At the end of her study, Russell (1982a) concluded that obtaining "disclosure of unwanted sexual experiences in marriage was more difficult than disclosure of sexual abuse by all other categories of people, including the victims of incestuous abuse" (p. 32).

Findings from Within-Group Studies

The lack of within-group studies relevant to minority groups also leaves a particularly serious gap in our knowledge, because factors may differentially affect specific cultural groups when compared to the dominant culture (Hawkins, 1986, pp. 103–107; Lockhart & White, 1989). Attitudes toward assault, definitions of abusive behaviors, and meanings given to violence differ markedly across culture groups (e.g., Torres, 1991) and are critical areas for scientific inquiry. Those inquiries that have been conducted on violence against women in ethnic minority populations have tended to look at African-American or Hispanic women and compared their experiences to those of Caucasian women, rather than comparing with-in group experiences of individuals. Past studies have also suffered from poor problem conceptualization, faulty data collection procedures, inappropriate data analyses, and ideologically biased interpretations of findings. In one of the only reviews of the literature, Coley and Beckett (1988) found just 17 studies on partner violence against African–American women. These studies variously included both African Americans and Caucasians and either (a) used the race variable as a major focus of the analyses, (b) analyzed only a few variables by race, (c) reported the composition of African Americans in the sample but did not analyze the data by race, or (d) discussed the applicability of findings to the entire sample, even though one-quarter or more of the respondents were African American.

Apart from nationally representative or random samples, much of the research on partner violence has used indirect measures of woman abuse such as the percentages of homicides that involve intimate partners, the number of wife abuse claims handled by family courts, the number of physically assaulted women treated in hospital emergency rooms, and the number of domestic calls responded to by the police. Lockhart (1985) noted that indirect measures such as estimates from police records or clinical populations do not provide an accurate basis even for racial (or intergroup) comparisons, because African Americans and individuals of lower socioeconomic status (SES) are overrepresented among cases known to the police and to hospital emergency rooms (e.g., Coley & Beckett, 1988). Moreover, women who become known to public and private agencies are not representative of abused wives in the general population (Frieze & Browne, 1989; Straus & Gelles, 1990). Lower SES respondents tend to use more of these help sources than middle- or upper-class Americans. Additionally, upper- and middle-class respondents keep marital problems hidden more often than lower-class respondents (Gelles, 1980; Lockhart & White, 1989).

To date, data on partner violence among minority populations are so incomplete that they preclude meaningful generalizations. This "selective inattention" (Hawkins, 1986) to violence against minority women is of serious concern, because violent assault is one of the most serious problems facing women and their families in many minority communities.

INTERPRETIVE ISSUES IN UNDERSTANDING VIOLENCE BETWEEN WOMEN AND MEN

Definitional Issues

In discussing physical aggression between adult partners, empirical conclusions are typically presented as findings on domestic, family, or dating violence. Yet only rarely have violence researchers paused to engage in a thoughtful analysis of their applications of this term and the reliability with which their stated definitions match their methodology and interpretation of findings. Others in related fields have engaged in such definitional struggles. In a discussion of "The Concept of Violence" from the perspective of peace research, Pontara (1978) suggested several "conditions of adequacy" that a definition of violence should satisfy in order to have theoretical and practical utility: (a) normative adequacy, (b) theoretical adequacy, and (c) descriptive adequacy. Pontara's third criterion has particular relevance: His requirement for *descriptive adequacy* demands that "the meaning [the definition] lays down does not depart too much from the meaning in which the term is, at least sometimes, used in common political discourse" (p. 21).

As professionals, we have a particular responsibility to present our knowledge in ways most likely to be understood accurately by the audience with whom we are communicating. Thus, it is important to consider what those outside the scientific and clinical community take the term violence to mean. Webster's *New World Dictionary of the American Language* (Guralink, 1984) defines *violence* as

> physical force used so as to injure, damage, or destroy; extreme roughness of action; intense, often devastatingly or explosively powerful force or energy, as in a hurricane or volcano; great force or strength. (p. 155)

By that definition—and from what we know about the potential to injure and the severity of actual outcomes in intimate relationships—this sort of violence is directed by parents against children and by men against women.

Contextualizing the Violence

To know very much about the violence of an action, it is necessary to have some information on (a) the force with which an action was carried out, (b) the relative size and strength of the perpetrator versus the target, (c) the point of impact of the action, if contact was made, and (d) the outcome of any impact in terms of discernable damage. Gender-neutral measures that *equate* the potential of an unarmed man and an unarmed woman to seriously harm, physically menace, or physically control an opposite sex partner run the risk of equating "fender benders" with head-on collisions. Imagine, for example, trying to assess car accidents—or, worse yet, equate them— without knowing the types of vehicles involved, the velocity of each vehicle, and the point of impact. Similarly, the potential to "injure, damage, or destroy" of being kicked, punched with a fist, or "beat up" by a typical unarmed man versus a typical unarmed woman cannot be simply equated. In using the term violence indiscriminately, we foster misimpressions among those with a more general interpretation, and add confusion and error—both within the scientific community and outside of it—that obscures an understanding of the phenomenon we purport to explore.

Women's Aggression as Precipitant to Male Violence

One theory that has been offered recently for the prevalence of male violence in couple relationships includes the supposition that physically aggressive acts by women toward their mates may be one cause of the violence against them (Straus, 1989). Certainly, abused women in city and regional samples report that "fighting back" worsens, rather than deters, their partners' violence (Browne, 1987; Dutton, 1992a; Frieze et al., 1980; Walker, 1984). Yet it is important to think carefully about the implications of such a premise lest it carry with it the assumption that, if women were not aggressive (i.e., if they did not initiate or respond to aggression with aggression), their partners would cease to be violent. Such an assumption runs counter to the growing literature on patterns of perpetration and desistance (or the cessation of abuse) for men who physically assault female intimates. Among other factors, this literature suggests that these patterns may be quite different for different couples, depending on characteristics of the male perpetrator (see Dutton, 1988a, for a review) and his overall patterns of aggression against others in addition to his wife (e.g., Fagan & Browne, in press; Fagan, Stewart, & Hansen, 1983; Shields, McCall, & Hanneke, 1988).

Such a proposition also runs uncomfortably close to suggesting that women should take abuse without action and hope that this passivity will somehow lessen the aggression against them. Given classic experimental findings that aggressive behaviors escalate once they have begun—*regardless* of the positive or negative behaviors of the target—such an assumption would offer false hope to many victims (Bandura, Underwood, & Fromson, 1975; Geen, Stonner, & Shope, 1975; Goldstein, Davis, & Herman, 1975; Goldstein, Davis, Kerns, & Cohn, 1981). Further, it fails to take into account the experience of women who remain passive in the face of repeated attacks with no discernable positive effect. There are findings on the perpetration of aggression that suggest some risks in passivity. For example, Berkowitz' (1973, 1974) early work indicates that aggressive tendencies are often *stim-*

ulated or reinforced when a victim indicates pain or submits to an aggressor. It is the dilemma of not being able to do anything "right"—that is, fighting back escalates the violence against them, remaining passive escalates the violence against them—that contributes so powerfully to the sense of hopelessness and despair reported by so many assaulted women (Browne, 1987; cf. Jones & Schechter, 1992).

The Importance of Gender-Based Analyses

The Question of Mutuality

The predominant debate in the literature on spouse abuse has been on the question of mutuality of aggression between adult relational partners. Both women and men can be verbally or physically aggressive. However, in terms of the definition of *violence* used in this discussion, men are the primary perpetrators of violence in intimate relationships.

Contentions of evidence for an equality of violence between partners have been based primarily on responses to the Conflict Tactics Scale (CTS) by women and men (Straus, 1990a). The conclusions on "equality" are drawn solely from *participation rates*. That is, in national surveys, about as many women as men report that they have perpetrated at least *one* of the behaviors listed on the CTS (push, shove, slap, kick, hit, beat up, choke, threaten with or use knife or gun) at least *one* time during their relationship. Based on these data, some researchers have concluded that women are about "as violent as men" in couple relationships (e.g., Straus, 1990b, p. 11; Stets & Straus, 1990, pp. 157–163).

Several oversights led to error in these conclusions. First, although definitions for violence have been at times clearly stated by researchers (e.g., "intent to cause harm," Straus et al., 1980), parameters of those definitions are *not* measured by the CTS (e.g., intent), nor are outcomes indicating harm specifically assessed (e.g., injuries resulting from assaultive incidents). Second, these conclusions are based on only one respondent per couple, which is not a clean test of mutuality. Third, even with these limited measures, *offending rates* (types of aggressive actions and frequency of these actions) for men are much higher than for women (Fagan & Browne, in press). The 1985 National Family Violence Survey found that even for couples in which the woman perpetrated at least one aggressive action, frequencies (Lambda's) for assaults by male partners were 21% greater than for women. This differential rose to 42% for the perpetration of "severe" actions such as punching, kicking, choking, beating up, or using a knife or a gun (Straus, 1989). The same national surveys used to conclude that women and men are equally violent in couple relationships indicate that:

1. Men perpetrate *more* aggressive actions against their female partners than women do against their male partners.
2. Men perpetrate more *severe* actions, such as punching, kicking, choking, beating up, or using a knife or gun.
3. Men are more likely to perpetrate *multiple* aggressive actions during a single incident than are women (Straus et al., 1980; Straus & Gelles, 1990).
4. Women are much more likely to sustain injury during attacks by male partners than men are during attacks by female partners (Stets & Straus, 1990).

Because it is based on the same methodology as survey research on marital assault, literature on dating violence also gives an impression of equality in the perpetration of aggression (Sugarman & Hotaling, 1989). Again however, in the aggregate, types of behaviors and severity of outcomes are quite different for women and men. For example, in studies with college populations, Makepeace (1989) found that men were more likely than women to have used each type of aggressive action listed on the survey in a dating context, and that women were four times as likely to sustain moderate to severe injuries in assaults by dating partners. Moreover, in both marital and dating violence literature, those researchers whose conclusions suggest that the aggression is equal for both men and women have failed to take into account male perpetration of sexual and forcible sexual assault—a behavior with often dramatic physical and emotional consequences for their victims.

In addition to definitional vagueness and conclusions that go beyond what the data will support, other omissions that contribute to confusion regarding the mutuality of partner violence include: (a) failure to contextualize behaviors, (b) lack of a recognition of gender-based physical differences, and (c) lack of attention to resulting differences in the perception of risk. What is being reported on scales such as the CTS are merely the names of specific behaviors. The measures do not gather information on (a) the *context* of these behaviors (e.g., what preceded the actions or whether the actions were in self-defense), (b) the *outcomes* of these behaviors (e.g., whether injuries occurred linked to specific actions or whether an individual acquiesced to a demand or a request based on the fear of harm), (c) the *clustering* of actions together, (d) the *escalation* of aggression over time, or (e) *threats* that may have accompanied aggression and changes in these threats over time.

Moreover, these gender-neutral analyses of violent behaviors have ignored the practical realities of physical differences between most men and women. One of the most determinative aspects in assaults between persons, physically and psychologically, is the target's ability to resist, escape, or physically restrain the aggressor. As Pagelow (1984) observed:

> Men are, on the average, larger and muscularly stronger than women, so if they choose to strike back they can do greater physical harm than is done to them, they can nonviolently protect themselves from physical harm, or they can leave the premises without being forcibly restrained. (p. 274)

Gender-blind analyses also ignore the role that perceptions of risk play in psychological responses of victims and in processes such as decision making and choice. It is unlikely that very many unarmed women, simply by physical menace, put their mates in fear of severe bodily harm or death. Yet the aspect of physical menace—the ability of a potential assailant to do damage, coupled with a perception of their willingness to do so—is a powerful dynamic in assaultive male-to-female interactions. In contrast to men, recognition of the potential for severe bodily harm deeply affects women's responses to actual or threatened physical assaults by a partner of the opposite sex.

The tendency to ignore the potential for differences by gender, and thus to render invisible the realities of women's lives, is well-illustrated in studies of homicide in the United States. Although patterns of homicide victimization for women are quite different from those of men, until recently, gender-based analyses of homicide were nonexistent (Browne & Williams, 1993). Some studies disaggregated homicide into various subtypes, such as family, acquaintance, or stranger homicide (Loftin & Parker, 1985; Parker & Toth, 1990), but none disaggregated rates by gender. Such exclusions suggest one of two implicit, but erroneous, presuppositions: Either that the conditions of women's lives are essentially the same as those of men making an analysis primarily reflecting men's experience sufficient to develop a theory applicable to both women and men; or that even though the conditions of women's lives may differ sharply from those of men, these differences are not germane to general theories or concerns. These assumptions reflect an implicit devaluing of women's experiences—even those experiences that are life-threatening—and foreclose the opportunity for grappling with alternative explanations if significant differences were to be found (Browne & Williams, 1993). An examination of empirical findings on the physical outcomes of partner violence for women is informative in understanding the severity of the danger many women face in romantic and marital relationships.

4

Physical and Psychological Outcomes of Partner Violence

Injuries sustained by women assaulted by male partners range from bruises, cuts, black eyes, concussions, broken bones, and miscarriages to permanent injuries. These include damage to joints, partial loss of hearing or vision, scars from burns, bites, or knife wounds, and even death. Bruises, contusions, and minor lacerations to the head, face, neck, breasts and abdomen are typical. Stark, Flitcraft, and Frazier (1979) found that the victims of partner violence seen in an urban hospital were 13 times more likely to sustain injuries to the breasts, chest, or abdomen than were accident victims. Women assaulted by male partners are also more likely to have multiple injuries than accident victims, as well as medical evidence of prior injuries such as old and new fractures, strained or torn ligaments, and bruises in various stages of healing (Burge, 1989).

When this pattern of injuries is seen in a woman—particularly in combination with evidence of old wounds and vague complaints of physical aches and pains—physical violence should be suspected regardless of the explanation given for the current complaint. The force with which an act is carried out, the number of repetitions of the act, and the clustering of different acts together play a major role in determining the amount of injury sustained during assaultive incidents (Browne, 1987). Both the repetition of violent acts and a clustering of acts within a single assaultive incident increase the potential for injury, as victims are psychologically and physically overwhelmed by the rapidity of events and are unable to recover in time to protect themselves from the next blow (cf. Patterson, 1982; Reid, Taplin, & Lorber, 1981).

INJURIES PRESENTED TO MEDICAL SETTINGS

Although questions about violence at home are not usually included when medical histories are taken, studies conducted in medical settings have provided some idea of how serious partner violence is for women. Having reviewed the medical records of 3,676 randomly selected patients of a Northeastern urban area emergency room during a one-year period, Stark et al. (1981) estimated that 21% of all women using emergency surgical services were there for the sequelae of partner violence. These researchers also concluded that one half of all injuries presented by women occurred in the context of partner abuse, and that over one half of all rapes to women 30 and over were partner rapes. More recent studies have confirmed these early findings, estimating that between 20% to 35% of women who present to hospital emergency rooms or community-based practices are there because of symptoms related to assaults by a husband or other intimate partner (Hamberger, Saunders, & Hovey, 1992; Randall, 1990).

Hamberger, Saunders, and Hovey (1992) conducted a thorough study in a large, community-based clinic that specialized in family practice residency-training in a medium-sized Midwestern community. All consecutive women patients who attended the clinic for regular appointments during a two-month period were asked to participate. The response rate was 83%—or 394 women. All ethnic, racial, and socioeconomic groups from the community were represented. Hamberger and his colleagues found a lifetime prevalence for assaults by a male partner of 39% and a lifetime injury rate of 25%. Women who had been assaulted in the year preceding the study ($n =$ 85) did not differ from nonvictims based on race or educational attainment; however, the victims were younger than nonvictims and were more likely to be separated or divorced. Women considered to be at risk during the year before the study (that is, those who were living with a partner, recently separated, or divorced), had a physical assault incidence rate of of 25%; their injury rate due to partner violence was 15%. Despite this level of victimization and physical trauma, Hamberger, Saunders, and Hovey (1992) found that only six women in the sample had ever been asked about partner violence by their physicians.

Because of the ongoing and injurious nature of violence toward women by male partners, abused women often visit physicians repeatedly with increasingly severe physical trauma (Health Care Systems, 1984; Koss, Koss, & Woodruff, 1991). In a study that documented the repeated nature of battered women's visits to health-care providers, Stark and Flitcraft (1988) reported that nearly one of every five women victims had presented at least 11 times with physical trauma. Another 23% had brought between six and 10 assault-related injuries to the attention of clinicians. As was found in the study by Hamberger et al. (1992), in most cases, no inquiries had been made into the cause of the injuries, and the history of victimization underlying physical trauma was never identified.

Comparative Risk of Injury for Women and Men

Although women as well as men may be verbally and emotionally abusive, women are at much greater risk to be severely physically assaulted and injured by their male partners than men are by their women partners (Brush, 1990; Koss & Heslet, 1992; Straus, 1989; Straus, Gelles, & Steinmetz, 1980; Stets & Straus, 1990). Using data from the 1985 National Family Violence Survey (NFVS), Stets and Straus analyzed the relationship between the perpetration of aggression and indirect measures of injury by gender. In this nationally representative sample, women victims were much more likely than men victims to require medical care, to need more time off from work because of injuries inflicted by the partner, and to be bedridden because of injuries. These findings held even when only the more severe levels of aggression by women and men (e.g., punch, kick, choke, beat up, use a knife or a gun) were considered.

Although her study lacked a detailed assessment of the physical sequelae of assaults, Brush's (1990) analysis of violent acts and injuries in a probability sample of 5,474 married couples also found women more likely than men to sustain injury as a result of assaultive acts between partners. Other research has found higher levels of reported injury than these national surveys by asking for responses to a detailed list of potential physical outcomes of assault (Frieze, 1983; Walker, 1984). To date, no nationally representative study has incorporated measures adequate enough to obtain reliable injury estimates for partner violence.

As with estimates of incidence, assessments of injury from the NFVS and other national surveys markedly understate the frequency of injury to women resulting from assaults by an adult partner. Responses to NFVS questions of "needing to see" or "actually seeing" a doctor are confounded with cultural and economic variations as well as with individual perceptions of how severe physical injuries must be to require formal medical care. Moreover, many abused women are known to refrain from actually seeing a doctor even when they are injured quite severely, due to shame, threats by the abuser against seeking outside help, and fear that seeking medical attention will identify them as the victims of domestic violence and thus will alert officials to the problems occurring within the family. In those states in which children can be removed from a mother's custody if she is found to be living with a violent partner, women's willingness to seek help is greatly affected.

Lethal Outcomes of Partner Violence

Homicide figures for the United States further demonstrate the severity of physical outcomes of partner assault for women compared to men in intimate relationships. In a study that analyzed all criminally negligent homicides from 1976 through 1987 using Supplementary Homicide Report (SHR) data, Browne and Williams (1993) found that the deaths of approximately 38,649 individuals age 16 and over during this period were the result of one partner killing another (this includes married, common-law, divorced, and dating partners). Of these deaths, 61% of the victims were women killed by male partners and 39% were men killed by female partners. For white couples, the difference was more marked: 70% of the victims were women. *In the United States, women are more likely to be killed by their male partners than by all other categories of persons combined.* For example, more than half of all women murdered in the United States between 1980 and 1985 (52%) were victims of partner homicide (Browne & Williams, 1989).

Of course, SHR data do not give us information about the prior interactions of specific couples; thus, no estimates are available on the numbers of partner homicides that involved a history of physical assault and threat. However, more specific studies have documented that, in addition to committing fewer homicides than men, a significant proportion of partner homicides committed by women occur in response to male aggression and threat (Chimbos, 1978; Daly & Wilson, 1988; Daniel & Harris, 1982; Totman, 1978; Wilbanks, 1983; Wolfgang, 1967).

Trends in Partner Homicides by Women and Men

One underlying factor of many homicides committed by women of male intimates appears to be their inability or perceived inability to protect themselves from the partner's aggression. In her study of incarcerated women homicide offenders, Totman (1978) noted that a major contributing factor to partner homicides by women was aggression by the eventual victim, coupled with a perceived lack of viable alternatives to an overwhelming and entrapping life situation on the part of the woman. Browne (1987) made similar observations in her study of women in abusive relationships who were charged with the death or serious injury of their mates. Browne indicated that homicides by women victims of a partner's violence tended to occur out of desperation, at a point when they felt trapped in an escalating and life-threatening situation without hope for either improvement or escape. Given the research establishing the link between male aggression and the perpetration of partner homicides by women, Browne and Williams (1989) theorized that simply the presence of resources that would enable women to escape or to be protected from a partner's violence might act to offset at least a portion of those homicides that occur in desperation and self-defense. They also contended that such resources might have symbolic as well as tangible significance by providing a social statement that confirms victims' perceptions of the seriousness of the violence and by lessening their sense of isolation and entrapment with the danger.

An analysis of all partner homicides for the years 1976–1984 did reveal a decrease—in fact, more than a 25% decline—in the rates of women killing male partners during this period (Browne & Williams, 1989). This decline began in 1979, at about the time that domestic violence legislation and extra-legal resources for abused women were becoming established in most of the 50 states (e.g., Kalmuss & Straus, 1983; Lerman, 1980; Lerman & Livingston, 1983; Schechter, 1982). Further analysis revealed that those states having more domestic violence legislation and extra-legal resources for abused women (e.g., funding for shelters for battered women, crisis lines, and legal aid) had lower rates of homicides by women in general against their male partners, and that the presence of these resources was associated with the decrease over time in partner homicides by women.

Unfortunately, the steep decline in partner homicides by women was not matched by a similar decline for men. Although there was a weak negative association between the presence of extra-legal resources—such as shelters—and male-perpetrated partner homicide, no association was found with the presence of domestic violence legislation. The years 1976–1987 do show a slight decrease in the rates of men killing their wives or ex-wives; however, during this same time period, rates of men killing current or former girlfriends or cohabiting partners increased sharply (Browne & Williams, 1993). The early 1990s have seen a dramatic increase in the rates of partner homicide against women in some states, despite domestic violence legislation and other community provisions for sanctions and protection.

PSYCHOLOGICAL OUTCOMES

Early literature on women assaulted by male partners included clinical speculation about pathology or specific traits believed to predispose them to abuse (Kleckner, 1978; Schultz, 1960; Shainess, 1977; Snell, Rosenwald, & Robey, 1964; see Symonds, 1978, 1979 for early responses). However, empirical investigations over the past 15 years have not substantiated these early speculations (Hotaling & Sugarman, 1986). Although studies from some special populations have stressed symptomatology, these characteristics appear to be sequelae of partner assaults, rather than antecedents (e.g., Margolin, 1988; Romero, 1985).

Human Responses to Trauma

Research during the past 30 years has documented a range of typical human responses to threats as diverse as natural disasters, war, captivity, and personal attack. When faced with immediate danger, most victims focus primarily on self-protection and survival, or on the survival of loved ones. Victims experience initial feelings of shock, denial, disbelief, and fear, and reactions of withdrawal and confusion (Chapman, 1962; Herman, 1992; Mileti, Drabek, & Haas, 1975; van der Kolk, 1987). The primary fear is of injury or death. Victims may deny the threat, leading to a lag in accurately defining or responding to the situation, or, overwhelmed by the enormity of the threat, become unable to respond at all (Bahnson, 1964; Miller, 1964; Peters, 1973).

When the threat is perpetrated by another person and is ongoing, the assailant or captor has a major influence on how their victims appraise the situation and analyze alternatives (Arnold, 1967; Biderman, 1967; Lazarus, 1967). Such appraisal involves an evaluation of whether a particular coping method would further endanger the victim and to what degree. As defensive strategies are employed and the individual becomes more and more involved with internal defense mechanisms, external activity may diminish, giving the appearance of extreme apathy (Withey, 1962). In situations of extreme helplessness such as concentration camps, surprisingly little anger is shown toward the captors, and this may be a measure of the captors' perceived or demonstrated ability to control and to harm (Lazarus, 1967). Symonds (1978) discussed the implications of a "state of terror" that may occur as a result of this appraisal.

Survivors of all kinds of threats report long-term reactions of fearfulness, anxiety, and confusion (Figley, 1985; Herman, 1992; van der Kolk,

1987). A survivor may become extremely suggestible or dependent and find it difficult to make basic decisions or function alone, yet may minimize the damage and personal loss (Bard & Sangrey, 1986). Long-term reactions to physical assault victimization include fear, anger, guilt, shame, feelings of powerlessness or helplessness, a sense of failure, and a sense of being contaminated or worthless (e.g., Bard & Sangrey, 1986; Frieze, Hymer, & Greenberg, 1987). Survivors of personal attack often react with intense anxiety and acute feelings of loss of control, vulnerability, and self-blame (Burgess & Holmstrom, 1979b; Janoff-Bulman & Frieze, 1983; Kilpatrick, Veronen, & Best, 1985; Resick et al., 1981). Other effects of physical attacks include mistrust of others that can disrupt personal relationships and functioning, development of phobias, manifestations of depression and hostility, and somatic symptoms (e.g., Burge, 1989; Finkelhor & Browne, 1985; Resick, Calhoun, Atkeson, & Ellis, 1981). In particular, women who have been raped tend to score high on a range of psychological measures postassault (e.g., Davidson & Foa, 1991; Resick, 1983).

During recovery, some survivors remain relatively withdrawn and passive and continue to exhibit symptoms of depression and apathy (Chapman, 1962; Peterson & Seligman, 1983). Chronic fatigue, tension, intense startle reactions, medical symptomatology, and disturbed sleeping and eating patterns are often noted in survivors as well (Davidson & Foa, 1991; Herman, 1992; van der Kolk, 1987). For victims of crime, even normal recoveries can take months (Bard & Sangrey, 1986). Other survivors evidence relatively little pathology immediately after a trauma, yet become extremely symptomatic years later in response to major life changes or other stressors (van der Kolk, 1987). Some effects may persist for years. In one study, rape victims evidenced consistently higher levels of fear and anxiety than women who had not been raped for as long as 16 years after the rape incident (Ellis, Atkeson, & Calhoun, 1981).

Abused Women's Responses to Trauma

Alexandra Symonds proposed, in 1979, the "psychology of catastrophic events" as a useful model with which to view the emotional and behavioral responses of abused women to the violence directed at them (see also Browne, 1980, 1987; Symonds, 1978). Although little subsequent work has been done to integrate the literature on the psychological reactions of victims across traumas as it relates to battered women (see Dutton, 1992a and Herman, 1992, for recent exceptions), *women's reactions to violence by male partners closely parallel reactions of survivors across a variety of traumatic events.*

As with other types of victims, the primary focus of women assaulted by their partners is usually on self-protection and survival (Kerouac & Lescop, 1986). Reactions of shock, denial, withdrawal, confusion, psychological numbing, and fear are common (Browne, 1987; Dutton, 1992a; Symonds, 1979; Walker, 1979). During—and even after—an assault, a victim may offer little or no resistance in an attempt to minimize the threat of injury or renewed aggression (Browne, 1987; Symonds, 1975, 1978; Walker, 1979).

In one of the earliest published studies of women victims, Hilberman and Munson (1977–1978; Hilberman, 1980) found severe levels of stress in a sample of 120 women who were referred to a rural medical clinic for psychiatric evaluation. Of this sample, half were victims of repeated violence by their partners. In this sample of mostly African-American women, stress was related both to basic survival needs and to the violence they were experiencing. Victims of ongoing abuse lived with the knowledge that an assault could occur at any time. In response to the potential for danger, some women reported experiencing anxiety to the point of panic (Hilberman, 1980). Most of the victimized women suffered from feelings of incompetence, unworthiness, guilt, shame, and fear of losing control. In this clinical sample, the most common diagnosis was depression (Hilberman, 1980).

The first extensive exploration of the psychological responses of women involved in abusive relationships was published by Walker in 1979. In this ground-breaking work, Walker described potential long-term effects of male violence in an intimate adult relationship based on more than 120 in-depth clinical interviews with abused women. The women she interviewed reported feelings of low self-esteem, depression, generally severe stress reactions, and helplessness; these were compounded by psychophysiological complaints. Walker subsequently reported empirical findings from 8-hour interviews with a sample of 432 women assaulted by their partners, obtained through referrals from medical and mental health facilities, advertisements, and shelters for abused women in six states (Walker, 1984). Her findings confirmed assaulted women's sense of helplessness in controlling their abusers' violent behaviors. Abused women also scored significantly higher than the norm on a "chance" scale of locus of control (Levenson, 1972), a finding that indicated a perception in abused women that many occurrences in life are beyond their control. However, contrary to expectations, abused women reported a high internal locus of control, perhaps because they were so actively engaged in managing their own responses to violence and threat while still balancing the needs of family and other responsibilities. Depression scores for abused women were twice as high as standard norms for that measure, however, and well above high-risk cut-off scores (Center for Epidemiologic Studies—Depression Scale, Radloff, 1977). Younger women (aged 18 to 24) were the most severely depressed of this group.

In her analysis of trends over time for a sample of 400 women victims, Browne (1980) noted other patterns in abused women's responses to violence by male partners that paralleled findings in the more general literature on victims' reactions to trauma. Of the women in this sample, 60% felt they had no control over their abuser or his behaviors and focused primarily on self-protection during attacks. Less than one quarter (23%) left the relationship even temporarily after the first major assault; this figure increased to only 29% after the third (or one of the worst) assault(s). Even after the third attack, only 31% sought outside help, and only 15% took offensive action against their mates. Although there was an initial reaction of shock, other emotional reactions intensified over time. Fear, anxiety, depression, anger, and hostility were reported at higher levels after the third battering incident, whereas shock at being victimized decreased (see also Walker, 1984). Browne (1980, 1987) noted that women victims often develop survival rather than escape skills and focus on strategies to mediate or dissociate from the violence (cf. Herman, 1992; Walker, 1979).

Consonant findings are noted in more recent clinically based work (e.g., Dutton, 1992a). Kerouac and Lescop (1986) found comparable symptoms of depression and anxiety in a descriptive study of the health perceptions of battered women. (Kerouac and Lescop also noted dominant symptoms of depression and anxiety in children under the age of 12 who were living in shelter settings with their abused mothers.) Clinical and other nonrandom samples of physical assault survivors also reveal a high prevalence of depressive symptomatology in abused women, as well as suicide ideation or attempts (McGrath, Keita, Strickland, & Russo, 1990; Stark & Flitcraft, 1988).

Cumulative Effects

Although just one assault can have permanent negative effects, the severity and repetition of violence clearly affects resulting psychological adjustment (Follingstad, Brennan, Hause, Polek, & Rutledge, 1991). In a comparison study that used in-depth interviews with 42 abused women charged with either the death or serious injury of their mates and 205 abused women who had not used lethal force against their spouses, Browne (1987) noted that both groups described feelings of anxiety and fear. However, women victims of severe violence—those who were frequently assaulted, had sustained physical injuries, were sexually assaulted, or had experienced death threats—were much more likely to express extreme levels of distress, including an overwhelming sense of danger, intrusive memories or flashbacks, and thoughts of suicide. Gelles and Harrop (1989) found similar effects for levels of violence in a study that used a nationally representative sample of 366 abused women and 2,622 nonabused women. Their multivariate analyses indicated that the more violence a woman experiences, the more she suffers from various forms of psychological distress.

Other studies have suggested that women who are victims of both physical and sexual aggression in a marital relationship are at risk of more severe psychological sequelae (Browne, 1987; Frieze, 1983; Pagelow, 1984; Walker, 1984). In their comparison study of women whose partners' aggression included sexual violence, women who were physically but not sexually assaulted, and nonvictimized women, Shields and Hanneke (1983) found that those respondents who were both physically and sexually assaulted exhibited the most severe sequelae, including lower levels of self-esteem and greater use of alcohol in response to depression. Earlier studies had found that women who experienced more frequent sexual assaults by their spouses reported more severe self-blame (Frieze, 1983; Frieze et al., 1980).

Long-Term Effects

Long-term reactions in women who are physically assaulted and threatened by male partners include fear, anxiety, fatigue, sleeping and eating disturbances, intense startle reactions, nightmares, and physical complaints (Goodman, Koss, & Russo, 1993a; Herman, 1992). Postattack women may become dependent and suggestible, and find it difficult to make decisions or carry out long-range planning (cf. Bard & Sangrey, 1986). In an attempt to avoid becoming psychologically overwhelmed, these women may voice unrealistic expectations about recovery, persuading themselves that they can "rebuild"— somehow, everything will be all right (Walker, 1979, 1984; cf. Mileti, Drabek, & Hass, 1975). As in all types of trauma victims, abused women fear a force that is out of control. Like other victims of interpersonal violence, women assaulted by male intimates learn to weigh all alternatives against their perception of the assailant's ability to control or to harm. Although these findings parallel those on responses to interpersonal attacks or captivity, the effects for women assaulted by an intimate partner are compounded by the fact that the assailant is someone they may love, someone they are supposed to be able to trust, and someone on whom they may depend for shelter and other components of survival (Browne, 1991; Jones & Schechter, 1992). In such cases, perceptions of vulnerability, loss, betrayal, or hopelessness may be especially pronounced (Walker, 1979).

Noting the similarities in the reactions between battered women and prisoners of war, Romero (1985) compared the patterns of abuse and response of male prisoners of war in Korea with women in violent adult relationships. Romero identified three dimensions as common to both types of experiences: (a) psychological abuse that occurs within a context of threatened physical violence leading to dread and debilitation in victims; (b) isolation of victims from past support systems (e.g., friends and family) and outside activities that results in dependency on the abusers and validation of the abusers' actions and points of view, and (c) intermittent positive reinforcement in the face of fear and personal loss that strengthens the emotional victims' dependency of victims on their abusers. Experienced in combination, these dynamics appeared effective in diminishing self-agency and psychological well-being across both male prisoners of war and physically assaulted women. These dimensions parallel the cycle of violence, first described by Walker (1979), in which abusive episodes are followed by kindness or contrition (or at least by the cessation of aggression) and accompanied by the implicit threat of renewed violence if certain demands or expectations are not met (see also Herman, 1992, pp. 77–87; and Walker 1984, p. 27 for a discussion of the principles of torture and experiences of abused women).

Realistic Appraisals of Danger

Repeated assaults by male partners take abused women through a progression of emotions and attributions as they attempt to reinterpret their lives and their interactions with others in light of a pattern of continued attacks (Browne, 1987, pp. 128–130). Therefore, the effect of both psychological responses to trauma and the realities of danger must be considered when evaluating the posttrauma responses of women victims. For example, posttrauma psychological responses may cloud a woman's perceptions and impede her ability to make decisions or take effective action to improve her situation. At the same time, for a woman who is reasoning clearly, social realities may in themselves engender a sense of entrapment and helplessness. With the removal of psychological responses of denial or unrealistic hopes for improvement, women at risk from their male partners may become even more frightened by the lack of viable alternatives for safety and well-being. Unlike the victims of strangers, victims of marital violence have a legal, financial, emotional, and role relationship with their assailants. Especially for women who are married to their assailants, decisions about their relationships are complicated by legal and financial ties, overlapping family and support networks, and issues related to the care and custody of children (Browne, 1991).

Violence at home typically leaves no place in which defenses can be let down—a condition the human organism is ill-equipped to bear. Ongoing experiences of victimization may produce long-term manifestations of emotional numbing, extreme passivity, and helplessness (Dutton, 1992a, 1992b; Frieze et al., 1987; Herman, 1992; Walker, 1979, 1984). As levels of threat and violence escalate, a woman's perception of alternatives becomes increasingly restricted and taking action on any of those alternatives may seem too dangerous to pursue (Blackman, 1989; Browne, 1987). Conversely, states of heightened arousal, hostility, or aggression may occur (e.g., Herman, 1992; see also section on "Psychopathy Versus Trauma," this chapter, p. 83). Some women may also respond by abusing alcohol or other substances following the onset of chronic or severe violence as a way of dealing with the physical and psychic pain (Dutton, 1992a; Jones & Schechter, 1992); although, in studies of general populations, alcohol abuse does not distinguish abused women from nonbattered women (Hotaling & Sugarman, 1986).

Finally, it is important to note the potential effect of even a single incident of physical agression in an intimate relationship. Although women who are assaulted "only once" are rarely labeled as battered and are studied even less often, *any* use of violence in a relationship can dramatically alter the balance of power destroying a sense of openness and trust on the part of the woman and resulting in a permanent sense of inequality, threat, and loss.

Recovery from Trauma

A few studies have suggested that negative psychological responses to physical violence and threat may improve once the survivor is no longer in danger. For example, Follingstad et al. (1991) studied 234 battered women, of whom more than three quarters (77%) reported feelings of depression and 75% reported anxiety. Most of these women reported healthier stages before the onset of violence. The 26% of the sample who had experienced a total of three or fewer assaultive incidents reported a return to a healthier psychological condition after the assaults ended. The same was true for women who had no assaultive experiences for at least two years prior to the study. Walker's (1984) clinical observations also suggested that acute negative responses may decrease fairly rapidly once the danger is removed. However, some survivors manifest chronic reactions of depression, withdrawal, and posttraumatic stress disorder years after becoming free of a violent relationship (Dutton, 1992a, 1992b; Herman, 1992; see also Walker, 1991, 1994a).

PSYCHOPATHY VERSUS TRAUMA: BATTERED WOMAN SYNDROME AND THE CONCEPT OF LEARNED HELPLESSNESS

Several theories specific to abused women were developed during the late 1970s and 1980s in an effort to explain reactions of women to physical and sexual attacks by male partners. One of the most influential of these was Lenore Walker's construct of the *Battered Woman Syndrome*. By structuring her theory around the *effects* of physical assault and threat by intimate partners, Walker established a conceptual base for viewing abuse as the cause rather than the result of later symptomatology. Walker (1979, 1984) took strong exception to early hypotheses that abused women derive enjoyment from their suffering, feel a need to be punished, or seek out abusive treatment in adult intimate relationships. She contended, however, that living in constant fear of violent attack and experiencing ongoing physical assault from an intimate partner creates sufficient stress to affect women's responses in significant ways. The battered woman syndrome was developed to describe emotional, cognitive, and behavioral reactions noted in women who have experienced physical assault and threats of assault by an adult partner with whom they share an intimate relationship. As such, battered woman syndrome does not describe a character disorder or specific personality traits, but rather is a situationally based construct that describes "psychological changes that occur in abused women after exposure to repeated abuse" (Walker, 1992, p. 326).

Walker's application of the concept of *learned helplessness*—or loss of the ability to predict whether behaviors will have any effect on an outcome and a corresponding restriction of behaviors—is typically viewed as the core feature of battered woman syndrome. Walker (1979, 1984) stressed that abused women's affective, cognitive, and behavioral responses may become impaired by their concentrated focus on survival. Further, they may exhibit other trauma responses such as hypervigilance, acquiescence toward the abuser, lack of trust and fearfulness resembling paranoia, denial of the seriousness of the abuse, and a strong protection of the inner self while appearing suggestible or easily manipulated by others. Many of these characteristics resemble symptoms of personality disorder and would be maladaptive if there was no threat of harm. They are, however, understandable for an individual faced with ongoing and unpredictable assaults. Walker proposed learned helplessness (together with the concept of a cycle of violence) as a theoretical construct to explain why women experiencing physical and sexual assault from their male partners might find it difficult to leave abusive relationships or, in some cases, to seek help or take other actions in their own behalf.

This conceptualization of learned helplessness was an adaption of earlier constructs by Seligman (1975). In studies on the genesis of exogenous depression, Seligman and some of his colleagues found that when laboratory animals were repeatedly and noncontingently shocked, they lost the ability to predict the efficacy of their actions and eventually ceased in their attempts to escape the aversive situation, even when escape was possible and apparent to animals who had not experienced aversive stimuli. Seligman likened this learned helplessness to human depression and theorized that the two conditions have similar cognitive, motivational, and behavioral components. On the basis of clinical interviews with abused women, Walker (1979) contended that battered women's experiences with noncontingent violence in their intimate relationships could, over time, similarly produce learned helplessness.

Walker (1979) conceptualized learned helplessness as beginning when repeated battering incidents, perceived as occurring in a random and variable pattern, lead a victim to believe that the effect of her responses cannot be predicted. The victim then learns to believe that she has no control over experiences as vital as those threatening her life and well-being. That is, she believes there is little she can do to reliably bring about a positive result or lessening of the danger. This, in turn, mitigates against future planning, escape attempts, or help-seeking, and a self-perpetuating cycle may ensue. In the 1980s, Walker (1992, 1994a) linked the theory of Battered Woman Syndrome and learned helplessness to the *DSM-III* diagnosis of posttraumatic stress disorder (PTSD), although her conceptualization of Battered Woman Syndrome highlighted components of trauma responses not included in PTSD criteria.

Critiques of the Theory

Although the concepts of learned helplessness and battered woman syndrome help to explain the responses of some abused women, they have been criticized on a number of grounds. First, some posit that these concepts rely too heavily on individual psychology rather than social forces to explain why women sometimes remain with violent and threatening mates (Flannery & Harvey, 1991). Critics have contended that the apparent helplessness of some battered women may simply reflect the reality of inadequate resources, such as police responsiveness and protection, employment and educational opportunities, child care, and financial and legal support (Jones, 1994; Okun, 1986; Pagelow, 1981; Strube & Barbour, 1983). In fact, a growing body of research indicates that women in assaultive relationships show a high degree of resourcefulness and persistence in their responses to their violent situations (Bowker, 1983; Dutton, 1992a; Gondolf, 1988; McHugh, Frieze, & Browne, 1993; Walker, 1991).

Others have noted the reality, and often the severity, of risk involved in leaving a violent and threatening man, including the potential for reprisals based on abusers' perceptions of abandonment and rejection (e.g., Browne, 1987, 1993; Dutton, 1992a; Mahoney, 1991). Behaviors that could be interpreted as helplessness—such as not separating from the abuser or refraining from initiating legal actions against him—may simply be the result of common-sense evaluation of the assailant's potential for violent response and others' inability to intervene in time to guarantee safety. Short of extreme medical or criminal justice measures, forcing a violent individual to stop aggressive behavior is virtually impossible. Orders restraining the assailant from the home or from proximity to the victim only work if the assailant respects those orders, or at least does no harm during times of violation. Living in hiding is incompatible with maintaining gainful employment, raising and educating children, and other components of normal life.

Economic circumstances also play a major role in the choices facing an abused woman. If, for example, a woman lacks adequate financial resources and is forced to live in an unsafe dwelling in a crime-ridden community, only the type of danger to be braved may change if she chooses to leave a violent mate. Moreover the risk of assaults by strangers will be added to the risk of reprisal by her partner. Although Walker's work has consistently stressed the multiple coping mechanisms used by abused women in the face of danger and debilitation, an over-generalization of an assumption of helplessness by uninformed laypersons or therapists can, and often does, obscure an understanding of the realities of danger and of abused women's strengths and abilities in attempting to survive.

Legal Pitfalls

Battered Woman Syndrome was not intended to be used as an excuse or as a diminished-capacity defense, although legal applications err too frequently in this direction (Browne, 1987; Dutton, 1994; Maguigan, 1991; Schneider, 1986; Walker, 1986). Walker (1992) described the application of the battered woman self-defense in cases that involve assaulted women who killed their partners as providing "a legal defense that rests on the justification of the act they have committed as necessary to protect themselves or someone else . . . from further harm or death" (p. 321). Although sometimes billed as a new defense in homicide and other legal cases, battered woman syndrome, without the theory of learned helplessness, is a logical extension of the much larger literature on human responses to harm and the threat of harm. As such, the primary focus (as is Walker's consistent emphasis) should be on the reactions of victims to trauma and on abused women's reactions as understandable in light of known human responses (Browne, 1987; Walker, 1986, 1992).

Presenting battered woman syndrome as a totally new construct decontextualizes both the theory and the victims; leaving victims open to the charge of requesting special treatment. It also leaves the theory open to questions of bias and scientific merit. Requesting or presenting evidence of battered women syndrome in trial settings should not be framed as a request for a unique defense for battered women. Rather it should be viewed as an assertion of the defendant's right to present the psychological effects of cycles of violence and threat by an intimate partner and the relationship of those effects to her subsequent behaviors and perceptions (Dutton, 1994).

DSM-IV Diagnoses

Clinical studies have identified a high incidence of PTSD, depression and, in some studies, an elevated use of alcohol and other substances in women victims of violence. These are seen particularly in women treated in emergency medical and inpatient settings. These symptoms sometimes lead to *DSM* Axis I diagnoses (e.g., Kilpatrick, Veronen, & Best, 1985; Stark, Flitcraft, & Frazier, 1979). Diagnoses of personality or developmental disorders (Axis II) are also frequently assigned to women with histories of rape, child sexual molestation, and battering despite much controversy over their potential misuse (Herman, 1992; Walker, 1994a). The approach taken in the *DSM* is supposedly atheoretical: For most disorders, etiology is not emphasized and definitions are limited to descriptions of the clinical features of the disorder. For cases in which individuals have undergone or are currently undergoing severe physical threat and violation, however, a structure that ignores etiology as well as extrinsic realities presents grave challenges for the clinician.

Unfortunately, most mental health-care providers rarely incorporate the potential for childhood or adult family violence in routine intake procedures, ongoing assessments, or treatment interventions. As Koss (1990a) noted:

> Standard procedures of psychological history-taking, evaluation of suicide risk, assessment of psychopathology and personality, and measurements of life events, all routinely fail to include questions about victimization by violence. (p. 376)

In their incisive discussion of the "victim to patient process" based on their review of inpatients records in a psychiatric facility, Carmen, Rieker, and Mills (1984) concluded:

> Psychiatric patients are more likely to have experienced physical or sexual violence than to hear voices, yet clinicians are systematic in their inquiries about hallucinations while overlooking the reality and importance of violent assaults." (p. 383)

Many studies have documented this oversight. Gondolf (1990), in his discussion of clinical responses to family violence when such histories are known, noted the lack of data on experiences of victimization as well as a lack of interventions that incorporate an understanding of its potential effects. In one study of adult women with sexual molestation histories, two thirds met diagnostic criteria for posttraumatic stress disorder. However, none of these women received that diagnosis, and none received any treatment specifically addressing these childhood traumas (Craine, cited by Gondolf, 1990).

Applicability of Personality Disorder

Diagnoses of personality disorder are especially likely to be applied to women, based on interpretations of the concept of dependency. Yet, as Walker (1994a) has noted that the definition of dependency used to make diagnostic decisions includes the ways in which *women* express dependency upon men and not the ways in which men express dependency. For example, men who rely on others to maintain their homes and take care of their children are not considered to be expressing personality-disordered or dysfunctional behaviors. Further, as Walker pointed out, other cultures (such as Hispanic, Native American, and Asian) have quite different definitions of dependent behaviors than do European-oriented societies. Thus, assignments of pathology in this area need to take into account both gender and cultural differences.

Critique of the Diagnosis

Personality disorder, in particular, is a diagnosis based on indices of social dysfunction. It does not take into account the influence of environmental factors *extrinsic* to the organization of the personality such as poverty, racism, victimization, and gender-bias (Bassuk, Rubin, & Lauriat, 1986). Although commonly assigned to women and to women victims, diagnoses of personality disorder are especially problematic for cases in which a trauma history is present, *particularly if that history is not known to the clinician* (Browne, 1992; Walker, 1994a). Herman (1992) has suggested that the effect of violent victimization on individuals over time may constitute a different kind of interference with personality expression, one that is more similar to a severe form of PTSD than to character disorders. Rosewater (1988), whose research identified a profile for women victims using the Minnesota Multiphasic Personality Inventory (MMPI), discovered marked similarities between the profiles of individuals usually diagnosed as borderline personalities and women facing violent assault by male partners (cf. Dutton, 1992a). Assaulted and threatened women frequently were misdiagnosed because their reactions to the violence approximated behavioral descriptors for borderline or other Axis I and Axis II disorders. An adapted interpretation of the MMPI is now available for the assessment of battered women to accommodate the presence of real danger in their lives (Dutton, 1992a; Rosewater, 1988).

Posttraumatic Stress Disorder (PTSD)

Applicability of PTSD

The diagnostic construct of PTSD provides one way of systematizing some of the psychological responses evidenced by women victims of partner violence (Browne, 1992; Burge, 1989; Dutton, 1992b; Goodman, Koss, & Russo, 1993b; Harvey & Herman, 1992; Kemp, Rawlings, & Green, 1991; Walker, 1991, 1992). Posttraumatic stress disorder has been used as a framework for understanding a range of psychological responses to traumatic experiences that may be discrete and clearly bounded, such as natural disaster or rape, or prolonged and ongoing, such as military combat or battering (Davidson & Foa, 1993; Figley, 1985; Herman, 1992; van der Kolk, 1987). Horowitz (1976a, 1979), who argued for a dynamic model of traumatic stress response, posited that victims respond to trauma through an alternative, or phasic, sequence of intrusion and denial. Intrusions are experiences in which the trauma is in some sense relived. Denial designates victims' attempts to insulate themselves from reminders of traumatic events and thus avoid becoming emotionally overwhelmed.

Based on the work of Horowitz and other PTSD theorists, the *DSM-III-R* characterizes PTSD as consisting of a set of responses to an event that is outside the range of usual human experience and that would be markedly distressing to almost anyone. The *DSM-IV* has dropped the requirement that the event be outside the range of usual human experience and defines PTSD as

> an extreme traumatic stressor involving direct personal experience of an event that involves actual or threatened death or serious injury, or other threat to one's physical integrity; or witnessing an event that involves death, injury, or a threat to the physical integrity of another person; or learning about unexpected or violent death, serious harm, or threat of death or injury experienced by a family member or other close associate." (1994, p. 424).

Responses suggested as indicative of PTSD include symptoms of intrusion and denial as well as symptoms of dissociation, increased arousal such as irritability and hypervigilance, and sleep disturbances. PTSD is highly likely to coexist with depression or substance abuse or both, although these conditions are more apt to appear after a major trauma than to exist before (Davidson & Fairbank, 1993; National Victims Center, 1992). Symptoms of posttraumatic stress disorder are sometimes misdiagnosed as adjustment disorder, major depression, or closed head injury (Lyons, 1987; Pitman, 1993).

Based on clinical and empirical inquiries, a growing number of clinicians now suggest that a diagnosis of posttraumatic stress disorder may be the most accurate primary diagnosis for many survivors of interpersonal and family violence (Browne, 1992; Bryer, Nelson, Miller, & Krol, 1987; Burge, 1989; Davidson & Foa, 1991; Dutton, 1992a, 1992b; Gelinas, 1983; Gondolf, 1990; Herman, 1986, 1992; Koss, 1990a; Koss & Harvey, 1991; van der Kolk, 1987; Walker, 1991, 1992). The "extreme traumatic stressors" noted in the PTSD definition are known to characterize the lives of women in relationships with violent mates. Human-made events are particularly likely to cause acute psychological distress (Davidson & Baum, 1990). Factors most often associated with the development of PTSD include perception of life threat, threat of physical violence, physical injury, extreme fear or terror, and a sense of helplessness at the time of the incident (Davidson & Foa, 1993; Herman, 1992; March, 1990). Human-made violence seems particularly likely to lead to extreme sequelae (Davidson & Baum, 1990); in the *DSM-III-R*, the presence of ongoing physical or sexual abuse was listed under the *Extreme Stressors* category (Category 5) on Axis IV classifications of severity of stressors. The only category more severe (Category 6) was reserved for *catastrophic* events and includes captivity as a hostage or in concentration camps. Women who have been held captive by virtue of the severity of violence and threat or who have experienced psychological torture by their abusers would also meet criteria for this most extreme category (Herman, 1992; Walker, 1991). Some researchers have also suggested that PTSD is most likely to develop when traumatic events occur in an environment previously deemed to be safe (Foa, Rothbaum, & Olasov, 1989); this is another dimension clearly applicable to violence occurring at home.

Many of the psychological aftereffects of violence against women can be understood as elements of a PTSD diagnosis. Women survivors of severe partner violence respond over the long term with fear and terror as well as flashbacks during which past abusive incidents are reexperienced. Marked expressions of denial and avoidance, loss of memory for parts of traumatic episodes, constricted affect, psychic numbing, chronic anxiety and hypervigilance, difficulty sleeping, nightmares, and marked physiological reactivity are also often noted (Dutton, 1992a). Providers may be particularly confused when periods of denial—an integral part of survival for most individuals faced with ongoing aggression—are interspersed with expressions of extreme fear or desperation at the dangers being faced. Recognizing the potential for at least *some* posttraumatic stress responses to be present in any individual exposed to physical attack, threat, or rape gives clinicians and researchers a basis from which to evaluate seemingly contradictory or inconsistent responses.

Several recent studies have documented high rates of PTSD among women victims of partner violence (Dutton, 1992b; Kemp et al., 1991) as well as among victims of rape (Davidson & Foa, 1991; Foa, Rothbaum, Riggs, & Murdoch, 1991; Foa, Steketee, & Rothbaum, 1989; Koss & Harvey, 1991). The PTSD construct has the advantage of providing a framework for recognizing the severity of events external to the individual, thus validating the presence of even dramatic responses to those events. It also enables clinicians and scientists to draw from a rich body of literature on psychological trauma to aid women survivors of male violence (Goodman et al., 1993b). However, *for reactions to be seen as understandable responses to severe stressors, the trauma must be known.* Unfortunately, in most mental health settings, routine screening for a history of family violence is almost never done and serious or chronic conditions are "treated" without knowledge of the core trauma underlying the presenting symptomatology.

It is vitally important for PTSD sufferers to become aware of the potential links between the symptoms that plague them and the exposure to an extreme stressor external to themselves. Clinical researchers have consistently noted that assaulted women internalize the derogatory attributions and justifications of the violence against them (Browne, 1987; Pagelow, 1984; Walker, 1979, 1984). An enhanced understanding of the range of responses manifested by all types of persons who are faced with physical or sexual danger or attack expands the interpretations of symptoms beyond internal or gender explanations. It therefore empowers both survivors and providers to proceed with focused goals of safety, symptom mastery, reintegrations, and healing (Herman, 1992; Leibowitz, Harvey, & Herman, 1993).

Failure to identify the presence of posttraumatic stress disorder can have tragic consequences. For example, current studies suggest that drug treatments alone have only limited utility in alleviating the effects of PTSD, providing some improvements in intrusive symptomatology, depression, and panic attacks, but having little effect on avoidance and numbing (e.g., Fairbanks & Nicholson, 1987; Solomon, Gerrity, & Muff, 1992). Recent prospective studies have indicated "supportive counseling" that emphasized nonjudgmental acceptance and focused on problem-solving techniques *without* discussing the trauma was less effective in alleviating the symptoms of PTSD suffers over time than interventions specifically designed to deal with traumatic experiences and their effects. In fact, victims in the supportive counseling condition were *more* symptomatic at followup than the wait-listed control subjects (Foa et al., 1991). Current empirical and clinical results indicate that, for individuals suffering from PTSD, the trauma must be dealt with directly in order for interventions to be effective (Dutton, 1992a; Foa et al., 1991; Herman, 1992; van der Kolk, 1987).

Pitfalls in Application

Gender-neutral or male-based assessments have long failed to capture predominant patterns of life experiences for women (McGrath et al., 1990). For example, the *DSM-III-R's* description of traumatic events as "outside the range of usual human experience" excluded the assessment of posttrauma responses in women and children for whom physical or sexual attacks may be a weekly reality. (This restriction was revised in *DSM-IV* so that the event is no longer required to be outside the range of usual human experience.) Similarly, introductory paragraphs to PTSD assessment protocols, with their emphasis on primarily male experiences such as war and heavy combat, cause many professionals to overlook the potential for similar responses in survivors of experiences more typical of the lives of women and girls. (See Dutton, 1992b; Herman, 1992; National Victims Center, 1992; and Walker, 1991 for exceptions).

Finally, criteria for PTSD—structured for situations in which the primary stressor is no longer present—do not always fit for individuals who are faced with ongoing threat or danger. Women who are still living in abusive situations or who are separated from their abusers but fear their retaliation may demonstrate clinical symptoms related to prior traumas as well as to the anticipation of future danger (Dutton, 1992a; Walker, 1991). The PTSD diagnosis as currently framed also may fail to account for the complexity of effects of chronic abuse that women victimized by intimates typically suffer (Dutton, 1992a; Herman, 1993; Walker, 1991). However, as a basis for understanding responses to physical or sexual attacks and threats or attempts to kill, the potential for posttraumatic stress disorder should be evaluated whenever a history of violent aggression by intimates is identified.

5

Intimate Violence: Treatment Issues and Policy Initiatives

COMMUNITY-BASED SERVICES

During the past 15 years, the battered women's movement, characterized in large part by grass-roots efforts, has developed a variety of community-based interventions for women who have experienced assault and threat from intimate male partners. These interventions have focused mostly on crisis intervention with the safety of women and their children the primary goal. Focus has been on the transition of women from violent homes to nonviolent settings and on the provision of auxiliary social services necessary to sustain a woman's move away from a violent partner. Services typically include legal advocacy, social services and welfare system referral, job assistance, and financial aid. (Refer to Schecter, 1982, for a history of the development of the battered women's movement.)

These services are premised on a model of the battered woman as a mentally healthy adult who is experiencing a severe and life-threatening crisis she did not create, but does have the power to ameliorate or change (Dutton, 1992; Walker, 1979, 1984). During this period of crisis, the battered woman may manifest psychological distress, but is not considered psychologically unhealthy at the core. Many such services reflect an explicitly feminist analysis of male violence as a social and cultural phenomenon (Schechter, 1982); others, arising from religious or other conservative social groups, tend to see violence as a problem, but not as an expression of a more general societal trend. Services are generally offered through shelters for battered women and their children, or, in some rural areas, through networks of safe homes organized and directed by a more central agency. Traditional help agencies such as the Salvation Army and the YWCA also operate community-based shelters for battered women and their children.

Nonshelter services available at the community level tend to take the form of information and suppport groups for women not yet able or willing to leave a violent relationship, as well as more general community information and referral resources. In some circumstances, these nonshelter programs combine services to several different types of women violence survivors (NiCarthy, 1982).

Although such services are necessary and valuable, they are chronically underfunded and suffer from severe staff turnover (burnout among staff is common due to low pay and high work demands). In short, these services are never sufficient to serve the needs of the battered women population. Shelter beds are full in almost every community where they exist, yet government funding to shelters was drastically reduced under the Reagan Administration (Walker, 1989). Additionally, community support systems do a poor job of serving certain groups of battered women, including minorities, immigrants (both documented and undocumented), lesbians, and women with mental and physical disabilities (Lobel, 1986; White, 1990). Women from some religious groups also have difficulty using community shelter resources. For example, Orthodox Jewish women who need Kosher food and Orthodox Muslim women who have similar hallal eating restrictions need shelter settings that reflect their unique cultural and other needs. In some larger cities, community interventions for special populations have been developed to fill this gap. For example, the Abused Deaf Women's Advocacy Services of Seattle is a community intervention, referral, and safe-home network designed to meet the needs of deaf and deaf-blind women; staff are either deaf or hearing women fluent in sign language.

Psychologists need to be aware of community-based services in their area (for both the general population of battered women and for special population groups), so client referrals can be made when needed and appropriate. Although community organizations rarely use psychologists for the delivery of services, they may be called on as consultants when particular issues and problems arise for shelter staff or residents.

CLINICALLY ORIENTED SERVICES

Women survivors of male violence often recover completely from their experience without professional intervention (Walker, 1984). However, those women who do seek psychological services present to treatment with a variety of concerns including depression, panic, vocational difficulties, and parenting problems (Dutton, 1992a; Walker, 1984). But as stated earlier, the abused woman is, first and foremost, a trauma survivor. Like survivors of other traumas, the abused women may have had factors in her life before the violence that may have affected her functioning negatively or may have had significant exposure to factors that increase her resilience. These prior risk and resiliency factors influence the meaning of being battered for some women, as well as their capacity to cope with it. They can also affect the nature and severity of the psychological consequences she experiences as a result. However, absent careful study and extended contact with a woman survivor of violence, clinicians should avoid assuming that any currently observable psychological distress is either a cause of, or contributing factor to, the abuse. Rather, unless and until careful assessment demonstrates otherwise, the survivor's symptoms are most reasonably attributed to the effects of her exposure to a repetitive, life-threatening trauma in a context that is severely undermining to her expectations of an intimate loving relationship. Therapy that seeks to assist a woman in understanding why she has unconsciously "chosen" a violent partner, or labels her as *codependent* or *enabling* of a partner's violence will be inefficacious and harmful and represents strategies to be avoided by the ethical psychologist (Bograd, 1984; Dutton, 1992a; Walker, 1984).

As Rosewater (1985a, 1985b) noted, women survivors of partner violence who seek psychotherapy rarely self-identify as such. Standard assessment instruments, such as the Minnesota Multiphasic Personality Inventory–2 or the Millon Clinical Multiaxial Inventory, are likely to misdiagnose battered women as psychotic or personality disordered (Rosewater, 1985a, 1985b). Therefore, an essential aspect of psychotherapy for such women includes careful queries during intake about current and past exposure to partner violence in order to avoid misdiagnosis and inappropriate treatment. Such inquiries are especially pertinent when the woman in question is of color, lesbian, disabled, non-native English speaking, or in some other way affected by social or cultural factors that may increase the difficulty of her coming forward to initiate a report of being beaten by a partner. Psychological test results should be viewed with caution and in the context of current research on battered women. Computerized test interpretations are especially inappropriate for the assessment of battered women because the context of violence is never factored into such materials (Rosewater, 1985a, 1985b).

Many women survivors of male violence have sustained repeated blows to the head over time. Such women may, therfore, suffer from the long-term consequences of minor head injuries, including depression, difficulties in concentration and performance, and problems of judgment and impulse control (McGrath, Keita, Strickland, Russo, 1990). Referral for neuropsychological assessment should always be considered if a woman describes such abuse as being hit in the head, having her head slammed against something, being shaken, or being choked into unconsciousness repeatedly (Dutton, 1992a).

When treating a woman who is being abused, a psychologist should pay careful attention to matters involving her safety (Dutton 1992a; NiCarthy, 1982; Walker, 1979, 1984, 1989). This includes developing safety and escape plans with her, informing her about community shelter and legal resources, and aiding her in the assessment of risk to herself and her children. It is important for therapists to take the initiative in developing such strategies with the client, even if the client has yet to identify a need. Often, women in battering relationships need support from a therapist to use what are otherwise adequate internal resources for planning and problem solving. The psychologist must also be aware of any legal mandate to report children who may be at risk because of the battering relationship. He or she must be sensitive to the ways in which a report will affect the client's safety. A psychologist needs to be especially attentive to issues of countertransference at this juncture because battered women are at the highest risk of being killed at the time of separation (Browne, 1987). Leaving the batterer must be the client's decision; a therapist must strenuously respect the client's judgment and timing on this matter despite genuine concern for the client's safety.

Dutton (1992b) provides one of the most thorough descriptions of the treatment needs of women violence survivors currently available. Her work, *Treating PTSD: Cognitive and Behavioral Strategies,*, is essential reading for psychologists working with this population. It describes the various components of working with women who are or have been battered. It also presents an overall philosophical framework for working with survivors, detailing both protective and cognitive interventions and describing the course of posttraumatic therapy.

In her work, Dutton noted that self-care, grief, and recovery from trauma can be complex and lengthy for some women survivors of intimate violence, even after the initial crisis has been resolved. Minority women, lesbians, religiously committed women, and women who are not part of the dominant culture may find these tasks particular challenging if ending the violent relationship is construed as a betrayal of their reference group or as an assimilation into the mainstream. Although *no* cultural group sanctions violence (Ho, 1990, Kanuha, 1990), the avenues available to the battered woman for remediation of its mental health consequences often take her far afield from her culture of origin. Thus, therapists working with these women need to ensure that their interventions are not only specific to the issues of surviving violence, but also carefully embedded in the norms and symbolism of the women's culture of origin. In other words, interventions must be culturally sensitive. (Refer also to Walker, 1994, for a generalist's guide to therapy with this population.)

If a woman is involved in a child custody struggle with her former batterer, an evaluating psychologist must take special care not to overpathologize her for demonstrating the effects of trauma. Conversely, psychologists should be careful not to underestimate the pathology of the batterer, who may appear more mentally healthy and functional because he has *not* been the target of repeated, severe interpersonal violence (Walker & Edwall, 1987). Chesler (1986) and Walker & Edwall (1987) have documented the harmful effects of participating in custody evaluations on battered women when the evaluator failed to take the context of battering into account. Battered women are often, quite reasonably, angry and hostile toward the men who beat them, and many are reluctant to expose children to a person known to be violent and controlling even when he is their father. This is not an attempt to alienate chidren from a parent, but rather to protect them from danger. The evaluator in such a circumstance needs to cautiously consider the accuracy of the battered woman's assessment of her spouse's risk of violent behavior toward children and avoid penalizing her for lack of equanimity toward the person who harmed her. (Readers are directed to Walker and Edwall, 1987, for a thorough discussion of the issue of custody evaluations with battered women.)

In general, therapists working with women survivors of violence must take an attitude of belief, support, and alliance (Dutton, 1992a; Walker; 1979, 1984, 1989). Although Ochberg (1988) recommended this position for working with all trauma survivors, it is especially important when working with women violence survivors who have had their power stripped from them in an intimate interpersonal relationship. Therapists must be sensitive and attentive to the ways in which their own power in the therapeutic exchange can be used to inadvertently exploit clients who have histories of abuse. Male therapists working with this population also need to be sensitive to ways in which they may inadvertently trigger fears of violence and dominance, such as the invasion of personal space, shaking a finger to make a point, or raising their voice to emphasize an issue. Women therapists working with this population need to attend to the risks of secondary victimization inherent in identification with the battered woman or in possible retraumatization if the therapist has a personal history of being a target of violence (McCann & Pearlman, 1990b).

POLICY RESPONSES TO VIOLENCE AT HOME

Although there have been earlier periods in U.S. history when the victimization of women and children were topics of special concern (Pleck, 1987), the past two decades represent the first time that systematic data on prevalence and outcomes have been collected and that responses have been so wide ranging. Advocacy groups, medical mental health, and criminal justice organizations, and governmental and academic communities have all been involved in these efforts (Fagan & Browne, in press; Schechter, 1982). Since 1975, major research and policy initiatives have been developed to address aggression occurring within families. The redefinition of violence against wives as an appropriate area for social intervention has been accompanied by a profusion of pro-arrest policies and other statutory provisions (Fagan & Browne, in press; Sherman & Cohen, 1989). Rape laws throughout the nation have been amended to protect victims, in some cases removing the exemption offered for assaults committed by husbands and ex-husbands against their current and former spouses. Nearly every state now has legislation dealing with violence between adult partners; federal legislation on violence against women is pending.

History: The Context of Reform

As noted earlier, many investigations have indicated that women in the United States are more likely to be assaulted, raped, or even killed by a male partner than by any other type of assailant. Yet, until the recent past, women received little legal protection from this type of danger. Until the late 1970s, assaults against wives were considered misdemeanors in most states, even when the same actions would have been considered felonies if perpetrated against strangers or acquaintances. In addition, social and cultural norms related to family privacy have kept many women from revealing their experiences to anyone (Pagelow, 1984). Those women who did report such violence found that the police went to great lengths to avoid arresting the abuser (Bard & Zacker, 1971; Dutton, 1987). In most jurisdictions, police were not empowered to arrest a suspect on a misdemeanor charge unless they had witnessed a part of the action, and virtually no other legal resource was available (Browne & Williams, 1989). Usually a wife could not file for a restraining order against a violent husband unless she was filing for divorce at the same time (Fleming, 1979; U.S. Commission on Civil Rights, 1978, 1982). Additionally, in some states, a single violent assault by a husband was not considered adequate grounds for divorce action (U.S. Commission on Civil Rights, 1978). Orders of protection were typically not available on an emergency basis and often carried no provisions for enforcement or penalties for violation. Even when cases of violent assault were considered in court, judges failed to apply criminal remedies appropriate to the seriousness of the offense, preferring probation, admonitions, counseling, or mediation (Dobash & Dobash, 1979; Field & Field, 1973; Lerman, 1981). Marital rape exemptions specifically excluded the sexual assault of women by their husbands from criminal statutes, and, until the mid-1970s, women who killed their mates to protect themselves or a child found the traditional plea of self-defense unavailable for their cases (Browne, 1987). Thus, women, supposedly under the protection of men in the home and in the courts, were left unprotected by them and were not allowed to protect themselves.

Before the 1970s, social service agents, operating within their mandates to protect children and preserve families, did little to aid women victimized by a partner's violence (Pizzey, 1974). Worse still, many mental health professionals pathologized victims of spouse abuse, calling them frigid, domineering, and masochistic and recommended therapy to help uncover supposedly unconscious conflicts that led them to provoke or tolerate the aggression. Physicians joined their mental health colleagues in denying men's responsibility for their assaults against women by focusing solely on victims' symptoms without regard to the source of their injuries (Browne, 1992; Randall, 1990; Stark, Flitcraft, & Frazier, 1979). Additionally many clergy, in their counseling capacities, subtly reinforced traditional attitudes that create and foster abuse between intimate partners (Alsdurf, 1985; Dobash & Dobash, 1979). It is not surprising that abused women still experience difficulty interpreting the meanings of their assaults and deciding on a course of action, given the fact that society—particularly in the case of marital rape and other assaults against wives—has traditionally offered more protection to the perpetrators than to the victims (Fiora-Gormally, 1978; Lerman & Livingston, 1983; U.S. Commission on Civil Rights, 1978, 1982).

The Battered Women's Movement

The antirape and battered women's movements of the early 1970s initiated what was to become a transformation in public policy responses to violence against women. By conceptualizing violence as a form of male power and control over women, newly formed women's groups across the country helped abused women realize that they were not alone in their experiences (Herman, 1992; Schechter, 1982). The activities of these early grass roots organizations initiated a wide range of responses that continue today (Fagan & Browne, 1993; Koss & Harvey, 1991; Schechter, 1982).

Since the mid-1970s, a variety of legal and extra-legal resources have become available to threatened or assaulted wives. Because the most pressing need of women faced with life-threatening violence at home is refuge, advocates—many of whom organized themselves into state coalitions—began taking abused women into their own homes. Others began the longer-term task of developing and maintaining emergency shelters in communities across the country.

The first facilities to house abused women were established between 1974 and 1976 (Schechter, 1982). These shelters were designed to provide temporary homes, free food, and clothing for abused women and their children; they also offered social support and legal and social advocacy services. In many cases, their locations were kept secret in order to protect residents from further danger. Most shelters operated under a philosophy that emphasized consensus decision making, individual empowerment, and self-help rather than mental health treatment or counseling. Newly developed shelter programs worked collaboratively to write funding proposals and mission statements as well as to identify problems, create solutions, and celebrate successes (Pence & Shephard, 1988; Schechter, 1982). Other resources, such as emergency crisis lines, counseling services, support groups, and children's services also developed out of shelters during the late 1970s (Pagelow, 1984).

Shelters also became agents of social change. Staff people educated shelter residents, community members, and the general public about the social context of violence against women and its roots in patriarchal ideologies. Within the health care arena, battered women's advocates helped develop standardized protocols for identifying and working with battered women in emergency rooms, primary care clinics, and physicians' offices. These protocols enabled practitioners to measure the extent and potential lethality of the violence, validate victims' experiences, avoid victim blaming, and provide referrals to other needed services. To facilitate quick and efficient referrals, advocates also helped health care providers forge ties with local criminal justice systems (McCambridge, 1989).

Possibly the most noticeable changes were seen within the legislative and criminal justice arenas. By 1980, 47 states had passed some form of domestic violence legislation (Kalmuss & Straus, 1983). This legislation emphasized assuring victims' rights, increasing victims' legal options, and protecting victims and those near them from further assault (Schechter, 1982). For example, courts were empowered to issue civil protection orders for women who were in danger of further abuse. Protection orders could be issued in any number of situations, including harassment or abuse of the victim at home, school, work, and other locations. They could also be used to stop unauthorized contact with any children involved and to curtail telephone threats or harassment. Such orders could be used to enjoin abusers from contacting their victims, if necessary by forcing them to leave home or to provide financial support to victims and other family members. Moreover, such orders did not have to be served on the perpetrators before they could be enforced. Other state legislative efforts focused on increasing arrest rates by broadening the arrest authority of police in misdemeanor assault cases or by providing guidelines for preferred responses.

Attempts to change legislation gained momentum when, in the mid-1970s, class-action suits were brought against police departments for failure to arrest in domestic violence cases (Gelles & Straus, 1988). Today, at least 15 states and many cities have laws or policies mandating arrest for felony assault. In every state except West Virginia, it is no longer necessary for police to witness an assault in order to arrest a suspected assailant without a prepared warrant. In addition to promoting legislative changes, advocates worked to educate police, prosecutors, and judges. These efforts led to the creation of special prosecution units in some jurisdictions, the expanded use of victim advocates, and the establishment of court-mandated treatment programs for abusers (Dutton, 1987; Gelles & Straus, 1988; Heise & Chapman, 1992).

Shortfalls in Application and Protection

Despite significant policy gains and increased options for victims of spouse abuse and sexual assault, rates of violent and lethal victimization against women remain high. Indeed, much work remains to be done. Many criminal justice personnel—including police, prosecutors, and judges—continue to view physical and sexual assaults by men against their women intimates as less serious than other types of assault. For example, approximately two thirds of reported incidents of domestic violence are classified as "simple assaults," placing them in the misdemeanor category, even though 50% of these assaults are as serious or more serious in terms of physical injury than 90% of all other rapes, aggravated assaults, and robberies (Bureau of Justice Statistics, 1986). Thus, it comes as no surprise that arrest remains the least frequent response to male aggression against relational partners. Indeed, by 1990, only 110 cities had domestic violence intervention programs that mandated arrest (Miletich, 1990).

The attitudes of police officers and their supervisors are directly related to the actions of responding officers in domestic violence situations (Independent Commission of the Los Angeles Police Department, 1991). In their study of police responses, Saunders and Size (1986) concluded that:

> Attitudes determine the extent of officer action, with stronger sexist attitudes and greater general approval of marital violence associated with a lessened tendency to arrest, counsel, or refer in domestic violence cases. (p. 37)

Even when arrests are made and charges filed, judges are often unwilling to treat male aggression against women, included life-threatening aggression, seriously. They often choose not to pursue protective actions and sometimes even blame the woman for clogging up the court system with family matters. Many times they suggest that the parties discuss their differences and work out their problems on their own (Browne, 1987; Gillespie, 1989). A case in point: 49 states and the District of Columbia have laws that enable judges to evict violent and threatening family members from the household, yet many judges do not exercise this option because they are concerned that summary eviction violates alleged abusers' rights of due process (Family Violence Project, 1990). In New York, the remedy of ordering a violent or threatening husband out of the residence is almost never pursued, particularly if the husband owns the home or has his name on the lease (Finn & Colson, 1990). Even when an order of protection includes an order to vacate, police often fail to respond to complaints or to enforce the vacate order when violations occur (Family Violence Project, 1990).

The low rate of conviction in domestic violence cases—in the face of high rates of assaults leading to injury and death for women—further illustrates the trivialized status of male violence against female intimates. In many jurisdictions, prosecutors contribute to these low conviction rates. Prosecutors often discourage victims from going forward with their cases or even dismiss cases at the misdemeanor level, often without advance notice to the victim. When prosecutors place a low priority on these cases, extensive delays often result, during which time a victim may be repeatedly reassaulted and threatened or may simply give up. Until recently in most jurisdictions, women who eventually took the defense of themselves or their children into their own hands were not allowed to enter evidence of physical violence or threat as a legal defense for their actions. However, there has been a gradual acceptance of such evidence on a state-by-state basis over the past decade (Browne, 1987; Gillespie, 1989; Maguigan, 1991; Thyfault, 1984; Walker, 1992; Walker, Thyfault, & Browne, 1982).

The social service system also remains underfunded and is inadequate to meet the needs of women victims (Zorza, 1991). Many of the women who attempt to escape a violent partner by seeking public shelter are turned away because of lack of space. In more than one half of all U.S. counties, no formalized resources exist for women assaulted by male partners (Jackson, 1990). Indeed, a Senate Judiciary Committee report noted that there are nearly three times as many animal shelters in the United States as there are shelters for abused women (McCarthy, 1991). Even when women are able to find temporary shelter, alternative permanent housing is often unavailable, a situation which leads in some cases to homelessness or a forced return to a violent situation (Zorza, 1991). In either case, a woman may lose custody of minor children for failure to protect them from exposure to a mate's violence or for inadequate care and housing. This adds a powerful impediment to women's ability to flee from or disclose violence perpetrated against them.

Federal Initiatives

Because both rape and violence by male partners, like most crimes, fall primarily under the jurisdiction of states and localities, the federal government's response to violence against women has been slow. Nevertheless, several important programs have been created and supported by persevering lawmakers and dedicated advocacy groups. Although not exhaustive, the following description provides a sampling of the different types of federal programs targeting violence against intimate partners.

Family Violence Prevention and Services Act

First enacted in 1984, the FVPSA provides states with grant money to establish, maintain, and expand shelters, child care programs, and related services for domestic-violence victims and their children. Although funds are also allocated for training and technical assistance to law enforcement agencies, a National Clearinghouse on Family Violence Prevention, and family violence research, most of the money is used for state-run domestic-violence programs and is earmarked for immediate shelter-related assistance.

Immigration Reform

Foreign nationals who are married to American citizens are required to remain married for two years before being granted residency status. In the past, this policy has resulted in victims of violence being "held hostage" during the time period necessary to establish residency. As part of the Immigration Act of 1990, however, Congress approved a provision to waive this two-year period for foreign individuals in abusive marriages with American citizens. Previously, such foreign nationals were unable to leave their abusers without risking deportation.

Sense of Congress Resolution

Typically, issues of child custody are considered separately from charges of physical assault and threat by one partner against another. In many cases, women who fled a violent mate and, in so doing, reduced her financial and residential stability lost custody to her assaultive partner. This congressional resolution—introduced by Rep. Constance Morella (R-Md) and passed in 1990—expresses the sense of the Congress that evidence of spouse abuse should create a statutory presumption that it is detrimental for a child to be placed in the custody of the abusive parent. Although this resolution does not *require* states to enact legislation, its purpose is to encourage them to do so by indicating strong congressional support from for such legislation. However, to date, only 10 states and the District of Columbia have such laws on the books.

Violence Against Women Act

This act is the most comprehensive legislation proposed to date to address the physical and sexual abuse of women. This bill is discussed in detail in chapter 11, but it should be noted here that Title 2 of the act (*Safe Homes for Women*) creates the first federal laws barring spousal abuse.

PART 3

Violence at Work

6

Sexual Harassment: The Last Great Open Secret

The unnamed should not be taken for the nonexistent.
MacKinnon, 1979

In a society in which the sexual victimization of women is so widespread it has been rendered effectively invisible, sexual harassment remains the last great open secret. Although all women know of it and many will experience it, until recently sexual harassment had no name or legal existence. Even now, there are no official statistics or national surveys; its existence is ignored in studies of both sexual victimization and workplace behavior, and women's stories of their experiences are routinely disbelieved.

Despite the silence that has surrounded it, sexual harassment has existed since women first sold their labor in the marketplace. In 1908, *Harper's Bazaar* published a series of stories by young women who had come to the city to find

This chapter is dedicated to the "Ladies of Dyersburg," in recognition of their courage and dignity in making their community a better place to live and work. Portions of the Incidence and Prevalence section first appeared as part of a science seminar presented by the author under the sponsorship of the Federation of Behavioral, Psychological, and Cognitive Sciences, Library of Congress, May 1992. A much abbreviated form of this chapter appeared in Fitzgerald, 1993a.

Because the focus of this report is violence against women and because the overwhelming majority of victims of sexual harassment are female, victims are referred to throughout the chapter as "she."

work, stories that read like yesterday's newspapers. A similar tale was told by Elizabeth Hasanovitch (1918), who was so afraid of her boss after he attempted to rape her that she never returned to collect her pay:

> I felt what that glance in his eyes meant. It was quiet in the shop, everybody had left, even the foreman. There in the office I sat on a chair, the boss stood near me with my pay in his hand, speaking to me in a velvety soft voice. Alas! Nobody around. I sat trembling with fear. (p. 110)

In a society in which a woman is raped every minute (National Victim Center, 1992) and more than 2,000 women are murdered annually by their husbands or partners, it is perhaps not surprising that sexual harassment has been so widely ignored, dismissed, and trivialized, becoming as banal as evil in other times and places (Arendt, 1951). Yet, as has recently become evident, the harassment of women in the workplace is a social problem of enormous proportions, affecting as many as one out of every two women over the course of their working lives (Fiske & Borgida, in press; Fitzgerald & Ormerod, 1993; Fitzgerald & Shullman, 1993; Pryor & McKinney, in press; see, more generally, Fitzgerald, 1992, 1993a; Tinsley & Stockdale, 1993).

The belief that harassment is a natural, if sometimes unfortunate, extension of normal heterosexual sexuality is sufficiently pervasive to necessitate a rationale for the inclusion of this topic in a discussion of violence against women. Analyses suggesting that harassment results from the misperception of sexual signals (e.g., Stockdale, 1993), arguing for the sociobiological necessity of male heterosexual intitiation (Studd & Gattiker, 1991), or warning against the inhibition of positive sexuality in organizations (Lobel, 1993) seem to imply that harassment is more akin to seduction than rape, and has more to do with romance than violation.

This view of harassment as romance gone astray influenced early legal opinions, such as *Miller v. Bank of America* (1977), in which the court declared "The attraction of males to females and females to males is a natural sex phenomenon and it is probable that this attraction plays at least a subtle part in most personnel decisions"(p. 236). More recently, a plaintiff in an Alabama court lost her case when a photograph of the defendant's wife was introduced; the judge ruled that the plaintiff was simply too unattractive to compete with the wife because she wore no makeup and didn't color her hair (Bravo & Cassedy, 1992). Research confirms that plaintiffs are more likely to be believed when they are attractive (Castellow, Wuenisch, & Moore, 1990), particularly if the harasser is not.

Research has also begun to confirm what has long been suspected, however, and that is the intertwining of sexuality, dominance, and misogyny in those men who are most likely to harass (Pryor, LaVite, & Stoller, 1993; Pryor & Stoller, 1992; Reilly, Caldwell, & DeLuca, 1992). It is not necessary to argue that harassment has nothing to do with sexuality to demonstrate that it has everything to do with violation. Research reviews, clinical reports of victims, and transcripts of court cases counter the natural or romanticized view of harassment with graphic stories of pain and degradation: The 25-year-old single mother who was orally raped during a job interview (*U.S. v. Lanier*, 1992); a workplace decorated with pornographic posters—one showing a meat spatula pressed against a woman's pubic area—and a dartboard with a drawing of a female breast, with the nipple as the bull's-eye (*Robinson v. Jacksonville Shipyards*, 1991); the women subjected to group assault by a crowd of drunken Navy pilots during the Tailhook Convention. Even what begins as love can become obsession, a psychological stalking as terrifying as any physical threat (see, for example, the recent case of New York Judge Sol Wachtler). Although most harassment is not physically violent, examples such as these are common enough to support the argument that harassment is a form of violence against women, differing from other forms mainly in venue rather than essence. Women subjected to sexual harassment demonstrate elevated fears of rape (Holgate, 1989) as well as fear of crime more generally (Junger, 1987). They also constrict their activities to avoid places and people where they have been or may be harassed further.

Like other forms of sexual victimization, harassment is a structural phenomenon, rather than one of individual deviance. Sexual harassment operates as an instrument of social control, as demonstrated by studies showing that women are most at risk in occupations traditionally reserved for men (Baker, 1989; Gutek, 1985; Gutek & Cohen, 1987; Gutek & Dunwoody, 1988; LaFontaine & Tredeau, 1986) and that women who report harassment commonly experience retribution, including being fired or forced to quit

(Caruthers & Crull, 1984; Coles, 1986; Fritz, 1989; Martin, 1984; Maypole & Skaine, 1983; Parmerlee, Near, & Jensen, 1982; Terpstra & Cook, 1985). Lesbian women may be at particular risk; if their identity is not known, they are generally perceived as single heterosexual women and face all of the dilemmas that this implies. Such situations may also compound any struggles they have in managing their identities as lesbians. Prejudice and homophobia may place openly lesbian workers at greater risk for harassment, possibly accounting for Schneider's (1982) findings of elevated levels of harassment among lesbians. Added to the danger of physical and emotional victimization is thus the threat of economic vulnerability, embedding the woman in a matrix of increasingly oppressive forces, with few viable choices and often no way out. This section of our report examines the phenomenon of sexual harassment in both the workplace and institutions of higher education, including its extent, nature and possible causes as well as its consequences for the women who experience it. As with acquaintance rape, perhaps the phenomenon to which it bears the closest resemblance, our review reveals that harassment has been routinely ignored, denied, or mystified as natural sexual behavior; society has blamed women for its occurrence and, sadly, women have blamed themselves.

DEFINITIONS, PERCEPTIONS AND LEGAL CONTEXT OF SEXUAL HARASSMENT

Attempts to study sexual harassment have been plagued since their inception by the lack of a generally accepted definition. Not only has the legal definition evolved over time, but also society's willingness to construe instances of harassment as problematic. This chapter outlines the legal definitions of sexual harassment within the context of society's evolving perceptions and concludes with a discussion of behavioral and operational definitions of the problem.

Legal and Regulatory Framework

Originally thought to be limited to situations in which women are threatened with their jobs to extort sexual cooperation, harassment is increasingly more broadly understood to include any deliberate or repeated sexual behavior that is unwelcome to the recipient, as well as other sex-related behaviors that are hostile, offensive, or degrading to women. Although theoretically illegal since the passage of the Civil Rights Act of 1964, a legal definition of harassment did not exist until 1980, when the Equal Employment Opportunity Commission (EEOC) issued its now well-known guidelines:

> Unwelcome sexual advances, requests for sexual favors, and other verbal or physical conduct of a sexual nature constitute sexual harassment when
>
> 1. submission to such conduct is made either explicitly or implicitly a term or condition of an individual's employment;
> 2. submission to or rejection of such conduct by an individual is used as the basis for employment decisions affecting such an individual; or
> 3. such conduct has the purpose or effect of substantially interfering with an individual's work performance or creating an intimidating, hostile or offensive working environment. (EEOC, 1980, p. 45)

This definition is generally understood to prohibit two broad classes of behavior: (a) any attempts to extort sexual cooperation by means of threats (either subtle or explicit) of job-related consequences (*quid pro quo* harassment), and (b) any sex-related verbal or physical conduct that is unwelcome and offensive (*hostile environment*), even if the woman suffers no tangible job consequence such as termination or loss of promotion. These two types of harassment were originally distinguished by MacKinnon (1979) in an influential book that first articulated the theory of sexual harassment as illegal sex discrimination. This book provided for the first time a basis upon which sexual harassment could be challenged legally.

The EEOC (1993) supplemented its original Sex Discrimination Guidelines (1980) with a statement emphasizing that Title VII's prohibition of a hostile environment include offensive, sex-related conduct that is not specifically sexual in nature (*i.e., gender harassment*). According to the EEOC, gender harassment is "verbal or physical conduct that denigrates or shows hostility or aversion" (p. 51269). Examples of such conduct include epithets, slurs, taunts, and gestures; the display or distribution of obscene or pornographic materials; gender-based hazing; and threatening, intimidating or hostile acts. As Gelfand, Fitzgerald, and Drasgow (unpublished manuscript) observed, "such behavior is not easily accounted for by (psychological) theories that insist on the role of heterosexual sexual interest as the essential stimulus for harassment (e.g., Stockdale, 1993; Studd & Gattiker, 1991). It is thus frequently ignored in psychological writings on this topic, despite its prevalence and centrality in many celebrated legal cases."

Although the Supreme Court has affirmed that both *quid pro quo* and *hostile environment* harassment are illegal because they violate Title VII (*Meritor Savings Bank v. Vinson*, 1986), research has demonstrated that many people simply do not believe that behaviors other than direct job-related coercion constitute sexual harassment (Adams, Kottke, & Padgitt, 1983; Fitzgerald & Ormerod, 1991; Gutek, 1985; USMSPB, 1981, 1987). Studies have also emphasized that the likelihood of any behavior being labeled as harassment is heavily influenced by questions concerning the victim's behavior, the nature of her relationship to the perpetrator and so forth (Reilly, Carpenter, Dull, & Bartlett, 1982; Rossi & Weber-Burdin, 1983; Weber-Burdin & Rossi, 1982). Questions concerning what the woman was wearing, what she said and did, and whether she previously had any romantic relationship with the harasser continue to influence how individuals evaluate any particular situation. Such personal theories serve to inhibit understanding of the seriousness of this issue, as well as to implicate the victim as responsible for causing it in some way. Research on attitudes and beliefs about the nature and causes of harassment has revealed a significant gender gap, with women being far more likely than men to label a given behavior as harassing (Fitzgerald & Ormerod, 1991; Gutek, Morasch, & Cohen, 1983; Hartnett, Robinson, & Singh, 1989; Koenig & Ryan, 1986; Padgitt & Padgitt, 1986; Powell, 1986; Valentine-French & Radtke, 1989; Workman & Johnson, 1991). The gap is particularly large with respect to less explicit situations and those situations involving hostile-environment behaviors. Because of the importance of this gender gap and its implications for the evolving legal framework of sexual harassment, we examine this research in some detail in the following section.

Gender Differences in Perceptions and Reactions

The body of literature supporting the assertion that men and women react differently to situations involving potentially sexually harassing behavior is both large and consistent, involving three separate but complementary lines of research: evaluation and labeling of specific behaviors; laboratory analogue research examining responses to written scenarios describing potentially harassing interactions; and the direct assessment of attitudes and beliefs about sexual harassment as a social problem.

Evaluation of Specific Behaviors

With regard to specific behaviors, considerable data exist to support the assertion that women have broader definitions of sexual harassment than men and are more likely to recognize a variety of specific situations as being sexually harassing in nature. This line of research generally involves presenting participants with a list of behaviors (e.g., sexual propositions, sexual bribes and threats, repeated sexual comments or jokes, leering, touching, cornering, etc.) and asking them which of these behaviors constitutes harassment. In variation of this paradigm, subjects rate behaviors in terms of offensiveness, seriousness, threat, and so forth. Research in this tradition includes Fitzgerald and Hesson-McInnis (1989); Fitzgerald and Ormerod (1991); Gutek (1985); Padgitt and Padgitt (1986); USMSPB (1981, 1987). Although women are more likely to assign higher ratings to all forms of harassing behavior, the gap between men and women is particularly large with respect to the less explicit situations and those involving hostile-environment behaviors.

Experimental Analogue Research

The most widely used paradigm for researching sexual harassment involves presenting research participants with written scenarios of potentially harassing behaviors and requiring them to rate the scenarios with respect to whether they represent harassment, the degree of perceived offensiveness or harm, responsibility of the perpetrator, and so forth. The advantage of this paradigm is that it allows the researcher to systematically vary salient aspects of the situation (e.g., status of perpetrator, reaction of victim) and examine the effects on the subsequent ratings. Virtually every study in this body of research has found substantial gender differences in the responses of men and women, with women being significantly more likely to evaluate the scenarios as harassing, offensive, threatening, and so forth. Research in this tradition includes Adams et al. (1983); Castellow et al. (1990); Gutek et al. (1983); Gutek and Morasch (1982), Hartnett et al. (1989); Hunter and McClelland

(1991); Jones and Remland (1992); Koenig and Ryan (1986); Lester, Banta, Barton, Elian, MacKiewicz, & Winkelried (1986); Malovich and Stake (1990); Mazer and Percival (1989); McKinney (1990, 1992); Popovich, Gehlauf, Jolton, Somers, and Godinho (1992); Powell (1986); Pryor and Day (1988); Reilly et al. (1982); Valentine-French and Radtke (1989); and Weber-Burdin and Rossi (1982). In a variation on the usual written scenario read by the research participants, Marks and Nelson (1993) constructed videotapes of potentially sexually harassing interactions and had them rated by both men and women. As with all the studies already cited, the women in Marks and Nelson's study interpreted the situations as more harassing than did the men. (For one of the few exceptions to this finding, see Terpstra & Baker, 1986.) As with many of the studies that involved direct ratings of behaviors, the scenario research demonstrated not only that women react more negatively to virtually all types of harassing behavior, but also that the gender gap is particularly notable with respect to less explicit situations and those involving hostile environment behaviors.

Attitudes and Beliefs

The final line of research examining the effect of gender on reactions to sexual harassment involves the direct assessment of individual attitudes and beliefs about harassment, its seriousness, and its perpetrators and victims. This paradigm involves the construction of an attitude scale containing statements such as "I believe sexual harassment is a serious social problem;" "Most people who file complaints of sexual harassment are just trying to get the person in trouble;" "Most complaints of sexual harassment are false;" or "Much of what is called sexual harassment is just normal sexual interplay between adults."

Studies in this tradition include those of Adams et al. (1983); Gutek (1985); Lott, Reilly, and Howard (1982); Mazer and Percival (1989); Reilly et al. (1992); Reilly, Lott, and Gallogly (1986); and USMSPB (1981, 1987). Such research has consistently demonstrated that women are more likely to believe that harassment is a serious problem, to hold perpetrators responsible for their behavior, to believe that reports of harassment are likely to be true and should be taken seriously, and so on. Men, on the other hand, are more likely to disbelieve reports, to hold the woman responsible for the situation, and to blame the woman for its occurrence or for not handling it properly. An interesting variation on this research was provided by Workman and Johnson (1991) who showed participants photographs of women wearing differing amounts of cosmetics; the male participants in this study were significantly more likely than female participants to rate *all* the women as likely to provoke harassment.

Possible Explanations

There are at least two possible explanations for such findings. First, women are (by far) more likely than men to be victims of sexual harassment and other forms of sexual victimization. Research has documented that approximately one in four women will be the victim of a sexual assault in her lifetime (Koss, 1992) and that one in approximately every two women will be subjected to some form of sexual harassment over the course of her academic or working life (Fitzgerald & Shullman, 1993). This does not include the millions of women who are battered and assaulted by their intimate partners (Browne, 1993). Virtually all perpetrators of sexual harassment are men. Given the extent of this victimization, it is not surprising that women are more sensitive to this issue, see it more seriously, and attribute to it more importance. Men, influenced no doubt by their own experiences and those of other men, are uniformly more likely to downplay the issue, to attribute it to women's behavior or to think that the problem is simply exaggerated.

A second explanation has to do with the fact that men are much more likely than women to hold traditional sex role attitudes and beliefs about women and their roles. Such traditional sex role attitudes have been implicated in studies of sexually harassing behaviors (Pryor, 1987; Pryor et al., 1993) as well as in studies related to beliefs about sexual harassment (Brooks & Perot, 1991; Pryor, 1985; Reilly et al., 1992) and other forms of sexual victimization (Burt, 1980; Lonsway & Fitzgerald, in press). Some studies have shown that traditional sex role attitudes account for the major variability in beliefs about sexual harassment (Malovich & Stake, 1990) and that when gender role is held constant, gender differences per se virtually disappear. To the degree that men as a group are almost uniformly more likely than women to hold traditional sex role attitudes, it is not surprising that they also hold more victim-blaming attitudes and beliefs about sexual harassment. There is also a large body of literature indicating that men frequently sexualize women's behavior and see sexual invitations when none in fact exist (Abbey, 1982, 1987a; see Stockdale, 1993, for a review).

The argument that there are consistent and substantial gender differences in perceptions of and attributions about sexually harassing behavior is supported by three separate bodies of research demonstrating remarkably consistent findings. Regardless of what approach is taken, how the question is asked, or what outcome variables are examined, women are consistently more likely than men to take this issue seriously; to see harassing behavior as offensive, threatening, and the like; to believe victims; and to hold perpetrators responsible for their behavior. As with all behavioral science research, counter examples can be offered; however, they are very few and far between.

This perceptual gender gap recently stimulated the establishment of the so-called *reasonable woman* standard as the appropriate legal criterion for determining whether sexual harassment has occurred. In *Ellison v. Brady* (1991), the U.S. 9th Circuit Court ruled that the law must take into account the victim's perspective, noting that:

> Conduct that many men consider unobjectionable may offend many women. Because women are disproportionately victims of rape and sexual assault, women have a stronger incentive to be concerned with sexual behavior....Men, who are rarely victims of sexual assault, may view sexual conduct in a vacuum without a full appreciation of the social setting or the underlying threat of violence that a woman may perceive. (p. 878–879)

It is thus unclear at this point whether the difference argument will ultimately survive judicial review. Even feminist legal scholars are divided about the desirability of codifying gender differences, some arguing that it is preferable to declare particular behaviors illegal, independent of individual perceptions. However, the ruling does not differ appreciably from the ordinary tort standard (which requires that injury be evaluated from the perspective of the victim); is congruent with the research data; and constitutes an important advance over the reasonable *person* standard, generally considered to reflect male perspectives and standards. The Supreme Court's recent decision in *Harris v. Forklift Systems, Inc.* (1993) was widely expected to resolve this issue, as urged in several amicus briefs (including that submitted by the American Psychological Association). The Court, however, restricted itself in this case to clarifying the standard of severity; rather than addressing directly the reasonable woman issue, it retained the standard "reasonable person" language while, at the same time, emphasizing that it is also necessary to take the perspective of the victim into account. It is unclear what effect this dual test will have on cases such as Ellison and many observers expect the Court to revisit the issue sometime in the future.

Conceptual, Behavioral, and Operational Definitions

In addition to legal and legislative definitions, scholars have proposed more theoretical or conceptually based definitions of harassment, the most influential of which was offered by MacKinnon (1979): "Sexual harassment...refers to the unwanted imposition of sexual requirements in the context of a relationship of unequal power. Central to the concept is the use of power derived from one social sphere to lever benefits or impose deprivations in another" (p. 1; cf. Cleveland & Kerst, 1993). Similarly, Benson and Thomson (1982) asserted that sexual harassment is broader than sexual coercion and can only be understood as the confluence of authority relations and sexual interest in a society stratified by gender. LaFontaine and Tredeau (1986) proposed that sexual harassment can be defined as "any action occurring within the workplace whereby women are treated as objects of the male sexual prerogative. Furthermore, given that women are invariably oppressed by these actions, all such treatment is seen to constitute harassment, irregardless of whether the victim labels it as problematic" (p. 435). Farley (1978) asserted that "sexual harassment is...unsolicited non-reciprocal male behavior that asserts a woman's sex role over her function as worker" (p. 14). Also, Fitzgerald, Swan, and Fisher (in press) asserted that sexual harassment can be defined *psychologically* as unwanted sex-related behavior at work that is appraised by the recipient as being offensive, exceeding her resources, or threatening her well-being. Thus, such theoretical conceptions have defined harassment as an act of violation and have situated the experience within a socially constructed nexus defined by the intersection of sex and power, rather than by either in isolation.

Finally, a variety of behavioral definitions of harassment have been proposed; the original list proposed by Working Women United Institute (WWUI) is typical: "Sexual harassment can be any or all of the following: verbal sexual suggestions or jokes, constant leering or ogling, 'accidentally' brushing against your body, a 'friendly' pat, squeeze, pinch or arm around you, catching you alone for a quick kiss, the explicit proposition backed by threat of losing your job, and forced sexual relations" (WWUI, 1978, p. 1). Similar lists have been proposed by others (see, for example, Betts & Newman, 1982; Project on the Education and Status of Women, 1978; for a review, see Fitzgerald, 1990).

A widely used classification scheme was proposed by Till (1980) who classified the responses of a national sample of college women into five general categories that covered a wide spectrum of experiences from verbal abuse to sexual assault. His analysis yielded a five-fold classification of behaviors, including *gender harassment* (generalized sexist remarks and behavior, similar in many ways to racial harassment); *seductive behavior* (inappropriate and offensive sexual advances); the solicitation of sexual activity by promise of reward (*sexual bribery*); the coercion of sexual activity by threat of punishment (*sexual coercion*); and *sexual imposition* or assault. Although early studies of harassment generally employed simple lists of researcher-generated behaviors, Fitzgerald et al. (1988) developed a survey instrument, the Sexual Experiences Questionnaire (SEQ), which had items designed to tap Till's categories and to meet generally accepted standards of reliability and validity.

Gelfand et al. (unpublished manuscript) proposed a tripartite psychological model of sexual harassment that parallels but is distinct from current legal formulations. Their work demonstrated that Till's (1980) original five categories can be more parsimoniously accounted for by three stable factors, that is, *gender harassment, unwanted sexual attention* (both verbal and physical), and *sexual coercion*. On the basis of confirmatory factor analyses of the SEQ across multiple settings, samples and cultures, they argued that these related but nonoverlapping categories are necessary and sufficient to classify any particular instance of sexual harassment. Although multiple, disparate examples of each category abound, the categories themselves appear to represent an exhaustive classification of sexual harassment behaviors.

Incidence and Prevalence

Because the study of workplace harassment is in its infancy, large scale formal studies are rare. Therefore, incidence and prevalence rates must be estimated from those investigations that are available. Unlike other forms of sexual violence, there are no centralized records or reports of sexual harassment comparable to the data available on rape or domestic assault. The Equal Employment Opportunity Commission compiles statistics reflecting the number of federal complaints filed annually with the federal government. Separate figures are also available for the 18 states that prohibit harassment under their own statutes.

As with the *Uniform Crime Reports* (UCR) data, which report annual figures for the number of crimes reported to local authorities, such figures represent only a fraction of the true incidence of harassment in the population. The best evidence available suggests that less than 5% of victims ever report their sexual harassment experiences (Fitzgerald et al., 1988; Livingston, 1982) to anyone in authority; only a small subset of that 5% file formal complaints with their employers or institutions. A smaller percentage still brings charges under state or federal legislation. Although recent public attention to this topic suggests that these percentages have or will likely increase, even such increased percentages have little to say about the actual incidence and prevalence of sexual harassment.

Because harassment is legally a civil rights violation rather than a crime, it is not included in national victimization surveys, and there are currently no national data that estimate its extent. The most reliable evidence concerning incidence and prevalence rates can be drawn from a handful of major investigations conducted in the 1980s and early 1990s. Although studies of convenience samples and specialized populations abound (e.g., Baker, 1989; Culbertson, Rosenfeld, Booth-Kewley, & Magmusson, 1992; Grieco, 1987; Gruber & Bjorn, 1982; Martindale, 1990; Mazer & Percival, 1989; Roscoe, Goodwin, Repp, & Rose, 1987; see also Fitzgerald & Shullman, 1993, for a summary and review), it is from these that we obtain our most reliable information.

Employed Women

In 1980, Congress commissioned the largest and probably the best known study of sexual harassment conducted to date. In this study, the U.S. Merit Systems Protection Board (USMSPB, 1981) surveyed a stratified random sample of 23,964 federal workers. Of the female respondents, 42% reported experiences of sexual harassment, a figure projecting to 294,000 women in the federal workforce who were harassed over a two-year period. The researchers reported that, rather than experiencing isolated occurrences, many women were victimized repeatedly over a considerable period of time. They noted that incidents occurred repeatedly, were of long duration—many continuing for six months or longer—and had a sizable economic effect, costing the federal government nearly $200 million over the two-year period covered by the study.

The Merit Systems study (USMSPB, 1981) examined the frequency of seven types of harassing behaviors, classified in three categories of severity. In the "less severe" category, 33% of the women reported being the target of unwelcome sexual remarks; 28% reported suggestive looks; and 26% had been deliberately touched. When more severe behaviors were examined, 15% of the women reported being pressured for dates, 9% (or nearly one in 10) had been directly pressured for sexual favors, and a similar number had received unwelcome letters and telephone calls. One percent of the sample reported actual or attempted rape by coworkers (a figure that projects to 12,000 victims of sexual assault during the period covered by the study), again refuting the popular assumption that harassment is a trivial or nonserious form of behavior. A follow-up investigation conducted six years later yielded essentially similar results (USMSPB, 1987).

The second major harassment study was conducted by Gutek (1985) who studied a representative sample of the Los Angeles area workforce ($N = 1,232$). Based on telephone interviews generated through a random digit dialing procedure, the study found that 53% of the female participants reported at least one experience that they considered harassing during their working lives, including insulting comments (19.8%); insulting looks and gestures (15.4%); sexual touching (24.2%); and being expected to socialize as part of the job (10.9%). In addition, nearly one in 12 (7.6%) of the women reported they had at some point been expected to participate in sexual activity as part of their job. Although differences in methodology make comparisons between the Gutek and Merit Systems studies difficult, their overall estimates are fairly comparable—that is, approximately half the female workforce experiencing some form of sexual harassment.

The National Victim Center included questions on sexual harassment in its latest study of sexual assault. This survey of 3,020 women, of whom 2,720 had been employed at some point in their lives, provides prevalence data in a nationally representative sample (Kilpatrick, 1992; Saunders, B. E., 1992). Preliminary results (Saunders, B. E., 1992) indicated that approximately 17.5% of the U.S. adult female population had been sexually harassed in the workforce, an estimate significantly lower than that reported by other investigators. Given that this survey inquired only about harassment by supervisors and bosses, and counted as harassment only those instances that the respondant herself labeled as harassment, the results likely represent a significant underestimate. Still, even this conservative assessment yields an estimated figure of nearly 17 million women who have been harassed during the course of their working lives.

Women Students

Studies of women university students provide similar figures. In the first published survey of the sexual harassment of students, Benson and Thomson (1982) studied the experiences of 269 randomly selected seniors at the University of California–Berkeley. Nearly one in three of the women surveyed had experienced some form of harassment during their college careers. In a survey of women students at East Carolina University conducted by Wilson and Kraus (1983), 33% reported being harassed by male teachers. A study done at Michigan State (Maihoff & Forrest, 1983) found that 25% of the female students surveyed had experienced at least one incident of sexual harassment. A variety of other university-based studies have been reported (see Fitzgerald, 1992, and Rubin & Borgers, 1990, for reviews). Most of these employed some version of the Merit Systems methodology and typically reported figures in the 30% range.

In the largest study of college women conducted to date, Fitzgerald et al. (1988) surveyed more than 2,000 students using the behaviorally based SEQ. The SEQ is an objective inventory designed to sample multiple instances of the original five categories developed by Till (1980) from his national qualitative survey of college women. Each category is assessed by multiple items, all items employ behavioral terms, and the words *sexual harassment* do not appear until the end of the instrument. Participants respond to each item on a 3-point scale (*never; once; more than once*), and results are reported in terms of frequencies for each item. These frequencies can be averaged to provide an estimated mean frequency for each of the categories. The SEQ appears to possess psychometric characteristics comparable to those of other psychological inventories (e.g., reliability and stability coefficients in the .80s, reasonable content validity, and promising estimates of criterion-related validity). Thus, it represents an advance over the simple checklist methodology used in previous studies (see Fitzgerald, 1994, for an update and revision).

Fitzgerald and her colleagues (1988), who used the SEQ, reported that approximately half of the women in their multicampus sample had experienced some form of harassment from their professors or instructors during their undergraduate or graduate careers. The most frequently reported behavior was some form of gender harassment (e.g., hostile or degrading verbal remarks or similarly negative behaviors directed at them simply because they are women). However, 28% reported unwanted sexual attention. One in 20 said they had been bribed or threatened to induce sexual cooperation, and nearly one in 10 reported some form of sexual imposition, ranging from unwanted touching and fondling to outright sexual assault.

Factors Influencing Detection of Harassment

Examination of the prevalence literature suggests a substantial degree of agreement despite considerable methodological variation. Still, a variety of factors influence the incidence and prevalence estimates that have been compiled thus far, including operational definitions, the wording of surveys, method of data collection, and sample composition.

Type and Wording of Surveys

With regard to the wording of questionnaires and surveys, data will be only as complete as the operational definition allows. Measurement issues have been almost completely ignored until recently and are still seriously neglected (Fitzgerald & Shullman, 1993; Gelfand et al., unpublished manuscript).

The simplest (and least satisfactory) method of obtaining prevalence estimates is to ask participants, "Have you ever been harassed?" Although not typically used by behavioral researchers, such a procedure is prevalent in newspaper surveys and opinion polls. This was true of many surveys and polls conducted during the Supreme Court confirmation hearings of Clarence Thomas in which less than 30% of respondents said that they had been harassed. This rate found by the surveys should be considered an underestimate. In addition to the psychometric problems posed by the use of single-item measures to assess complex, multidimensional phenomena, the use of the term *sexual harassment* introduces additional difficulties. A wide range of studies have demonstrated that substantial individual differences exist in perceptions of what behavior constitutes sexual harassment and under what conditions (e. g., Castellow et al., 1990; Fitzgerald & Ormerod, 1991; Gutek & Morasch, 1982; Harnett et al., 1989; Koenig & Ryan, 1986; Lester et al., 1986; Padgitt & Padgitt, 1986; Powell, 1986; Reilly et al., 1982; Valentine-French & Radtke, 1989; Workman & Johnson, 1991). Thus, asking respondents if they have been sexually harassed, or labeling behaviors as harassment and asking respondents if they have experienced such behaviors introduces considerable error into the procedure. Most women have been socialized to accept many forms of sexual exploitation as jokes, compliments, or "just the way things are." Fitzgerald and her colleagues (1988) reported that almost 50% of the women in their sample had been victims of unwanted sexual attention—ranging from verbal behavior to rape—yet only 8% responded on a separate item that they had been sexually harassed. Thus, estimates produced by such single-item screens cannot be considered valid estimates of the prevalence of sexual harassment.

More typical methods involve presenting the respondent with a list of behaviors and asking her whether she has ever experienced them (prevalence) within a particular timeframe or organization (incidence). The seven types of behavior used by Merit Systems and Gutek's (1985) list of six similar types are examples of this methodology, as are the seven items derived by Saunders (1992). Gutek asked respondents whether they thought the behavior was intended to be complimentary or insulting, and Saunders asked respondants whether they considered their experiences to be harassment. Although a considerable improvement over a simple one-item measure, such lists can be criticized as *ad hoc* and atheoretical, as little if any rationale is offered for the particular behaviors chosen and many of them are relatively vague (e.g., "insulting looks or gestures"). Because there has been little agreement on such issues, the target behaviors often vary from study to study, making cross-sample comparisons virtually impossible.

Although most of the major forms of harassment have been included in the majority of investigation done to date, some studies have only asked participants about a narrow range of fairly severe behaviors (e.g., Maihoff & Forrest, 1983). Such studies have produced marked underestimates. Still other studies have asked respondents to report not only behaviors they themselves have experienced, but also whether they have ever heard of such incidents happening to others (Lott, Reilly, & Howard, 1982). Some studies, as noted previously, have also asked respondents to assess the intentions of the perpetrator. Such procedures confound different types of information, inappropriately inflate or depress estimates, or require judgments that are likely to be unreliable.

Fitzgerald and Shullman (1993) offered the following suggestions for improving the quality of harassment surveys:

1. Assess the full range of potentially sexually harassing behaviors, from gender harassment to sexual assault.
2. Write items in behavioral terms and in enough detail to ensure that all respondents interpret them similarly.
3. Separate items assessing respondents' judgments concerning whether they have been sexually harassed from those asking about their experiences of actual behaviors; in general, the words sexual harassment should be avoided when assessing incidence and prevalence.

4. Add supplementary scales to assess the frequency, duration, and perceived offensiveness of the behaviors assessed. Such assessments, generally accepted as indicators of stressor severity, are important because of individual differences in tolerance for hostile environment behaviors. Such individual differences imply the necessity of collecting victim-based measures of severity when individuals (as opposed to environments or organizations) are being assessed.

Data Collection Methods

In addition to incommensurable definitions and questions, a variety of data collection methods have been employed to assess the incidence and prevalence of harassment among both employed and college women. Although mail surveys have clearly been the method of choice, both in-person surveys (Fitzgerald et al., 1988) and telephone interviews (Gutek, 1985; Kilpatrick, 1992) have been used. To date, no formal in-person interview studies have been reported, although Fitzgerald, Hulin, and Drasgow (1992) are implementing a computerized interview procedure in an on-going study.

A major concern with mail surveys is that response rate is likely to be influenced by subject matter interest; thus, those who have been harassed may be more likely to respond, leading to inflation of the estimates obtained. (A prime example of this problem can be seen in a reader survey conducted by *Redbook* magazine (Safran, 1976). *Redbook* included an informal survey in a regular issue of the magazine and reported that 90% of the more than 9,000 respondents had been sexually harassed. The biases introduced by such a procedure are obvious.) Although sophisticated methods to ensure a representative response are available and have been used successfully by some (Reilly et al., 1986; USMSPB, 1981), they are expensive and unlikely to be available to researchers without fairly substantial funding resources.

Despite such difficulties, there are some data to suggest that response bias has not been a serious problem in the major studies of harassment. USMSPB (1981) managed to achieve a response rate of 85% and reported that its sample was representative of the federal workforce. Similarly, Gutek (1985) reported a 77% acceptance rate in her telephone interview procedure, and

Fitzgerald et al. (1988) noted no systematic differences between their mail and in-person samples of college women (the later having virtually a 100% participation rate). Given that these studies report fairly similar estimates, it seems reasonable to assume cautiously that response bias has not been a major problem in the data base accumulated so far. Nationally representative surveys supplemented with in-person interviews (generally considered the gold standard in epidemiological research) are badly needed, however. Gordon and Riger (1989) report that such interviews produce dramatically higher prevalence rates in studies of other forms of sexual victimization. Although it is logical to suspect that this will also be true with respect to sexual harassment, confirmation awaits the appropriate data.

Sample Composition

The validity of any prevalence estimate depends heavily on the generalizability of the sample, and it is clear that the great majority of sexual harassment research has been conducted on small, local, or nonrepresentative samples. Given that the prevalence of sexual harassment is clearly influenced by a variety of workplace and occupational factors, the biases associated with such samples may be quite serious.

Early research (e.g., Crull, 1982) was based mainly on samples of self-identified victims, a situation which presents obvious problems. Although the Merit Systems data base (USMSPB, 1981, 1987) rests on large, stratified random samples, its conclusions cannot be generalized beyond the federal government, a workplace setting likely to differ in important ways from other organizations and institutions. Martindale's (1990) large-scale study of sexual harassment in the military presents similar problems of generalizability, as does Culbertson et al.'s (1992) Navy-wide survey. Gutek's (1985) sample is one of the most representative samples of the general workforce, although limited to a specific area (Los Angeles). Kilpatrick's (1992) nationally representative telephone sample may represent the most comprehensive sample of working women yet available. With the exception of Fitzgerald et al. (1988), studies of college women are typically limited to a single, often small, college campus. Even Fitzgerald et al.'s study—though it covered multiple campuses, diverse geographical areas and the majority of occupational and educational disciplines—was not truly national in scope.

There are two particularly serious problems with the available data base. First, even the large-scale studies lack adequate participation by women in blue-collar and other nontraditional jobs, a population that is clearly at increased risk. Second, there is virtually no information available concerning the harassment of ethnic and racial minority women, or those at educational institutions other than traditional four-year colleges and universities (e.g., technical schools, trade institutes, etc.), populations that are thought to be particularly vulnerable. The generalizability problems produced by dependence on such nonrepresentative samples place serious limitations on our knowledge of sexual harassment.

7

Responses to Sexual Harassment

D espite the widespread nature of sexual harassment and the seriousness of its consequences, most victims do not report it and in fact,
the modal response of women who are harassed is simply to endure the situation and hope it will somehow go away. Take, for example, the case of Law
Professor Anita Hill who told the Senate Judiciary Committee she had been
sexually harassed by then-Supreme Court Justice nominee Clarence
Thomas. The fact that she did not file a contemporaneous complaint against
Thomas, did not immediately quit her job, and in fact moved with him to a
different agency appeared inexplicable to many observers and was taken as
clear evidence that she was not telling the truth. During the confirmation
process, several senators cited these actions as a major basis for not believing her allegations, a suspicion echoed by large segments of the general public. Newspaper accounts published at the time made clear that many people
simply had great difficulty believing that a victim would behave in this manner. Such reactions conflict with the body of data indicating that this is how
victims of harassment have typically behaved.

Although rigorous examination of women's responses to sexual harassment is in its infancy, it is already clear, for example, that a notable discrep-

ancy exists between how individuals *say* they would respond to harassment and how victims actually *do* respond (Fitzgerald, Swan, & Fisher, in press). What little research exists on this topic demonstrates that (a) the great majority of individuals believe that women *should* respond assertively (Benson & Thomson, 1982; Collins & Blodgett, 1981; Gutek, 1985), and (b) the majority of women say they *would* respond assertively (Dunwoody-Miller & Gutek, 1985; Hogbacka, Kandolin, Haavio-Mannila, & Kauppinen-Toropainen, 1987). The overwhelming majority of victims, however, clearly do not respond in this manner (Fitzgerald, Gold, Brock, & Gelfand, unpublished; Gutek & Koss, 1993). When individuals have been asked what they would do if they were harassed, the majority have said they would speak up and tell the person to stop (Dunwoody-Miller & Gutek, 1985; Gutek & Koss, 1993). Research also indicates that, consistent with the cultural tradition of holding women responsible for controlling male sexuality, many individuals believe that women should be able to handle harassment themselves (Benson & Thomson, 1982; Collins & Blodgett, 1981; Gutek, 1985; Sheppard, 1989) and that women report that they feel confident they can do so (Gutek, 1985). The power of this cultural expectation is reflected in studies that demonstrate confronting the harasser or reporting him through formal organizational channels is one of the most important predictors of outcome in sexual harassment legal cases (Terpstra & Baker, 1989, 1992; York, 1992).

Despite the popularity of such beliefs, it is clear from the research that actual victims behave quite differently than survey respondents and analogue participants say they *would* behave if they were harassed. Merit Systems (1987) reported that the majority of victims in their second study either ignored the behavior or did nothing, and other studies confirm this finding (Benson & Thomson, 1982; Fitzgerald, Gold, Brock, & Gelfand, unpublished; Fitzgerald et al., 1988; Loy & Stewart, 1984). In their study of women auto assembly workers, Gruber and Bjorn (1982) found that 23% of victims said they simply ignored the behavior or put up with it.

If few victims actually confront their harasser, even fewer take any formal action such as reporting the problem to a supervisor or filing a complaint. Only 18% of Gutek's (1985) victims reported their harassment to anyone in authority; comparable figures were 24% for enlisted women and 12% for officers in the Navy study (Culbertson et al., 1992) and 7% in Gruber and Bjorn's (1982) sample of autoworkers. Filing formal complaints is less likely still, with estimates ranging from 2% of federal workers (USMSPB, 1981) to 12% of Navy enlisted victims (Culbertson et al., 1992). The Women's Legal Defense Fund (1991) estimated that only 1% to 7% of victims in the civilian workforce file a formal complaint or seek legal help.

When asked why they did not report the harasser, victims most commonly respond that they were afraid to do so—afraid of retaliation, of not being believed, of being shamed and humiliated (Fitzgerald et al., 1988; Fitzgerald, Gold, Brock, & Gelfand, unpublished). Ormerod (1991) found that harassment had to be quite explicit and severe before positive outcome expectations (i.e., that the behavior would stop) outweighed negative outcome expectations (i.e., fear of retaliation). In addition to such fears, other reasons for keeping silent include the belief that nothing can or will be done (Allen & Erickson, 1989; Fitzgerald et al., in press) and a reluctance to cause problems for the harasser (Gutek, 1985; Jensen & Gutek, 1982).

Not surprisingly, research has demonstrated that victims' fear of retaliation is frequently well-founded (Hesson-McInnis & Fitzgerald, 1992; Livingston, 1982). In contrast to the Merit Systems (1981) study in which the majority of victims who responded assertively believed that it "made things better," Livingston (1982) found that those who reported harassment to their supervisors actually experienced greater emotional distress. Although Livingston's finding may be at least partially an artifact of the positive correlations between severity of harassment and (both) emotional distress and reporting, other research indicates that this is not a complete explanation. Working with the second Merit Systems data set (USMSPB, 1987), Hesson-McInnis & Fitzgerald (1992) found that assertive responding was associated with more negative outcomes of every type—psychological, work-related, and health-related—independent of the contribution of harassment severity. Although there will clearly never be one right way to respond to harassment, such findings should give pause to those who recommend "just report him" as a matter of course.

The research on coping response strategies has begun to receive increased attention in the literature and has recently been reviewed in several places (Fitzgerald et al., in press; Fitzgerald & Shullman, 1993; Gruber & Bjorn, 1986; Gutek & Koss, 1993). Originally operationalized as simple checklists of common sense behaviors, such responses are now beginning to be conceptualized in a more complex, multidimensional fashion (Gutek & Koss, 1993) and can be assessed through psychometrically sophisticated instruments of known reliability and validity (Fitzgerald et al., in press). Although analogue research has contributed significantly to our knowledge in this area, the discrepancy between the reactions of experimental research participants and actual victims suggests that the results of such research must be viewed with skepticism. As Fitzgerald and Shullman (1993) noted, "the only way to understand women's responses to harassment, their effectiveness, and outcomes is to study them directly, despite the difficulties of doing so" (p. 15).

IMPACT AND CONSEQUENCES OF SEXUAL HARASSMENT

A number of studies have documented the high cost of harassment to women (Crull, 1982, 1984; Fitzgerald & Ormerod, 1993; Gutek & Koss, 1993; Hamilton, Alagna, King, & Lloyd, 1987; Hamilton & Dolkart, 1992; Hesson-McInnis & Fitzgerald, 1992; Koss, 1990b; Salisbury, Ginorio, Remick, & Stringer, 1986). Fitzgerald and Ormerod (1993) noted that the outcomes of the harassment/victimization process can be examined from three main perspectives: work-related, psychological or emotional, and physiological or health-related (cf. APA, 1992). It is this framework that we use here.

Work-Related Outcomes

In the original Merit Systems (USMSPB, 1981) investigation, nearly 10% of the women who were harassed reported changing jobs as a result. In its more recent study, Merit Systems (USMSPB, 1987) reported that more than 36,000 federal employees left their jobs because of harassment in the two-year period covered by the study. This included victims who quit, were fired, transferred or were reassigned because of unwanted sexual attention. Gutek (1985) reported that (a) 9% of the women in her sample had quit a job because they had been sexually harassed, (b) 5% had transferred, (c) 9% had given up on a job they wanted, and (d) 6.9% had lost a job due to a refusal to have sex with a supervisor. A study of women who had filed complaints with the California Fair Employment and Housing Department revealed that 50% had been fired and an additional 25% resigned as a result of either the harassment itself or pressures associated with the complaint process (Coles, 1986). Crull (1982) documented a similar level of job loss in a sample of victims who sought assistance from the Working Women's Institute. Hamilton et al. (1987), describing the price that women pay for leaving their jobs under the stress of harassment, noted not only the loss of income and seniority, but also the disruption of work histories, problems with references, and (frequently) a failure to qualify for unemployment benefits.

Although actual job loss is the most dramatic example of work-related damages, exclusive focus on this outcome seriously underestimates the work-related effect of sexual harassment. Other outcomes have also been documented such as decreased morale and absenteeism (USMSPB, 1987), decreased job satisfaction (Baker, 1989; O'Farrell & Harlan, 1982; Schneider & Swan, 1994), and damage to interpersonal relationships at work (Bandy, 1989; Culbertson et al., 1992; DiTomaso, 1989; Gutek, 1985). Shullman (1991) noted that the damage to women's careers and vocational development includes decreased job satisfaction, poor job performance (due to stress), loss of job or promotion, negative performance evaluations, absenteeism, job withdrawal, and changes in job plans or career goals (cf. APA, 1992; Scott, 1992). Gruber (1992) reported a negative correlation between sexual harassment and job satisfaction in an international sample of women engineers and production workers, paralleling findings reported among female blue-collar workers in the United States (Baker, 1989).

With respect to job performance, there was a positive relationship between harassment and lowered productivity and job withdrawal in the Merit Systems (USMSPB, 1981, 1987) samples. However, Gruber and Bjorn (1982) reported that women autoworkers reported little effect of harassment on their work behavior or sense of competence. Others have argued for an indirect effect on performance because victims are excluded from informal networks and thus denied performance feedback (Martin, 1978, 1980), as well as lack of information and support from others in the work environment (Gutek & Koss, 1993). There are obvious difficulties in studying the effects of harassment on job performance using the traditional performance evaluation paradigm. Additionally, self-reports of victims may be biased in unknown ways and in a variety of directions. Given the data indicating that sexual harassment costs the federal government more than $200 million in productivity losses and other costs in a two-year period alone, it seems safe to assume a nontrivial effect on job performance, at least at the organizational level. Anecdotal reports and clinical data support such an assumption, although formal research confirmation has yet to appear.

With respect to students, a 1983 study conducted at Harvard University and reported in the *Chronicle of Higher Education* noted that 15% of the graduate and 12% of the undergraduate student victims changed their major or educational program as an outcome of harassment. Similar results were reported by Adams et al. (1983). Fitzgerald et al. (1988) described similar percentages of women students who had either dropped courses, avoided courses, or avoided certain professors as a way of coping with unwanted sexual attention.

Glaser and Thorpe (1986) studied the retrospective reports of women clinical psychologists and noted, like Pope and his colleagues before them (Pope, Levenson, & Schover, 1979), that large numbers had experienced sexual advances from their professors while in graduate school. Among the 90% of women who declined such advances, 45% reported not only significant damage to important working relationships, but also punitive and vindictive reactions, including lowered grades, the withdrawal of support and professional opportunities, and derogation of their scholarly work. Many indicated that they had seriously considered dropping out of graduate school; the unknown number who did leave school are not, of course, represented in the sample and their stories—like their careers—are lost. As Dziech and Weiner (1990) noted, harassment "forces a student to forfeit work, research, educational comfort or even career. Professors withhold legitimate opportunities from those who resist, or students withdraw rather than pay certain prices" (p. 10).

It is difficult to overestimate the toll that harassment takes on women's lives. Women are disproportionately represented in the most economically vulnerable segments of the labor market. In addition to the millions of single women who support themselves, most married women work from financial necessity, and tens of thousands are the sole support of their families, including a large percentage with small children. Workplace harassment places these women in an intolerable situation. Virtually tens of thousands are forced to tolerate sexual exploitation or run a daily gamut of sexual and emotional abuse as the price of earning a living. Women and children constitute the fastest growing segment of the homeless population (U.S. Conference of Mayors, 1987) and for many women their job is the only protection from homelessness and utter poverty. Even for those who are less economically vulnerable, the price is extremely high. The links between unemployment and mental health are well established (Osipow & Fitzgerald, in press) as is the connection between occupational and general well-being. Although economic deprivation constitutes the most visible and dramatic loss associated with harassment, to focus solely on that loss trivializes the serious psychological and health-related outcomes of workplace trauma. It is to those outcomes that we now turn.

Psychological and Health-Related Outcomes

Research on the effect and outcomes of sexual harassment is still in the descriptive mode characteristic of immature fields and our information depends heavily on samples of self-identified victims (Koss 1990b). What data do exist, however, present compelling evidence that harassment represents a serious risk to women's health and well-being. Merit Systems (USMSPB, 1981) reported that literally thousands of female employees experienced a deterioration in their emotional or physical condition as a result of their experiences. As might be expected, negative consequences were more common among those who had experienced more severe victimization, such as actual or attempted rape or sexual assault; 82% of these women reported negative effects on their emotional or physical conditions. Still, even when harassment is not physically violent, many victims experience strong fear reactions (Holgate, 1989; Junger, 1987). These include lowered self-esteem (Gruber & Bjorn, 1982), lessened self-confidence (Benson

& Thomson, 1982), loss of control, and disruption of their lives (Alliance Against Sexual Coercion, 1976; Quina, 1990).

In one of the first studies in this area, Crull (1982, 1984) described physical symptoms (e.g., headaches, sleep disturbance, disordered eating, gastrointestinal disorders, nausea, weight loss (or gain), and crying spells) in a sample of self-identified victims who sought assistance from Working Women United. More recently, the Institute for Research on Women's Health (1988) underscored that sexual harassment constitutes a serious threat to women's psychological and physical well-being; this report stated that there is now reason to believe that a clinically significant depression can be associated with harassment and employment discrimination (see also Pendergrass, Kimmel, Joesling, Petersen, & Bush, 1976). The National Council for Research on Women (1991) noted that the American Psychiatric Association recognizes harassment as a severe stressor (see also Hamilton et al., 1987).

Most recently, Gutek and Koss (1993) reviewed the research on the outcomes of sexual harassment and reported findings of extensive stress-related physical symptoms, including gastrointestinal disturbances, jaw tightness and teethgrinding, nervousness, binge-eating, headaches, inability to sleep, tiredness, nausea, loss of appetite, weight loss, and crying spells (Crull, 1982; Gutek, 1985; Lindsey, 1977; Loy & Stewart, 1984; Safran, 1976; Salisbury et al., 1986). Emotional reactions included anger, fear, depression, anxiety, irritability, lowered self-esteem, feelings of humiliation and alienation, and a sense of helplessness and vulnerability (Gutek, 1985; Safran, 1976; Silverman, 1976-77; Tong, 1984). To this list can be added disruption of sexual adjustment (e.g., loss of desire, flashbacks during intercourse) and difficulties with interpersonal relationships with partners, families, and significant others.

As with other forms of sexual victimization, harassment is often viewed as shameful and unmentionable, an experience that reflects as much on its victim as its perpetrator. Combined with the fact that womens' reports of harassment have historically been denied, discounted, or trivialized, such a perception increases the likelihood that women will remain silent about their experiences. Victims are isolated from one another and from possible sources of support, and their experiences are personalized as each woman searches for explanations in the idiosyncratic features of her particular situation. This combination of circumstances exacerbates the stress of the original trauma and increases the probability of serious psychological aftereffects and consequences.

These and other similarities among harassment and the other forms of sexual victimization such as rape and incest suggest the usefulness of general models of trauma (e.g., McCann, Sakheim & Abrahamson, 1988) for understanding the effect of sexual harassment on womens' lives. Noting that prospective studies of victims are not yet available, Koss (1990b; Gutek & Koss, 1993) argued persuasively for the utility of the general Post Traumatic Stress Disorder (PTSD) model as a framework for understanding the psychological effect of harassment. Others have argued that workplace victims can exhibit a postabuse syndrome characterized by shock, emotional numbing, constriction of affect, flashbacks, and other signs of anxiety and depression (IRWH, 1988).

Kilpatrick (1992) presented the first formal data concerning the relationship among sexual harassment and both PTSD and depression. In his nationally representative sample of 3,020 women surveyed through a telephone interview procedure, Kilpatrick found that women suffering from PTSD and depression were more likely to have been sexually harassed than those who had never experienced these problems (cf. Schneider & Swan, 1994). In addition, respondents diagnosed as having PTSD or depression were more likely to report each of seven types of harassing behaviors than were employed women in general. Contrary to perceptions that appropriately assertive responding is the answer to being sexually harassed, Kilpatrick found that those women diagnosed with PTSD and depression were just as likely to have responded assertively to the harassment as employed women in general. However, those with PTSD were less likely than either depressed women or employed women in general to have filed a complaint. It is unclear how these results compare with those of Hesson-McInnis and Fitzgerald (1992) who found that more assertive responding (including filing formal complaints) was associated with self-reports of psychological distress; however, these latter results were based on the 1987 Merit Systems data, which did not include formal diagnostic criteria nor any assessment of PTSD.

Gutek and Koss (1993) noted that Kilpatrick's (1992) results are still preliminary, as no comprehensive report has yet been published. They emphasize, however, that if the initial results hold, they implicate sexual harassment in a variety of psychological and health-related problems encountered by women. Although prospective studies are clearly needed, the available data support the conclusion that harassment constitutes a serious risk to womens' health and well-being. Given the number of women who are victimized in this manner, the enormity of this problem becomes increasingly clear.

RISK FACTORS: WHO IS HARASSED?

Individual Factors

As harassment has become increasingly recognized as a social problem of significant proportions, researchers have attempted to identify individual and organizational factors that place individuals at risk for this type of victimization. Although much of the early work in this area was poorly designed and often contradictory, it did clearly establish that harassment is overwhelmingly a women's problem (see Vaux, 1993, for a different perspective). For example, Fitzgerald et al. (1988) demonstrated that virtually all the harassment reported by their sample of more than 2,000 college students was reported by women; other studies have reported similar results. Men who have reported occasionally receiving sexual advances at work, say generally that they find such advances flattering (Gutek, 1985) whereas women report the same behaviors to be insulting or frightening. In the Merit Systems' study (USMSPB, 1981), virtually all of the victims who reported serious job-related consequences of sexual harassment were women.

Such data underscore the critical importance of *context* for understanding research findings in this area. Although it is true that men are sometimes sexually harassed (most generally by other men), it is clear that harassment is overwhelmingly a situation in which men impose unwanted, offensive, and often frightening sexual behavior on women. In this, as in other ways, it resembles other forms of sexual violence. In this context, it is useful to recall Mills' (1959) distinction between *private troubles* and *public issues*. As Hoffman (1986) noted:

> Private troubles occur when isolated events cause personal difficulties for individuals—they are the vicissitudes of individual biographies, related peripherally at best to the location of the individual in the social structure. Public issues, on the other hand, are structurally induced problems affecting large numbers of individuals in particular social locations. Since they are the consequences on individual lives of the institutional arrangements within which individuals live, they are not amenable to individual solutions.... The sexual harassment of men by women is a private trouble, that of women by men a public issue. (p. 110)

Age and Marital Status

Individual factors that have yielded some correlation with victim status are age and marital status. It appears that younger women are more often the target of harassment (Gutek, 1985; USMSPB, 1981, 1987); the younger the worker, the more likely she is to be harassed. Both Gutek and Merit Systems reported that the victims in their studies were younger than the average worker; other studies have reported similar results (Baker, 1989; LaFontaine & Tredeau, 1986). Despite the relative consistency of such data, Fitzgerald and Ormerod (1993) pointed out that they represent an oversimplification, as it is clear that the experience of harassment is not limited to younger women. Women in all age groups have reported experiencing harassment. In addition, researchers have not typically examined what sorts of harassment are experienced by which groups of women. For example, gender harassment, the most common form of harassment, most likely demonstrates a weaker relationship to age than do other types of sexual harassment. Most studies confound the *experience* of harassment with the recognition or *labeling* of harassment, a variable that has been shown to bear differential relationships to age. Thus, although younger women do appear to be at greater risk for harassment, it is erroneous to conclude that the problem is limited to this group.

As with age, the data demonstrating a relationship between marital status and harassment are easy to misinterpret. Although unmarried women (divorced, separated, never married, and cohabiting) are likely to experience harassment somewhat more often than other women, it is likely that marital status represents a dummy variable standing in for more influential factors, such as perceived availability, lack of the protected status of wife, or, most probably, age itself.

Race and Ethnicity

There has been considerable speculation in the literature that race or ethnic minority status may increase the risk of being harassed (Defour, 1989; 1990). Although it is intuitively reasonable to believe that minority status heightens vulnerability (if only because it correlates with economic vulnerability in representative samples), such arguments remain largely unexamined. Of the major data sets available, Gutek's (1985) sample appears the best suited for testing this hypothesis, as approximately one third of her 824 women respondents were nonwhite. She reported that the ethnic minority women in this group were no more vulnerable to harassment than white women were. Gutek also found that minority women were less likely to quit a job because of harassment (a finding open to multiple interpretations). The first Merit Systems study (USMSPB, 1981) appeared to find no relationship between ethnicity and harassment, although there is some dispute about the exact nature of this finding (Fain & Anderson, 1987; Lach & Gwartney-Gibbs, 1993; Martin, 1984). The subsequent study conducted by Merit Systems did not include ethnicity as a variable (USMSPB, 1987). Thus, despite the intuitively reasonable argument (and several well-publicized legal cases) the relationship between racial/ethnic status and vulnerability to harassment remains an open question.

Organizational Factors

More powerful than the research on individual characteristics is the research demonstrating occupational differences in the likelihood of harassment. The most powerful and consistent finding to emerge from this research so far substantiates a strong connection between harassment and occupations in which women have traditionally been underrepresented and the content of the work has been traditionally considered masculine (Coles, 1986; Gutek, 1985; Gutek & Dunwoody, 1988; Lafontaine & Tredeau, 1986; USMSPB, 1981). Gold (1987) reported that her sample of blue-collar tradeswomen reported significantly and substantially higher levels of all types of harassment than did either white-collar professional women or pink-collar clerical women. LaFontaine and Tredeau (1986) also found higher rates of sexual harassment in male-dominated occupations.

The most carefully designed study in this area was conducted by Baker (1989), who examined both traditional and nontraditional blue-collar jobs; the results of this study clearly demonstrated that high levels of sexual harassment are associated with the existence of low numbers of women in the work group. Baker's work suggests that, as women approach numerical parity in various segments of the workforce, harassment may decline, a suggestion also supported by Gutek (1985).

Another organizational-level variable that might reasonably be expected to exert influence as a risk factor is organizational norms or climate. Although work has only recently begun in this area (Fitzgerald, Hulin, & Drasgow, 1992; Hulin, 1993), what data do exist support the intuitively reasonable notion that institutional or organizational norms exert an important effect on harassing behavior. For example, Bond (1988) found that the most important predictor of sexual harassment in a sample of graduate students was departmental norms regulating sexual contact between faculty and students. Organizational norms that communicated disapproval of such relationships apparently also served to inhibit harassment of women students. Similarly, Hesson-McInnis and Fitzgerald (1992) analyzed the second data set of Merit Systems (USMSPB, 1987) and found that organizational climate (operationalized as the presence of harassment policies and procedures) affected not only the extent and level of sexual harassment, but also the perceived effectiveness of victims' coping strategies and severity of outcomes.

The most powerful support for the idea that organizational norms can influence the prevalence of harassing behavior was provided by Pryor and his colleagues (Pryor, 1992; Pryor et al., 1993). Pryor (1992, 1993) studied a federal agency that employed more than 8,000 workers who were geographically dispersed in offices throughout the United States. Employees were asked about their experiences of sexual harassment as well as about their opinions concerning management's stance toward this issue. Female employees' reports of a variety of sexual harassment were significantly correlated with their impressions of organizational tolerance of harassment; the women who thought that their local office management had made reasonable efforts to stop harassment and provided good role models were less likely to have experienced harassment on the job. The reverse was true for those who believed that management ignored the problem, discouraged reporting, and so forth. Pryor et al. (1993) provided data that indicate his earlier results were not based on spurious correlations or response sets. Although research in this area is only beginning, studies such as these suggest the clear importance of ecological factors in predicting harassment, as well as providing some relatively unambiguous targets for intervention.

WHO IS THE HARASSER?

What kind of man sexually harasses women? As evidence accumulates that harassment represents a social problem of significant proportion, researchers have attempted to address this question, seeking to identify a pattern of easily identifiable demographic or interpersonal characteristics that characterize the typical harasser. Such attempts have been largely unsuccessful. Pryor (1992) noted that the majority of data concerning men who harass is drawn from descriptions provided by self-reported victims (Gutek, 1985; Perry, 1983; USMSPB, 1981, 1987). Such studies have suggested that the typical harasser is an older, white, married man—a description notably similar to that of the modal male employee. Gutek (1985) remarked on the problems presented by the fact that the profile of the harasser is similar to that of the typical worker. Similarly, Fitzgerald, Weitzman, Gold, & Ormerod (1988) noted that professors who admit to multiple sexual relationships with students are demographically indistinguishable from those who do not.

So although popular stereotypes suggest that harassers are uncouth boors or "dirty old men," who are easily identified and presumably easily avoided, the data do not bear this out. Similarly, a deviance explanation for harassment, exemplied by Senator Orrin Hatch's assertion during the Clarence Thomas confirmation hearings, that such a person "would not be a normal person. That person...would be a psychopathic sex fiend or a pervert" founders on the data showing that harassers are mostly indistinguishable from the ordinary man, at least on the easily identifiable level of demographics.

Pryor (1992) discussed the limitations of knowledge drawn from victim descriptions as well as that derived from attempts to assess perpetrators directly, noting that such data may well not generalize to the majority of harassers. To address such limitations, he proposed a methodology for studying sexual harassment propensities in the general male population (Pryor, 1987). Noting that severe forms of harassment (i.e., quid pro quo, sexual imposition) bear a conceptual similarity to rape, Pryor developed a self-report methodology based on Malamuth's (1981, 1986) Likelihood of Rape Index (LRI). The LRI asks study participants to indicate the probability that they, personally, would rape if assured they would not be caught or punished; scores on the LRI are related in theoretically expected ways to variables that have been shown to differentiate between rapists and non-rapists.

Pryor's (1987) Likelihood of Sexual Harassment Scale (LSH) asks men to imagine various situations in which they control an important outcome for an attractive woman and to rate the likelihood of using this power to sexually exploit her. Thus, the LSH assesses the self-reported likelihood of engaging in quid pro quo sexual harassment. Pryor reported that college men who score high on the LSH can be characterized by adversarial sexual beliefs, authoritarianism, lack of empathy, and traditional sex role attitudes. Most importantly, such men have been shown to exhibit sexually harassing behavior, at least in laboratory situations. LaVite (1992) showed the important interaction of such personal characteristics with ecological factors such as organizational tolerance by demonstrating in a laboratory study that high LSH men were more likely to harass following the modeling of harassment behavior on the part of a confederate (cf. Pryor, LaVite, & Stoller, 1993).

The search for simple demographic-marker variables that can identify harassers in an easily operationalized manner seems unlikely to be successful. Although misogynistic attitudes and a cognitive connection between dominance and sexuality can discriminate harassers in a laboratory situation (Bargh & Raymond, 1992; Pryor & Stoller, 1992), the generalization of these results to actual harassers is yet to be demonstrated. Further, although gender harassment appears to be the most extensive type of sexual harassment, the LSH results have so far been limited to examination of unwanted sexual attention. Finally, it is currently unclear in what ways such research—although theoretically important—can inform practical applications (although, see Moorman & Mankin, 1992) and may inadvertently contribute to the perception that harassment primarily arises from individual deviance rather than structural societal support for male dominance more generally. Although it is difficult for most to accept, harassers are found in all types of occupations, at all occupational levels, among college professors as well as railroad workers, ministers, and business executives, and among individuals who live otherwise exemplary lives. The notion that there is a typical offender who can be easily identified by his blatant and obvious mistreatment of women is not supported by research and is a serious misreading of a complex issue. Everything we have learned tells us that there is no typical harasser.

8

Intervention, Prevention, and Treatment Issues for Sexual Harassment

A comprehensive approach to sexual harassment intervention must consider not only treatment and services for victims, but also prevention and remediation efforts in organizations and institutions. Ultimately, broadbased societal-level interventions in the guise of legal and legislative reform will be required for lasting change. Perhaps it is because of sexual harassment's legal status as a civil rights violation—with the recently established possibilities of corporate and institutional liability provided by the Civil Rights Act of 1991 and the Supreme Court's decision in *Franklin v. Gwinnett County* (1992)—that the more general organizational efforts have progressed more rapidly than traditional victim services.

INTERVENTIONS WITH VICTIMS

Very little is formally known concerning appropriate and effective treatment for victims of harassment. Most discussions of the topic rely on clinical and anecdotal data or extrapolate from discussions of other forms of victimization. Koss (1990b) noted the absence of any published guidelines for those treating sexual harassment victims, although two reports of group treatment approaches have been published (Hamilton et al., 1987; Salisbury et al., 1986). Hamilton et al. and the Institute for Research on Women's Health

(IRWH, 1988) have advised the clinician to adopt the following assumptions during the initial evaluation:

1. The client's reports of discrimination and harassment are based in fact.
2. She probably has an adequate or better work history prior to the harassment.
3. She has probably reacted in some way to the perceived discrimination in a way that others view as negative.
4. If she has complained, there has been retaliation.
5. Extreme affect and behavior should be interpreted in terms of a victimization model unless proven otherwise (although even "difficult" women can be harassed).

The core theme of these recommendations is that the clinician should provide support and validation for the victim. Koss (1990b) suggested that clinicians will be most effective by providing emotional support, encouraging the expression of feelings, monitoring physical symptoms and coping behavior, and assisting in specific problem solving. As with other forms of victimization, significant therapeutic progress cannot be expected while the client is still confronting a chronic, highly abnormal, and abusive environment because exaggerated self-protective behaviors are necessary for day-to-day psychological survival. Koss recommended that clincians validate feelings, assist in the search for meaning, allow the expression of anger, monitor damage, provide for the mourning of losses, and offer hope for the future. Similar suggestions have been offered by Pendergrass et al. (1976).

Such recommendations are consistent with a general model used for trauma, a treatment which seems most appropriate for use with harassment victims at this time. Specific considerations important to working with this population focus on managing reactions within the work setting and dealing with the often traumatic aspects of the complaint and litigation process (IRWH, 1988). The considerations outlined here are generally thought to be applicable to either individual or group approaches. Although no data exists on this point, it also seems reasonable to encourage the formation of all-female support groups (IRWH, 1988).

Interventions With Harassers

If little has been written concerning interventions with victims, virtually nothing has appeared concerning interventions with harassers. Yet, counseling is routinely recommended or required for individuals found to have engaged in the less egregious forms of harassment (Wagner, 1992). Scott (1992) provided clinical description of guilt, anxiety, anger, and fear in a sample of harassers referred for counseling. Being held accountable for harassment is no doubt a stressful experience with many negative practical and emotional consequences, however, what is of more concern here is the development of training interventions designed to inhibit sexually harassing behavior in men. No such studies have yet been attempted, but Pryor's (1987, 1992) work identified a logical starting point for interventions. Additionally, Gilbert, Heesacker, and Gannon (1991) reported success in changing attitudes that were supportive of sexual aggression using a group intervention based on Petty and Cacioppo's (1986) Elaboration Likelihood Model. Given the relationship between LSH and attitudes supportive of sexual aggression (Pryor, 1987), it seems reasonable to assume that a similar intervention might be effective with men who sexually harass. Lonsway's (1992) finding that hostility toward women contributed unique variance to rape-supportive attitudes in men provides another intervention target.

Organizational Interventions

Recent years have seen a virtual explosion of interest in organizational-level interventions designed to prevent sexual harassment. Strengthened federal civil rights legislation providing for compensatory and punitive damages virtually guarantees that this trend will continue. Although this is a positive sign, many training programs seem focused more on protecting the organization from liability than on protecting women from sexual victimization.

Some of the best work in this area has been developed within the context of higher education (see, for example, Fitzgerald, 1992; Paludi, 1990; and Paludi & Barickman, 1991, Barickman, 1991, for reviews and resources;

also the discussion by Biaggio, Watts, & Brownell, 1990, is particularly thorough), although excellent programs have also been developed in industry (e.g., Webb, 1991), and (particularly) by women's groups committed to providing a harassment-free workplace (e.g., Local 925, the IRWH, and the Alliance Against Sexual Coercion; an extensive list of resources is provided by the National Council for Research on Women, 1991).

Although a thorough treatment of organizational interventions is beyond the scope of this report, the elements of an effective prevention program have been identified (Fitzgerald, 1992, 1993b). These elements include a clear definition of sexual harassment, couched in clear and understandable language; a strong policy statement indicating that harassment will not be tolerated; an effective and accessible grievance procedure designed to encourage reporting and providing for both formal and informal resolution procedures; and effective information channels, including multiple methods for disseminating information. The goals of such an intervention, which requires strong support from management or the institutional administration, should include not only raising awareness and providing information, but also changing attitudes and effecting behavioral change.

Societal Level Interventions

Broad societal interventions designed to eliminate sexual harassment and eradicate its causes, although clearly desirable, are obviously the most difficult to effect. Social change is not easily mandated, and the roots of women's sexual oppression run deep in American society. Deeply held beliefs about proper roles for men and women, women's responsibility for male sexual behavior, and widespread misogyny and hostility to women combine to produce a social climate in which sexual victimization becomes an almost normative event in women's lives. The most effective interventions are often serendipitous and include events, such as the Clarence Thomas confirmation hearings, that arise from the chance collision of unpredictable events and influence the consciousness of an entire society. Such collisions can be neither predicted nor produced at will.

In a very real sense, Title VII legislation provided the first societal-level intervention for sexual harassment; recent strengthening of that legislation through the Civil Rights Act of 1991 provided another. The possibility of compensatory and punitive damages—limited though they are—has provided the first real incentive for organizations and educational institutions to provide a safer environment for women.

Such interventions have not, however, been uniformly positive. In particular, the current focus on litigation as a method of resolving sexual harassment issues is neither effective nor desirable. Although provision for damages is clearly critical, no financial compensation can recompense the victim for what she has endured, and its availability may suggest to many that the problem has been solved. More importantly, the tiny proportion of victims who file legal charges ensures that litigation can never be a comprehensive solution to the problem. Nor does the answer lie in convincing more women to file charges; quid pro quo harassment is relatively rare and difficult to prove without evidence and witnesses (who are often difficult to come by). The great majority of harassment—although degrading, offensive and frightening—may not reach the level required by law to constitute a hostile environment claim. Even truly egregious cases are often not considered to be so by judges and juries, and the legal process itself exacerbates the trauma of harassment, adding a second injury (Hamilton & Dolkart, 1992; Symonds, 1980) to the one already suffered.

It is critical that the legal system not continue to re-victimize harassment victims. Filing a harassment complaint and going through the adversarial legal process is often an extraordinarily punitive experience that compounds the original trauma (Hamilton & Dolkart, 1992). Although this may never be completely eliminated, it can and should be lessened. Current regulations and laws that safeguard against re-victimizing the complainant of rape and domestic assault (e.g., rape shield laws) should be expanded to include victims of sexual harassment. Evidence that seeks to make the victim responsible for sexual harassment (e.g., allegations of a promiscuous past, inappropriate conduct, provocative appearance) should be statutorily excluded in all states, as it is now in California. Additionally, if victims are to receive humane treatment, competent representation, and a fair hearing, personnel at all levels of the legal-enforcement system should be educated about sexual harassment; and this includes judges as well as attorneys and agency staff.

The potential for the legal system to retraumatize the victim is well-enough established to have received considerable attention in both the legal and psychological literature (Dolkart, 1992; Estrich, 1987; Hamilton & Dolkart, 1992; Wyatt, Notgrass, & Newcomb (1990). Lawyers routinely seek to win their cases by defaming the victim and even judges often show an amazing degree of misinformation and insensitivity. As noted previously, Katherine Young lost her case when the judge ruled she was unlikely to have been harassed because she "wore little or no makeup and didn't color her hair in any way" (Bravo & Cassedy, 1992). Other judges have been known to admonish victims that "at least you weren't raped" (see Bravo & Cassedy, 1992, for this and other examples) and similar incidents are far from unusual. If legal recourse is to provide relief rather than a second injury (Symonds, 1980), reform of the legal process is mandatory.

Primary Prevention

Finally, as with any critical social problem, primary prevention is the only true solution. In the case of sexual harassment, social policy initiatives must be formulated to elevate women's status in the workplace. Harassment thrives on women's inferior status, particularly in the world of work; it can be eliminated by improving that status. The data are clear that work sites with relatively equal numbers of men and women have significantly fewer problems with harassment (Gutek, 1985). Strong affirmative action programs and aggressive recruiting procedures are one of the most powerful strategies for eliminating harassment and are critical to any truly effective policy in this area. Actively helping women move into jobs traditionally held by men, eliminating discrimination in hiring and training, moving women into top management, and adopting truly profamily and prowoman policies such as family leave and child-care assistance are critical to primary prevention and social change. We have left it very late; we should start as soon as possible.

PART 4

Violence in the Community

9

Uniting All Women:
The Fear of Rape

W hen women step outside the "safety" of their homes, they can be victimized in many ways. Among people they know, women face the possibility of courtship violence and acquaintance rape. On the street, they face the risk of crimes such as purse snatching, mugging, stalking, frottage, shootings, and rape by a stranger. Such street crime disproportionally plagues ethnic minority and poor women (Bureau of Justice Statistics [BJS], 1992; Wyatt, 1992). Lesbian women may be additionally targeted for antigay violence that can include verbal epithets, physical assault, and even rape (Berrill, 1990; Garnets, Herek, & Levy, 1990). But, uniting all women is the fear of rape (Gordon & Riger, 1989; Riger & Gordon, 1988).

One third of women interviewed in several urban centers across the United States cited the fear of physical harm, especially rape, as their most

Support for the preparation of this section of the book was provided by a Research Scientist Development Award from the Antisocial and Traumatic Stress Studies Branch of the National Institute of Mental Health. The chapter is based in part on portions of material that appeared previously in *Applied and Preventive Psychology*, the *Archives of Family Medicine*, the *Journal of Interpersonal Violence*, the *Journal of Women's Health*, and *Violence Update*. The author acknowledges gratefully the research and technical assistance of Melinda Tharan and Rose Gordy.

common concern (Gordon & Riger, 1989). With the exception of rape, women are less likely than men to be victims of all the violent crimes that are monitored by the Federal Bureau of Investigation (FBI), yet women fear victimization more than men (FBI, 1991). This fear of crime appears to be based largely on women's perceived likelihood of rape (Riger, LeBailly, & Gordon, 1981). Among women younger than 35, rape is feared even more than murder, assault, or robbery (Warr, 1985). More than half of the women surveyed by Gordon and Riger reacted to their fear of crime with self-isolation; they stayed inside and avoided visiting friends or going out for evening entertainment. In contrast, an overwhelming majority of the men (90%) denied taking steps to reduce their vulnerability to crime, even though they lived in the same neighborhoods as the female respondents (Gordon & Riger, 1989). These findings suggest that contemporary women in the United States live their lives under the threat of sexual violation and this fear constitutes a special burden not shared by men (Thompson & Norris, 1992). Sadly, women truly have no safe haven from rape because they are at risk both outside their homes and within their intimate circle of acquaintances.

Despite the number of ways in which women can be victimized by both strangers and acquaintances, rape's unique status as a barometer of women's fear served as a primary reason for focusing exclusively on rape in this section of our report. A second rationale for limiting the discussion to rape is that, of all the forms of violence against women, the psychological scholarship on rape is the most extensive and well-developed. Consistent with the focus of the Task Force on male violence against women, this section considers the rape of adult women. Although rape of children is associated with some of the most severe mental health effects, a thorough review of this subject was beyond the scope of the Task Force. In this report, rape in childhood is considered only in its role as a risk factor increasing vulnerability to re-victimization as an adult. Marital rape, because of its close association with battering, was discussed in the earlier section on violence in the home. The subject of courtship violence, although qualifying as "outside the home" in the organizational schema adopted for this report, was also considered earlier because the methods used to study it grow out of research on battering. In the following chapters, rape of adult women is reviewed, including its frequency, causes, effects, and interventions.

The traditional offense of common-law rape has been defined as "carnal knowledge of a female forcibly and against her will" (Bienen, 1980, p. 174). The FBI used this definition in compiling its Uniform Crime Reports (UCR, FBI, 1991, p. 17), as did the Bureau of Justice Statistics (BJS) in its National Crime Victimization Survey (NCVS, BJS, 1992, p. 156). However, women's groups and feminist legal scholars have objected to it as overly narrow. They have lobbied across the 50 states for passage of reform statutes that have transformed the very acts that are considered rape, although those changes that survive the political process are often different from the original goals (Goldberg-Ambrose, 1992). Current statuatory definitions of rape no longer limit the crime to female victims, to vaginal penetration alone, and to forcible situations only. In contemporary legal usage, rape is defined as nonconsensual sexual penetration of an adolescent or adult obtained by physical force, by threat of bodily harm, or at such time when the victim is incapable of giving consent by virtue of mental illness, mental retardation, or intoxication (Searles & Berger, 1987). Sexual penetration includes "sexual intercourse, cunnilingus, fellation, anal intercourse, or any other intrusion, however slight, of any part of a person's body, but emission of semen is not required" (Mich. Stat. Ann., 1980). Social scientists have delineated several types of rape including stranger, acquaintance, date, and marital rape. However, the essential meaning of the word rape is unaffected by the relationship of the parties, except in the handful of states still maintaining a statutory spousal exclusion (Searles & Berger, 1987).

All the information from which generalizations about the scope of rape can be made hinge on information volunteered by victims themselves (Hindelang & Davis, 1977). Therefore, studies that aim to describe the true scope of rape must include methods to overcome the compelling forces that favor nondisclosure. Hesitancy to disclose rape is fostered by a historical tradition of skepticism toward rape victims and denigration of them as damaged goods. The desire to withhold information about victimization often can be quite high. For example, in one study, only 54% of acquaintance-rape victims who had reported an assault to the police would admit to an interviewer that they had been raped (Curtis, 1976).

RAPE INCIDENCE

Incidence refers to the number of new incidents that occur within a specified time frame—often a one-year period (Kleinbaum, Kupper, & Morgenstern, 1982).

Federal Estimates of Rape Incidence

The two federal sources of rape incidence data are the UCR (FBI, 1991), and the NCVS (BJS, 1992). The UCR is a compilation of crimes reported to local authorities. The NCVS is a nationwide, household-based crime victimization survey that is designed to determine the total amount of crime that is occurring including both reported and unreported cases.

Uniform Crime Reports

A total of 102,555 reported crimes qualified as rapes in 1990. All these rapes involved women because the UCR definition of rape is limited to female victims (FBI, 1991). This figure represents a victimization rate of 80 per 100,000 female Americans. Approximately 84% of the rapes reported in 1990 were completed by force, the remainder were attempts. There are several steps involved in the decision to report a crime to the police, and once reported there are discretionary points at which the data may be disqualified or lost from the system. Although improvements in procedures can minimize the loss at each step of the reporting process, as long as some percentage of victimizations go unreported, compilations of crimes will remain an inherently incomplete picture of the true scope of rape. Rape is considered one of the most (FBI, 1982, p. 14) to the most (Bowker, 1979) underreported crime of personal violence.

National Crime Victimization Survey

The NCVS is based on a "panel design," wherein respondents are recontacted multiple times. Once selected as a NCVS household, a given dwelling remains in the sample for three years with interviews occurring every six months. During each contact, occupants are asked to indicate only those criminal victimizations that have occurred since the last interview, a technique which serves to "bound" or delineate the recall period. The first and fifth contact with the household is in person; all other interviews are conducted by telephone. Approximately 74% of the interviews are by telephone under current procedures. The 18th NCVS report was based on a representative sample of approximately 97,000 inhabitants over age 11 living in 62,600 housing units in the United States (BJS, 1992).

Rape is detected at very low rates by the NCVS. Precursors of the current survey resulted in only 15 rapes being reported among 10,000 households (Hindelang & Davis, 1977). To obtain the 1,000 cases needed for a 1985 descriptive profile of rape, it was necessary to aggregate *all* the incidents of rape *and* attempted rape that were reported in *every* NCVS interview from 1973 to 1984 (BJS, 1985). Perusal of the current report reveals numerous instances in which asterisks next to rape figures indicate unreliability due to the low number of instances reported. In spite of this low rate of detection, the approach to measuring the number and kind of rapes has remained entirely unchanged for almost 30 years (1973–1991).

Estimated rape victimization rates in 1990 NCVS data are 1.0 per 1,000 women and girls and 0.2 per 1,000 men and boys (BJS, 1992). Of the 124,480 rapes that were projected to have occurred in 1990, only 49% were completed, the majority were attempts. All the perpetrators were male, and most often were acquaintances of the victim. Only 42% of rapes were perpetrated by strangers (BJS, 1992). Rape rates are highest for single, divorced, or widowed women, under 24 years of age, from families earning less than $25,000 per year, with less than a high school education, who reside in central cities of the west or south. Victimization rates for Whites and Blacks are equal. Rates for Hispanics are lower than for non-Hispanics although it cannot be determined whether this is a true difference or simply a reflection of reluctance to report crime to any governmental authority, including interviewers. It is unknown how many of the rape victims identified in the NCVS were lesbians because this information is not ascertained.

According to NCVS estimates, 54% of the rapes experienced by survey participants were reported to the criminal justice system. However, if the 102,555 rapes reflected in the UCR represent approximately half of all rapes that occurred, then more than 200,000 rapes should have been identified by NCVS. In fact, the NCVS detected only about the same number of rapes (124,480) as did the UCR. The inconsistencies between the UCR and the NCVS have been extensively documented (Biderman & Lynch, 1991; Jensen & Karpos, 1993). Many experts believe that NCVS estimates of rape are too low because the methodology used undermines the self-disclosure of relevant incidents (Eigenberg, 1990; Kilpatrick, Best, Veronen, Amick, Villeponteaux, & Ruff, 1985; Koss, 1992; Russell, 1984). There are at least 6 problems with the methodology used in NCVS to identify rape:

1. The surveys lack the important element of confidentiality because interviews may be conducted in front of other family members.
2. The rapport between respondents and interviewers may be less than optimal because the interviewers do not have special training to handle sensitive issues and are not routinely matched for ethnicity or gender.
3. The language of the survey questions may lead respondents to believe that only violent rapes involving strangers are of interest to the interviewer.
4. The screening question for rape is ambiguous. It reads, "Did anyone try to attack you *in some other way?*" (BJS, 1992, p. 108, *emphasis added*). In response to public criticism of this inadequate approach, a multi-item, branching approach with six rape questions was developed. Unfortunately, only one item is a clear-cut improvement over past practice (Koss, 1992).
5. The definition of rape underlying the survey is outmoded. It excludes those rapes in which (a) the offender was the legal or common-law spouse of the victim, (b) forms of penetration other than penile-vaginal intercourse were involved, and (c) no force was used, but the victim was unable to consent because of drugs, mental illness, or mental retardation.
6. The rape estimates exclude repeated victimizations by the same perpe-

trator. Elimination of multiple incidents (which tend to involve intimates) has the effect of exaggerating the extent to which rape is committed by strangers and across races.

Independent Estimates of Rape Incidence

Rape incidence also has been estimated in several specialized studies that
used national samples. Questions about sexual assault were included in the
National Youth Study (Ageton, 1983). The 1,725 adolescents age 11 to 17 in
this nationwide sample were interviewed once a year for five years. Two
questions were used to measure sexual assault including the following item,
"How many times in the last year have you been sexually attacked or raped
or an attempt made to do so?" (Ageton, 1983, p. 12). The estimated rape
victimization rates for adolescent girls were developed by extracting incidents involving violent force or the use of a weapon or both. Excluded from
estimates were attempted rape, and nonforcible forms of rape involving
threat of bodily harm or taking advantage of one incapable of giving consent. Some of these are significant exclusions. For example, 51% of the incidents included in NCVS estimates are attempts, not completed rape. Even
with this significant difference in criterion for rape, the rape incidence estimates from the National Youth Study (9.2 per 1,000 for 1978; 6.8 per 1,000
for 1979; and 12.7 per 1,000 for 1980) were much larger than NCVS data for
girls aged 13 to 19 for the years 1978 (3.5/1,000) and 1979 (4.2/1,000;
Ageton, 1983).

In another nation-wide study, Koss, Gidycz, and Wisniewski (1987)
administered 10 sexual victimization screening questions to a sample of
3,187 women college students at 32 colleges and universities selected to represent the total higher education enrollment in the United States. (The
study included students from universities, colleges, community and junior
colleges, historically Black colleges, and technical schools.) Six screening
questions for attempted and completed rape were used, including "Have
you had sexual intercourse with a man when you didn't want to because he
used some degree of force such as twisting your arm or holding you down

to make you cooperate?" The study found that 76 per 1,000 college women experienced one or more attempted or completed rapes (as defined by the UCR) in a 12-month period. (When a state statute definition of rape was used, the incidence doubled to 166 per 1,000 women). A total of 84% of these incidents involved an offender known to the victim; in 57% of the cases the perpetrator was a date (Koss, 1988a). Adjustments to the data were made to account for telescoping of incidents (a possibility in unbounded data collection) and to eliminate duplication (e.g., women who experienced both attempted rape and rape, and women who experienced multiple forms of rape). The adjusted incidence rate was 35 per 1,000 women. (The published figures are 76 and 166 per 1,000 women; Koss, Gidycz, & Wisniewski, 1987.) Although direct comparisons with NCVS data are difficult, these estimates were about 10 times higher than the 1985 NCVS estimates of 4.3 per 1,000 for women aged 16-19 and 3.4 per 1,000 for women aged 20-24 (BJS, 1987).

Incidence data are also available from a national sample of 4,008 adult women identified by random-digit telephone dialing (National Victims Center, 1992). Participation rate in this survey was 84% of eligible respondents. The study employed a panel design, and the incidence data were obtained at the second contact, during which the women recalled their experiences since the first interview held a year previously. Four screening items identified rape including the following item, "Has a man or boy ever made you have sex by using force or threatening to harm you or someone close to you? Just so there is no mistake, by sex we mean putting a penis in your vagina?" Preliminary data revealed a 12-month incidence of 7.2 per 1,000, but this rate excluded attempted rapes, rape while unable to consent, and assaults of adolescents aged 17 and younger (D. G. Kilpatrick, personal communication, November 13, 1990). These omissions are notable: As mentioned previously, attempts account for half of the rapes identified by the NCVS, and rape incidence is among the highest for girls aged 16-19 years (BJS, 1992). Also the sampling plan did not reach several high-risk groups for rape including women who were homeless, women too poor to own a telephone, women residing in places where telephone service may not be available (such as Indian reservations), women living in group-living quarters such as college residences, institutions, and prisons, and women serving in the military. Yet, even with these omissions from the sample frame and with a definition of rape narrower than many statutes, all of which would have the effect of lowering the resultant incidence rate, the National Victims Center estimate was six times larger than the NCVS rates (1.3/1,000) for the same time period (BJS, 1989).

An accumulation of data challenges the validity of NCVS victimization estimates, suggesting that rape incidence may be six to 10 times higher than the public has been told. Several data sources also directly contradict the NCVS conclusion that, "A woman is twice as likely to be attacked by a stranger as by someone she knows" (BJS, 1985, p. 2). These flawed data blunt social concern for rape victims and support myths that rape is a rare event predominately perpetrated by strangers. Six new questions to detect rape were introduced into the NCVS in July, 1991. However, other problematic NCVS procedures have remained unchanged, including the conducting of interviews under suboptimal levels of rapport and confidentiality. The revised questions do not promise rapid improvements in the validity of NCVS rape estimates because they are being phased in gradually in subsamples of respondents; the bulk of respondents continue to receive the old protocol. It may be several years before published rates fully reflect input from the new questions. Nevertheless, after 30 years of no change, the revisions are concrete steps in the right direction. They suggest that those responsible for the survey have accorded a higher priority to the measurement of rape than has been evident in the past. Continued monitoring and pressure from both the public and behavioral scientists is essential to ensuring that these first small steps are extended.

RAPE PREVALENCE

A woman raped 13 months ago is not a rape victim from the perspective of incidence research. Yet, many rape victims continue to experience the physical and emotional effects of rape for months or even years after the assault. Many wait this long to present themselves for medical or psychological care.

Rape prevalence data capture the cumulative toll of sexual victimization more effectively than incidence data do. Researchers have asserted that rape's impact remains active for a considerable time, if not indefinitely, and have presented prevalence rates that consider as active cases anyone who has been raped at any time during their life.

No federal rape prevalence estimates exist, but the literature contains many independently obtained estimates. Published studies that employed random or probability samples include those focused on adolescents (Ageton, 1983; Hall & Flannery, 1984; Moore, Nord, & Peterson, 1989), college women (Koss, Gidycz, & Wisniewski, 1987; Koss & Oros, 1982; Miller & Marshall, 1987); and adult women (Burt, 1979; Essock-Vitale & McGuire, 1985; George, Winfield, & Blazer, 1992; Kilpatrick et al., 1985; Kilpatrick, Saunders, Veronen, Best, & Von, 1987; National Victim Center, 1992; Russell, 1984; Sorenson & Siegel, 1992; Sorenson et al., 1987; Winfield, George, Swartz, & Blazer, 1990; Wyatt, 1992). Data are also available for special groups including psychiatric patients, medical patients, gay and lesbian individuals, and the homeless (Berrill, 1990; D'Ercole & Struening, 1990; Goodman, 1991; Jacobson & Richardson, 1987; Koss, Woodruff, & Koss, 1991). The prevalence rates of sexual assault or rape are summarized in Table 1 along with several major methodological characteristics of each study.

It is immediately apparent from Table 1 that there is variation among the figures. Prevalence of completed rape has been estimated at approximately 20% of adult women according to several different sources (Burt, 1979; Goodman, 1991; Kilpatrick et al., 1987; Koss et al., 1991; Russell, 1984; Wyatt, 1992). However, a group of studies have reported lower prevalence of between 6% and 14% (Essock-Vitale & McGuire, 1985; Gordon & Riger, 1989; Kilpatrick et al., 1985; National Victim Center, 1992). The rates of sexual assault among men and adolescent boys are far lower than the rates for women and girls (Sorenson et al., 1987), with the exception of gay and lesbian groups. Lesbian women report rates of sexual assault that are only about half as high as gay men experience (Berrill, 1990).

Despite the national scope of several of the studies, few have included sufficiently large numbers of minority participants to present group-specific

Table 1

Empirical Studies of Rape Prevalence Among Women

Study	Sample	Data collection method	Participation rate	Type of screening	Context of questioning	Measured phenomena	Prevalence rate
Adolescent Girls							
Ageton (1983)	1,716 national	Interview	73%	Single item with word "rape"	Delinquency	Forced sexual behavior	5–11% per year
Hall & Flannery (1985)	508 ages 14–17 years	Telephone	56%	Single item	Sexual aggression	Rape and sexual assault	12% lifetime
Moore et al. (1989)	565 ages 18–22 years national	Telephone	82% of Wave II	Single item	Family conflict	Nonvoluntary sexual intercourse	12.7% lifetime (Whites) 8.0% lifetime (Blacks)

(continues)

Table 1

(Continued)

Study	Sample	Data collection method	Participation rate	Type of screening	Context of questioning	Measured phenomena	Prevalence rate
College Women							
Koss (1985); Koss & Oros (1982)	2,016 Kent, Ohio	In-person survey	Not given	Scenario 13 items	Sexual aggression	Completed rape	12.7% lifetime
Koss et al. (1987)	3,187 National	In-person survey	99%	Scenario 10 items	Sexual aggression	Completed rape	15.4% lifetime from age 14 years
Miller & Marshall (1987)	323 North Carolina	In-person survey	Not given	Scenario 11 items	Sexuality	Coerced or forced intercourse	27% while at university
Yegidis (1986)	348 Tampa, FL	In-person survey	Not given	Not given	Sexual aggression	Forced sexual encounter	22%
Adult Women							
Burt (1979)	328 Minnesota	Interview	n/a	n/a	Rape attitudes	Completed rape	24% lifetime

				Gate	Sexuality/Reproduction	Rape	
Essock-Vitale & McGuire (1985)	300 ages 35–45 years Los Angeles	Interview	66%				8% from age 18 years
Kilpatrick et al. (1985)	2,004 Charleston, SC	Telephone	78%	Not given	Crime	Forcible rape including attempts	8.8% lifetime
Kilpatrick et al. (1987)	399 Charleston, SC	Interview	20% of 1985 sample	Not given	Crime	Completed rape	23.3% lifetime
Gordon & Riger (1989)	693 Chicago Philadelphia San Francisco	Telephone Interview and telephone (N = 299)	Not given	Single item with "rape"	Crime	Rape or sexual assault	2% telephone sample 6% of volunteers surveyed by telephone 11% of volunteers at interview
National Victims Center (1992)	2,008 nationally representative 2,000 over-sample aged 18–34 years	Random-digit dial telephone	85%	Scenario 4 items	Crime	Completed rape	14% lifetime, excluding rape when unable to consent
Russell (1984)	930 San Francisco	Interview	50%	Scenario 38 items	Sexual assault	Completed rape	24% lifetime

(continues)

Table 1

(Continued)

Study	Sample	Data collection method	Participation rate	Type of screening	Context of questioning	Measured phenomena	Prevalence rate
Sorenson et al. (1987)	766 Hispanics 678 non-Hispanic Whites	Interview	68%	Gate	Mental illness	Sexual assault	13.5% from age 15 years
Winfield et al. (1990)	1,157 North Carolina	Interview	77% of Wave I	Gate	Mental illness	Sexual assault	5.9% lifetime
Wyatt (1992)	126 Blacks 122 Whites ages 18–36 years Los Angeles	Interview	55%	Scenario 4 items	Sexuality	Completed rape	25% Blacks 20% Whites from age 18 years

Special Groups

Study	Sample	Method	%	Instrument	Focus	Definition	Result
Goodman (1991)	50 housed 50 homeless	Interview	65%	Scenario modification of Russell	Violence	Very severe abuse, including forcible and nonforcible rapes and attempts	56% housed 20% homeless
Jacobson & Richardson (1987)	50 psychiatric patients	Interview	42%	Not given 15 items	Violence	Sexual abuse	38% from age 16 years
Koss et al. (1991)	2,291 medical patients Cleveland	Mailed survey and interview	45% 18%	Scenario 5 items	Health	Completed rape	21% by survey 30% by interview

prevalence rates. Those studies that did offer data provided information for Hispanics, predominately of Mexican background (Russell, 1984; Sorenson et al., 1987; Sorenson & Siegel, 1992), African Americans (Russell, 1984; Wyatt, 1992), Asians, and Native Americans (Russell, 1984). Prevalence data by ethnicity are also available for college students (Koss et al., 1987). Except among college students, sexual assault is slightly more prevalent among African-American women than among Caucasian women, although the difference is not statistically significant (Koss et al., 1987; Russell, 1984; Wyatt, 1992). The lifetime prevalence rate of sexual assault among non-Hispanic Whites has been reported to be 2.5 times higher than that of Hispanics (Sorenson & Siegel, 1992). To support this finding as a true difference, the researchers pointed out that prevalence varies with acculturation. Sexual assault is 3 times higher among Mexican Americans born in the United States than among Mexican Americans born in Mexico. Although it is possible that traditional Hispanic culture is somewhat protective against sexual assault, the competing explanation that there is a culturally based reluctance to confide in authority figures about sexual assault that lessens with acculturation is also consistent with the data.

CRITIQUE OF RAPE DETECTION METHODOLOGICAL CHOICES

Of course, seeking a single number to represent rape prevalence is artificial because of the variation with age and sociodemographic characteristics (George, Winfield, & Blazer, 1992; Sorenson & Siegel, 1992). But in addition to these sources of variation, numerous methodological decisions affect the magnitude of the rape prevalence estimates across studies (Koss, 1993a). Some of these methodological differences are outlined here.

Definition of the Measured Phenomena

An obvious explanation for variation is differences in the criteria used to define what was counted as a "rape" or "sexual assault" (Muehlenhard, Powch, Phelps, & Giusti, 1992). A subset of the studies summarized in Table 1 presented formal, legally grounded definitions of rape (e.g., Kilpatrick et al., 1985; Kilpatrick et al., 1987; National Victims Center, 1992; Koss et al., 1987; Koss et al., 1991; Russell, 1982b; Wyatt, 1992). It is surprising that the data reveal no direct relationship between the breadth or narrowness of the definition and the magnitude of prevalence estimate.

Type, Text, and Context of Screening Questions

Several investigators have screened with questions that contain the word *rape,* thereby assuming that respondents (a) knew how rape is defined, (b) perceived what happened to them as rape, and (c) remembered the experience with this conceptual label (Ageton, 1983; Essock-Vitale & McGuire, 1985; Gordon & Riger, 1989; Moore, Nord, & Peterson, 1989). However, Koss (1988a) reported that only 27% of college women labeled as rape their experiences with forced, unwanted intercourse. An examination of the data in Table 1 reveals that studies in which respondents were directly asked whether they had been raped had generally low prevalence estimates.

Screening for rape has adopted two conceptually different strategies. A gate approach is a single item intended to identify respondents who have been victimized to any degree. These respondents may then be administered follow-up questions that request information about the specific victimizations that were experienced. In contrast, behaviorally specific screening involves presentation of multiple scenarios that describe in concrete detail the types of experiences that the respondent is asked to disclose. An examination of Table 1 reveals that use of the gate-item strategy has been associated with low-prevalence percentages for both sexual assault and rape. A single item appears unable to stimulate recall of the variety of guises under which rape can occur.

Many reports of prevalence estimates derive from larger studies in which questions about rape or sexual assault were piggy-backed. Some of these larger studies include the National Youth Study (Ageton, 1983), Epidemiological Catchment Area Studies (George & Winfield-Laird, 1986; Sorenson et al., 1987), the National Women's Study (National Victims Center, 1992), and the National Survey of Children (Moore et al., 1989). The context in which rape screening occurs may influence recall. Rape detection can be suboptimal if respondents believe they are being questioned only about assaults they perceived as crimes or about assaults that caused serious emotional repercussions.

Mode of Data Collection

All of the major data collection methods have been used in the measurement of rape prevalence, including face-to-face interviews, mailed surveys, in-person surveys, and telephone surveys. The studies summarized in Table 1 reveal no clear-cut tendencies for prevalence rates to covary by method except that telephone surveying has uniformly produced lower prevalence rates. It is the general consensus in the literature that telephone and in-person interviews are equivalent (e.g., Klecka & Tuchfarber, 1978). However, the only direct comparison of these methods for detection of rape revealed that the prevalence rate of those interviewed in person (11%) was double that of those interviewed by phone (6%). There were also some demographic differences between those who made themselves available for interview by each method (Gordon & Riger, 1989).

Confidentiality and Rapport

Guarantees of confidentiality are less persuasive when others are present during questioning. Failure to disclose rape in front of family members may occur because the assault has been kept secret or because the perpetrator is among those present. Sorenson et al. (1987) conducted the only study in which the effect of confidentiality on disclosure was examined. They reported no differences in prevalence rates according to the confidentiality of questioning. However, this finding may have been influenced by the non-specific single-screening item that was used in the investigation and by the low overall disclosure rates that were obtained. The gender and ethnic characteristics of interviewers may also contribute to the level of victimization that is detected. Respondents were 1.3 times more likely to reveal sexual assault to a female than to a male interviewer (Sorenson et al., 1987).

Selective Participation

The validity of prevalence estimates depends on how accurately the sample that was studied represents the group of women to whom the results are being extended. Even with random or representative sampling, it is frequently the case in rape research that those who agree to be interviewed are demographically different in age, education, and ethnicity from the larger population to which conclusions would apply. Another source of bias in this research that cannot be dismissed is the potential that victims of sexual assault volunteer disproportionally for interviews. The studies in Table 1 with the highest prevalence rates all derived from samples with participation rates between 50% and 70%. Therefore, these studies provided sufficient leeway for differential participation by various groups to have occurred.

RECOMMENDATIONS FOR IMPROVING RESEARCH ON RAPE FREQUENCY

Some of the lower prevalence rates clearly stem from a relative lack of success in overcoming the forces that foster nondisclosure of rape. The higher prevalence rates, on the other hand, raise concerns about differential participation by those who were younger, more educated, members of the majority culture, and by those who had experienced sexual assault. The 14% prevalence rate found by the National Victims Center (1992) has the advantage of a national sample and state-of-the-art techniques for questioning about rape. For the consumption of the general public, this study establishes a prevalence for rape that is high enough to command attention and to document a serious problem for U.S. women. But professionals should be aware that there are scientific reasons to regard this figure as a conservative estimate that would be higher but for certain methodological decisions. First, the sample was limited to those women with telephone service. Although telephone ownership on average is high in the United States, there remain people too poor to own telephones across numerous census tracts in the country, particularly in the south and west, where between 10% and 20% of households lack telephones (Doyle, 1993). Second, the sample excluded several potentially high-risk groups for rape that were detailed earlier. Third, the definition underpinning the study excluded nonforcible rapes that occurred when the woman was incapable of giving consent; these are considered legitimate rapes in the majority of states. Fourth, data collection was by telephone and it has not been demonstrated conclusively that rape detection is as high as can be obtained in person (Gordon & Riger, 1989). Currently, no alternate national estimates of rape prevalence based on non-telephone methodology are published in the literature, nor have there been any additional attempts to establish the equivalence of the data-collection methods with this subject matter. Furthermore, throughout this literature, insufficient attention has been paid to documenting variation in vulnerability to rape by ethnicity and class.

Enhanced Federal Data Collection Effort

An exemplary study of prevalence of multiple forms of violence in diverse populations is sorely needed. The Department of Health and Human Services and the Department of Justice should develop a joint strategy to conduct or contract for a national study that represents state-of-the-art sampling and face-to-face data collection. The sample must be designed so that the vulnerability of high-risk groups can be determined, the interrelatedness of various forms of violence can be revealed, and a full portrait of women's exposure to violence can be ascertained. Groups who have been particularly neglected in current research studies include adolescents, poor women, lesbians, physically disabled women, incarcerated women, and women from ethnically diverse backgrounds.

Continued Monitoring of the NCVS

Six new questions to detect rape were introduced into the NCVS in July, 1991, although other problem-laden NCVS procedures remain unchanged. The revised questions hold no promise of rapid improvement in the validity of NCVS rape estimates because they are being phased in gradually. The professional community must exert ongoing pressure until rape is measured with the same precision as other crimes.

10

The Physical and Psychological Aftermath of Rape

Experiencing sexual violence changes a woman's life forever. The immediate experience of rape and other crime victims includes disruption of daily routines; experiences of vulnerability, separateness, and helplessness; pervasive tuning in to the possibility of future victimization; reliving the victimization; and trying to get on top of the experience by taking further precautions and restricting the range of activities (Fischer & Wertz, 1979, p. 352). Successful return to a semblance of the survivor's former state requires an environment that responds with concern and respect for her attempts to make sense of the experience and that demonstrates over time that extreme vigilance is no longer necessary. Given the nature of rape, immediate distress is understandable. What is surprising, perhaps, is the longevity of its effects. Burgess and Holmstrom (1979b) interviewed victims four to six years after their rape experiences. The researchers asked these women if they "felt back to normal" (i.e., the way they felt prior to the rape). Of these women, 37% felt recovered from the rape within months; 37% felt recovered but said the process had taken several years; and 26% still did not feel recovered.

SOMATIC CONSEQUENCES OF RAPE

Information about the somatic consequences of violence is relevant to behavioral health practitioners because of their contributions to medical education and their provision of services within the health care system. The futility of making clear cut distinctions between mind and body effects of trauma is well-recognized and victim's assistance personnel uniformly attest to the high level of concern about physical health that is typical among victimized women.

Acute Medical Consequences

Approximately 40% of rape victims receive nongenital physical injuries and 54% of those injured seek medical treatment (Beebe, 1991; Geist, 1988). Between half and two thirds of all victims sustain no physical trauma (Beebe, 1991; Koss, Woodruff, & Koss, 1991; National Victims Center, 1992). Elderly victims are more likely to sustain genital injuries than younger victims (Muram, Miller, & Cutler, 1992). Several reviews detail the psychological and forensic protocol for the emergency examination of rape victims (Hicks, 1988, 1990; Hochbaum, 1987).

Sexually transmitted diseases (STD) are estimated to occur as a result of rape in 3.6% to 30% of victims (Beebe, 1991; Forster, Estreich, & Hooi, 1991; Jenny et al., 1990; Lacey, 1990; Murphy, 1990). The risk for contracting HIV during sexual assault is currently unknown, but cases have been reported in women with no other risk factors except rape (Clayton et al., 1991; Murphy, 1990; Murphy, Kitchen, Harris, & Forster, 1989). In interviews conducted within 3 months of rape, 26% of victims spontaneously mentioned AIDS as a concern; for half of these women it was their primary concern (Baker, Burgess, Brickman, & Davis, 1990). Pregnancy results from rape in approximately 5% of the cases (Beebe, 1991; Koss, Woodruff, & Koss, 1991).

The foregoing documentation must be interpreted conservatively because information from trauma centers may reflect only those who sought care and were identified as rape victims. Victims who did not reveal or were not asked about the origin of their injuries, who saw private physicians, or who sought no treatment in the immediate posttrauma period are not represented in the data base. Considering all victims together whether injured or noninjured, a rape examination was reported in 17% of cases (National Victims Center, 1992). Yet, even those who sought medical intervention may not have received the emergency care that rape protocols recommend. In a recent national sample, no pregnancy testing or prophylaxis was received by 60% of rape victims, and no information or testing for exposure to HIV was reported by 73% of victims (National Victims Center, 1992). Of course these retrospective data would have included some rapes that occurred before the present era of AIDS awareness, and it is possible that physicians may have skipped pregnancy testing because they determined that pregnancy was unlikely in certain cases such as premenarchial and postmenopausal victims. However, it is more difficult to rationalize the absence of information or testing for STDs that was reported by 39% of victims (National Victims Center, 1992). These findings point to a combination of two factors. On the one hand, they could suggest large-scale failure to provide mandated care. On the other hand, care could have been provided or deemed medically unnecessary, but the communication that accompanied the treatment for rape victims was insufficient for them to understand the care they received.

Chronic Illnesses

Unreflected in reviews of acute consequences would be those victims who sought no treatment in the immediate posttrauma period only to present themselves to the medical system later with delayed consequences of violence. There may be many such patients. Two studies have revealed that between 25% to 28% of female primary care patients have a history of rape or attempted rape (Koss, Woodruff, & Koss, 1991; Walch & Broadhead, 1992). Although women who have been raped may experience many pressures to keep their victimization silent, it does not appear that they avoid medical care. In fact, rape victims are more likely to seek care from their physician than they are to seek many specialty services including legal aid, mental health, or victim's assistance services (Koss, Woodruff, & Koss, 1991).

Pelvic pain is a major issue in women's health because it is the cause of 10% to 19% of hysterectomies performed in the United States (Reiter & Gambone, 1990). The incidence of physical and sexual abuse in both childhood and adulthood is elevated among women with chronic pelvic pain including both medically explained and unexplained cases (Rapkin, Kames, Darke, Stampler, & Naliboff, 1990; Reiter, Sharkerin, Gambone, & Milburn, 1991; Reiter, 1990; Reiter & Gambone, 1990). For example, women who had undergone laparoscopy for chronic pelvic pain had a higher prevalence of sexual assault in adulthood than women who had the procedure for tubal ligation or infertility, 48% and 13%, respectively (Walker, Katon, et al., 1988). Premenstrual syndrome is another gynecologic disorder associated with sexual victimization (Paddison et al., 1990; Steiger & Zanko, 1990; Stout, Steege, Blazer, & George, 1986). Many of the patients who meet diagnostic criteria for chronic pelvic pain also meet criteria for irritable bowel syndrome (Drossman et al., 1990; Whitehead & Crowell, 1991). For example, among a consecutive sample of women evaluated at a university-based gastroenterology clinic, 44% reported some type of sexual or physical victimization during childhood or adulthood (Drossman et al., 1990).

Victimization is associated with an array of chronic pain disorders such as headache, back pain, facial pain, temporal mandibular joint discomfort, and bruxism. For example, among women referred to a multidisciplinary pain center, 53% were either physically or sexually abused (Domino & Haber, 1987; Haber & Roos, 1985a, 1985b). Other neurologic disorders associated with victimization include psychogenic epileptic seizures (Shen, Bowman, & Markland, 1990; Wilkus & Dodrill, 1989). Victimization is also associated with health behaviors that can be life-threatening such as anorexia nervosa and bulimia. In one large group of bulimic patients, 23% had been raped, 29% had been sexually abused as children, 29% were physically abused as children, and 23% were battered (these categories are not mutually exclusive and some women experienced multiple forms of abuse; Root & Fallon, 1988; Root, Fallon & Friedrich, 1986). HIV infection is another behaviorally related illness that has also been found to be associated with a history of victimization. In a sample of New England adults selected on the basis of engaging in risk behaviors for acquiring or transmitting HIV infection, only 54% of the women lacked histories of sexual victimization compared with 81% of the men (Zierler et al., 1991). Among women in New York City who used crack, cocaine or both, 51% had been victims of at least one forced sexual encounter (Paone, Chavkin, Willets, Friedman, & Des Jarlais, 1992). Victimized women were 2.9 times more likely than nonvictims to engage in sex-for-drug transactions.

Given the relative recency of sexual assault as an explanatory variable in medicine, many of the studies of somatic consequences of rape have problems with methodological sophistication that are typical of a developing field. Most of the screening for sexual assault in this literature has been rudimentary and lacks connection to social science definitions of abuse categories. Furthermore, virtually all findings are based on retrospective designs that reduce confidence about causal linkages. Although it is plausible that a connection exists between victimization and the excess number of various diagnoses, it is also possible that a third variable such as neglect or violence in the family of origin has influenced both the likelihood of adult victimization and ill health. It is rare in this literature to measure other influences contemporary with sexual victimization. Both multivariate and prospective studies are needed in future work.

Stress-Related Health Effects

Rape is a risk factor for increased illness. Women with a history of victimization by rape and other crimes perceive their health less favorably than nonvictimized women and report more symptoms of illness across virtually all body systems except the skin and eyes (Koss, Koss, & Woodruff, 1991). In addition, victimized women are more likely to engage in destructive behaviors that have known associations with illness and premature death, including smoking, alcohol use, and failure to use seat belts (Koss, Koss, & Woodruff, 1991). Finally, victimized women make greater use of both medical and mental health services than do nonvictimized women (Golding, Stein, Siegel, Burman, & Sorenson, 1988).

These self-reported differences are corroborated by objective data on utilization taken from medical records (Fellitti, 1991; Koss, Koss, & Woodruff, 1991). For example, among adult woman enrolled in a health maintenance organization (HMO) who had a history of childhood molestation or rape, 22% visited a physician 10 or more times a year, compared with 6% among nonvictimized women (Fellitti, 1991). Likewise, women HMO patients who had been raped and assaulted during adulthood made physician visits in an index year twice as frequently—an average of 6.9 visits—than did nonvictimized women who made 3.5 visits (Koss, Koss, & Woodruff, 1991). The outpatient medical expenses incurred by the most severely victimized woman were 2.5 times higher than those of nonvictimized women ($401 vs. $161). In fact, victimization severity was the single most powerful predictor of total yearly physician visits and outpatient costs, exceeding the predictive power of age, ethnicity, self-reported symptoms, and morbidity-related injurious health behaviors. Finally, utilization data across five years preceding and following victimization indicated that the changes in use were temporally related to the violence (Koss, Koss, & Woodruff, 1991). The largest utilization changes were seen in the second year following victimization. Compared with their previctimization levels of yearly physician contacts, women who were raped increased their frequency of visits 56% in the second year following victimization (from 3.6 to 6.1 visits per year). This is in contrast to increases of 2% during the same period among nonvictimized women. Because the greatest increases in use occurred during the second year, chronic persisting complaints rather than acute injuries are suggested as the major health problems of victimized women.

Because elevated levels of victimization are seen among patients both with and without medical explanations for their illness, theoretical explanations of the somatic consequences of rape must go beyond somatization or psychosomatic theories to account for the induction of documented disease. One appealing model is stress-illness theory. As commonly understood, this theory suggests that stressful life events suppress resistance to illness by affecting immune function (Cohen & Williamson, 1991). Stress-triggered changes in immune functioning are plausible explanations for infectious diseases that follow shortly upon exposure to trauma. Although the repetitive nature of some intimate violence could be a source of continuing stress, health effects often persist far beyond cessation of the violence. Therefore, mechanisms are needed to account for prolonged stress effects. Behavioral alterations made in response to stress could create negative influences on health that far outlast the initial stress that triggered them (Cohen & Williamson, 1991; Kiecolt-Glaser & Glaser, 1987). Drinking more alcohol, initiating or increasing smoking, practicing poor dietary habits, and sleeplessness are a few examples of behavioral adaptations or coping responses to stress that may have deleterious effects on the immune response. Illness may also be associated with the PTSD that victims experience, a disorder which can result in chronic overarousal that induces disease (Baum, 1990).

A further mechanism that may contribute to the health effects of violence exposure is intensified focus on internal sensations. Victims of rape fear that they will be disfigured, injured, or killed during their assaults. Intense experiences of this type may focus attention on internal sensations and establish or heighten concerns about physical integrity (Wickramasekera, 1986). Once this focus of attention is established, sensations may be misperceived or labeled by the victim as symptoms of disease. There are several sources of distressing bodily sensations that can become the focus of attention and labeling, including undetected physical injuries, the physiologic concomitants of victimization-related emotional distress, physical sensations that occur as part of intrusive re-experiencing of trauma, and normal physiologic sensations present in everyone (such as the heartbeat) that are magnified when subject to attentional focus. When concerns about these symptoms exceeds some threshold of severity, people initiate visits to their physicians.

A final component of any model of victimization-related health effects is the interaction of the medical services system with traumatized victims (Gershman, 1991). In most cases, physicians focus on treatment of the physical symptoms alone and overlook environmental causes of distress. Routine screening for violence is rare even in psychiatric settings and emergency rooms (Jacobson & Richardson, 1987; Liese, Larson, Johnson, & Hourigan, 1989). If medical practitioners fail to elicit relevant contextual information, they are potentially responsible for misattributing physical sensations solely to organic pathology.

Negative Outcomes of Trauma

By failing to screen for victimization, the practitioner misses an opportunity to allow disclosure of trauma, to educate the patient about the significance of the discomfort, and to connect the patient with available support services. The simple act of disclosing a secret trauma has been linked to positive changes in indicators of immune response (Pennebaker, Kiecolt-Glaser, & Glaser, 1988). Misdiagnosis early in a woman's efforts to seek treatment may allow relatively mild problems to develop into more severe ones, may lead to distressing or harmful side-effects from medications, and may result in unnecessary invasive procedures (Katon, Ries, & Kleinman, 1984). Medical intervention within the first two years following victimization not only might reduce negative health changes, but also encourage the use of mental health services among a greater proportion of those in need if the stream of referrals is augmented by increased physician vigilance.

There is little likelihood that physicians currently realize their potential to help victims of rape. Many physicians respond to disclosure of rape the same way lay people do—by questioning the credibility or culpability of the victim. Medical service providers may be particularly unfamiliar and insensitive to the needs of lesbian survivors and may secondarily victimize them (Garnets, Herek, & Levy, 1990; Wertheimer, 1990). Other data suggest that rape victims frequently do not receive the care that emergency room protocols mandate (National Victims Center, 1992). These problems all reflect lack of attention to rape in the medical curriculum. Behavioral scientists clearly need to be involved in disseminating recent psychological literature on rape in medical education.

PSYCHOLOGICAL OUTCOMES OF RAPE

The psychological response to rape cannot be captured in a single snapshot. Rather, it is a process that unfolds across time. The magnitude of the response is predicted by both objective and subjective characteristics of the trauma and may be characterized by a range of psychological symptoms. The response is also sensitive to numerous personal and environmental influences. Many observers suggest that the reactions of rape victims follow a predictable sequence (for a review, see Frieze, Hymer, & Greenberg, 1987). However, the bulk of empirical evidence that has documented psychological status in the aftermath of rape has focused not on stages of response, but on assessing the severity of various psychological symptoms across time. These symptoms include anxiety, depression, sexual dysfunction, and interpersonal difficulties (for reviews, see Ellis, 1983; Hanson, 1990; Holmes & St. Lawrence, 1983; Lurigio & Resick, 1990; McCann, Sakheim, & Abrahamson, 1988; Resick, 1987, 1990; Roth & Lebowitz, 1988). More recently, increased empirical attention has focused on the cognitive changes that occur in the aftermath of trauma.

Cognitive Changes

Clinical work with victims has revealed the "overwhelming assault that victimization is to the child's and adult survivor's world of meaning" (Conte, 1988, p. 325). Much of the cognitive activity that occurs in the midst of life crises involves repetitive mental replaying of the traumatic event. A victim struggles with her understanding of why the event happened, attempts to evaluate whether the outcome was inevitable, and reconstructs multiple alternative scenarios for how the rape could have been stopped (Draucker, 1989; Janoff-Bulman, 1985a, 1985b; Taylor, 1983; Wortman & Silver, 1989).

The Relationship of Causal Attributions to Distress

Unexpected events like rape are especially likely to stimulate a search for any causes of the trauma that will satisfactorily answer the question, "Why did this happen to me?" The various responses to this question are called causal attributions, and one type of attribution is self-blame. Thus, a victim may explain that her rape occurred because she is too open and trusting of people. Psychological theory has held that even self-blame may be adaptive because it can satisfy deeply felt human needs to impose meaning on life, allows victims to preserve beliefs in a "just" world where bad things only happen to bad people (Lerner, 1980), and enhances illusions of control over life outcomes (Taylor & Brown, 1988; Wortman & Silver, 1989). Although several studies have suggested that those who blame their own actions for the occurrence of a trauma are better adjusted than those who do not feel responsible, rape victims break with this general pattern. Among them, self-blame repeatedly has been found to predict poorer adjustment and greater distress (Abbey, 1987b; Frazier, 1990; Katz & Burt, 1988; Meyer & Taylor, 1986; Wyatt, Notgrass, & Newcomb, 1990). In fact, the greater time spent considering any class of causes, whether self blame or external blame, is associated with more distress (Frazier & Schauben, in press). A rape victim's understanding of the forces that caused her victimization appear to exert a powerful influence on the psychological distress she experiences. In one study perceived control over negative events contributed as much to the prediction of postrape symptom severity as perceived life threat and the level of brutality involved in the assault (Kushner, Riggs, Foa, & Miller, 1993).

Alteration of Cognitive Schemas

After a sexual assault, the victim attempts to reconcile the violent, physical harm she has endured at the hands of a fellow human being, frequently someone who was known and trusted, with her previous assumptions about the world as a reasonably safe and predictable place. This shattering of inner models of reality is painful and destructive of psychological equilibrium. It is not unusual for victimization to precipitate a crisis in adult development. The crisis may be resolved positively or negatively depending on the nature of the changes made in the victim's central beliefs. Beliefs (or schemas) that may be affected by victimization include safety, power or efficacy, trust, esteem, and intimacy (McCann, Sakhein, & Abramson, 1988; McCann & Pearlman, 1990a). Each of these schemas involves beliefs about the self as well as the behavior of others. Under the best of circumstances, victimization can lead to a more personally-meaningful, better articulated, and more flexible belief system (Burt & Katz, 1987). In a less than ideal recovery environment negative alterations in schemas may lead to pervasive beliefs that one is bad, evil, destructive, responsible for bad events, and who cannot trust or be trusted. In addition to the schemas listed earlier, lesbian victims must confront the effect of victimization on their identity as lesbians. Lesbianism may become linked with the newly heightened vulnerability that normally follows victimization. Furthermore, victimization may be interpreted as a violation of one's self as a lesbian, may revive internalized homophobia, and may effect the coming-out process (Garnets et al., 1990).

Experiences like rape that effect self-identity stimulate people's needs to reaffirm themselves by seeking validation from others. Yet, a rape victim is less likely than other trauma survivors to receive the support she needs. No one blames hurricane victims for living in a storm-prone area, but rape victims face a culture in which prevailing beliefs at least partially implicate them for the provocation of their own sexual assault (Burt, 1980, 1991). In addition to being made to feel responsible, many victims learn painfully that people are not as helpful and open to victims as might be expected given the observance of Judeo–Christian ethics and a general orientation to help the powerless that characterize U.S. culture (Janoff-Bulman & Frieze, 1983). Empirical study of violent crime victims during the course of their recovery has documented the occurrence of negative changes in beliefs in the areas of safety, esteem, and trust (Norris & Kaniasty, 1991). These negative adaptations all predict increased psychological distress (Norris & Kaniasty, 1991). The degree of incongruity among the event and existing beliefs helps determine the amount of distress that is experienced. For example, rape victims who were following their personal safety rules at the time of the rape experienced greater fear and depressive reactions than women who perceived that they were in a dangerous situation (Frank & Stewart, 1984; Schepple & Bart, 1983). Negative change in self-schemas have been shown to persist for at least 18 months following assault (Murphy et al., 1988). Not yet examined in the literature are the spiritual consequences of rape including its potential to threaten belief in God and to stimulate an existential crisis characterized by loss of meaning and connection.

Psychological Symptoms

Both prospective and retrospective designs have been used to assess the severity of psychological symptoms seen in the aftermath of rape. Prospective studies follow victims forward in time from as close to trauma as humanely possible and involve measurements from several points during an individual's recovery process. Typically these studies document very high distress levels within the first week that peak in severity by approximately 3 weeks postassault, continue at a high level for the next month, then begin to improve by 2 to 3 months postassault. Most of the differences between victimized and nonvictimized women disappear after 3 months except for elevations in fear, anxiety, self-esteem, and sexual dysfunction, which persist for up to 18 months (Resick, 1987). Although prospective studies are in many ways ideal, they also have important limitations: Prospective research is expensive; it frequently includes only victims who have sought some form of formal service following rape; it often generates small samples due to difficulties recruiting women willing to enroll in research immediately following rape; and it is characterized by decreased integrity as follow-up continues due to the extensive attrition of participants that is uniformly reported by investigators (Briere, 1992).

Therefore, out of necessity the very-long-term aftereffects of rape have been measured crosssectionally, a methodology that allows more generalizable samples to be accessed and larger number of participants to be included. Here, a group of victims are studied who represent the range of elapsed times since assault from a few weeks to 50 or more years. These studies typically reveal that approximately one quarter of women who are several years beyond rape report continuing negative effects (Hanson, 1990). Data from the epidemiologic catchment area studies reveal evidence of continuing problems in victims—even when evaluated many years after sexual assault—as reflected by higher likelihood of receiving several psychiatric diagnoses including major depression, alcohol abuse/dependence, drug abuse/dependence, generalized anxiety, obsessive–compulsive disorder, and PTSD (Burnam et al., 1988; Winfield et al., 1990). However, cross-sectional studies also have many limitations that cannot be overlooked in assessing the quality of the data base (Briere, 1992). These limitations include the influence of contemporary adaptation on recall, unintentional biasing of responses in the direction of greater distress by participants, and the decreased ability of investigators to make definitive causal linkages.

In short, there is no single ideal approach to the study of rape outcomes. Rather, there are alternate approaches to visualizing the recovery process. Because prospective research requires participants to remain enrolled for a significant period of time, it may result in a sample of victims who are better adjusted than the typical victim. Also, continued involvement with a research project during recovery may alter the responses of those in the victim's social network, who become convinced by the presence of outside authorities that a legitimate trauma has occurred. For these reasons, prospective research may reflect the best possible outcomes that are seen in rape recovery. In contrast, cross-sectional studies, because of their broader range of participants and the potential effect of present circumstances on recall, may reflect the most pessimistic picture of recovery outcomes. The outcome for any given individual most likely lies within the range delineated by these two approaches. In the material that follows, the degree of distress and recovery course are described for several rape-related psychological symptoms that have been examined both prospectively and cross-sectionally.

Anxiety/Fears

Symptoms of fear and anxiety predominate in the immediate postrape clinical picture (Ruch, Gartrell, Amedeo, & Coyne, 1991; Ruch, Gartrell, Ramelli, & Coyne, 1991; Veronen, Kilpatrick, & Resick, 1979.) Within 72 hours of the assault, 86% of the victims reported having intense fear of their assailant and anxiety about their personal safety, as well as having *disclosure anxiety*, which is heightened concern about others' reactions to the assault (Ruch, Gartrell, Amedeo, & Coyne, 1991). The anxiety induced by rape reaches maximum levels in the third week but may not begin to decrease for some time. Victims score higher than nonvictims on measures of anxiety for up to 3 years (Calhoun, Atkeson, & Ellis, 1981; Resick, 1987). The degree of anxiety, fear, and stress experienced by victims of assaultive crime (including rape and physical assault) is significantly higher than the levels experienced by nonassaultive crime victims at both 1 and 6 months postattack (Wirtz & Harrell, 1987).

Depression

Although symptoms of anxiety predominate immediately after rape, precursors of depression are observed within a few hours to a few days of the assault; these precursors include sad feelings about the assault, apathetic feelings about life, and suicidal thoughts (Ruch, Gartrell, Amedeo, & Coyne, 1991). Within a few weeks, depressive symptoms and frequently a full-blown depressive syndrome become apparent. Interviews during this period reveal that 56% of the victims received scores within the moderately or severely depressed range on the Beck Depression Inventory; 43% met diagnostic criteria for major depressive disorder (Frank & Stewart, 1983, 1984; Frank, Turner, & Duffy, 1979). Victimization-induced depression lasts approximately 3 months (Atkeson, Calhoun, Resick, & Ellis, 1982; Foa, Rothbaum, & Kozak, 1989; Resick, 1987). Lifetime prevalence of major depressive disorder has been estimated to be 13% among victims of sexual assault compared with 5% in nonvictims (Burnam et al., 1988; Sorenson & Golding, 1990).

The frequency of suicidal ideation is also notable among rape victims. In the first month after victimization, reported rates of suicidal behavior have varied between 3% to 27% (Frank et al., 1979; Frank & Stewart, 1984). Suicidal ideation is reported by between 33% to 50% of rape victims examined in cross-sectional studies (Ellis, Atkeson, & Calhoun, 1981; Koss, 1988a; Resick, Jordan, Girelli, Hutter, & Marhoefer-Dvorak, 1989). Actual suicide attempts were reported by 19% of rape victims identified in a community sample compared with 2% among nonvictims (Kilpatrick, Best, et al., 1985).

Sexual Functioning

Rape victims experience less sexual satisfaction and more sexual problems than nonvictimized women (Becker, Abel, & Skinner, 1979; Becker, Skinner, Abel, & Cichon, 1986; Becker, Skinner, Abel, & Treacy, 1982; Burgess & Holmstrom, 1979b; Ellis, Calhoun, & Atkeson, 1980; Feldman-Summers, Gordon, & Meagher, 1979; Wyatt, Guthrie, & Notgrass, 1992). Disruption in sexual function immediately postrape, especially avoidance of sex, was reported by 61% of victims (Ellis, Calhoun, & Atkeson, 1980). At least one problem in sexual functioning was reported by 58% of sexual assault victims in a large cross-sectional sample (including rape, attempted rape, incest, and sexual molestation incidents) compared with 17% of nonvictims (Becker, Skinner, Abel, & Cichon, 1986). Even 4 to 6 years after sexual assault, 30% of raped women did not feel their sexual functioning had returned to prerape levels (Burgess & Holmstrom, 1979b). Most of the problems among victimized women were early response cycle inhibitions including lack of desire, fear of sex, and arousal dysfunction compared to complaints about sexual boredom or less frequent and intense orgasms among nonvictims (Becker, Skinner, Abel, & Cichon, 1986).

Social Adjustment

Despite evidence of considerable psychological distress, prospective studies of rape victims' abilities to carry out their social roles reveal only short-lived difficulties in most areas. Periodic monitoring of rape victims in the months following assault revealed the largest effect to be on work performance, which was found to suffer for 8 months following victimization (Resick, Calhoun, Atkeson, & Ellis, 1981). In social and leisure activities, victimized women differed from nonvictimized for only the first 2 months following trauma. Difficulties meeting responsibilities within the nuclear and extended family lasted just 1 month whereas marital, parental, and family unit adjustment were not impaired at all. However, the multiple contacts with a research team appear to have convinced those around the victim of the legitimacy of the trauma and changed their behavior toward the victim. Women who were given only an isolated assessment, either at 4 or 8 months postassault, showed more problems across the range of social roles than women who were regularly examined.

PSYCHOLOGICAL MODELS AND CONSTRUCTS OF THE AFTEREFFECTS OF RAPE

The psychological effect of rape is multifaceted, unfolds over time, differs according to a number of characteristics of the victim and crime, and is mediated by several cognitive variables. Given this complexity, it is not surprising to find a plethora of theoretical explanations for why rape survivors react the way they do and how they cope with recovery (for reviews, see Frieze et al., 1987; Kahn, 1984). It would not be possible to do justice to the range of conceptualizations that exist in this report, so we have chosen to focus on the theoretical explanations of a single conceptualization of posttraumatic effects, namely PTSD. This concept unifies much of the existing research on separate symptoms and is the dominant conceptualization in contemporary psychological and psychiatric literature on trauma. After a review and critique of the PTSD diagnosis, alternate theoretical explanations will be presented of the processes that create this complex of symptoms.

PTSD Construct

The *DSM-IV* (American Psychiatric Association, 1994) characterizes PTSD as a set of responses to a traumatic "event or events that involved actual or threatened death or serious injury, or a threat to the physical integrity of self or others..." (p. 427). The hallmarks of PTSD are intrusive reexperiencing of the trauma and cyclicity of symptoms. Recollections are in the form of daytime memories or nightmares and are accompanied by intense psychological distress including possible reactivation of the emotions and physiologic sensations experienced during the attack. To reduce the distress of reexperiencing, trauma victims often go to great lengths to avoid reminders of the trauma, this results in cyclic phases in which diminished responsiveness to the external world alternates with phases of intrusion characterized by an overload of psychic stimulation. Rape victims are thought to be the largest single group of PTSD sufferers (Foa, Olasov, & Steketee, 1987). In a prospective study of hospital-referred rape victims, 94% met PTSD criteria at initial assessment conducted a mean of 12 days after the assault; 46% still met the criteria 3 months later (Rothbaum, Foa, Riggs, Murdock, & Walsh, in press). The lifetime prevalence of PTSD in a national sample of rape victims was 31% (National Victims Center, 1992). Criteria for PTSD were currently met by 11% of the victims.

The major predictors of the presence of PTSD are experiencing life threat, physical injury, and rape (Kilpatrick et al., 1989). Victims whose incident included these elements were 8.5 times more likely than other crime victims to experience PTSD. Women appear to be more vulnerable to PTSD than men are, although this difference could simply reflect that women experience more traumatic events than men (Breslau, Davis, Andreski, & Peterson, 1991; Norris, 1992). PTSD is somewhat more likely to result from rape than from a number of other traumas including robbery, physical assault, tragic death, motor vehicle accident, and natural disaster (Norris,

1992). Rape continues to predict the presence of PTSD symptoms even after controlling for violence and dangerousness. Therefore, it has been suggested that rape is characterized by additional elements conducive to the development of PTSD that are not seen in other crimes (Kilpatrick, Saunders, Amick-McMullan, et al., 1989).

Theoretical Explanations for the Creation of PTSD Symptoms

Several comprehensive reviews are available of the psychological processes hypothesized to explain the development of PTSD symptoms in rape victims (Foa, Steketee, Rothbaum, & Olasov, 1989; Goodman, Koss, & Russo, 1993b; Jones & Barlow, 1990; Resick, 1990, in press; Resick & Markaway, 1991; Resick & Schnicke, 1991). PTSD has been addressed from both biological (see Van der Kolk, 1987) and psychological perspectives. We focus here on models of psychological processes including psychoanalytic, behavioral, and cognitive-behavioral perspectives.

Psychoanalytic Models

Noting the impoverished mental life of trauma victims, Freud (1955) theorized that a traumatic event produces such distressing emotions that victims are unable through conscious-thought processes to resolve the contradiction between their own egos and the incompatible material (for a review of psychoanalytic writings on trauma, see Herman, 1992). The incompatible material is then defended against or warded off from conscious experience. The exclusion process requires so much psychic energy that other psychological functions are diminished or even paralyzed, a process that would account for symptoms of psychic numbing. In spite of efforts to keep the trauma repressed, however, it intrudes into consciousness though unbidden memories or nightmares. Freud (1955) suggested that these memories are driven into consciousness by a *repetition compulsion*. Although formulated 5 decades later, Horowitz's (1975, 1976b) notion of *completion tendency* echos Freud's model and has been used to explain the alternating pattern of denial and intrusion central to PTSD. Among the criticisms of psychoanalytic models of PTSD are its nontestable nature and failure to account for the development of the depressive symptoms that equally characterize PTSD.

Behavioral Conditioning Models

Behavioral theories have relied on Mowrer's two-factor learning theory to explain PTSD symptoms. The theory holds that two types of learning occur in the acquisition of fear and anxiety. The first is classical conditioning that occurs when a previously neutral stimulus becomes associated with an unconditioned stimulus that innately evokes discomfort or fear. Through this pairing, previously neutral stimuli that were present during a sexual attack becomes conditioned stimuli that are able to evoke anxiety. Subsequently the conditioned stimuli may become further associated with events, words, images, and even thoughts. These stimuli then acquire the capacity to create anxiety, a process that is called higher-order conditioning. Stimuli that are similar but not identical to the conditioned stimuli may also evoke anxiety through a process known as stimulus generalization. The second factor of Mowrer's two factor theory is operant or instrumental learning. It occurs when an organism or person learns that certain behaviors allow him or her to avoid, escape, or decrease the discomfort arising from the presence of conditioned stimuli that trigger anxiety. Avoidance is reinforced by reduction in discomfort. But, avoidance is maladaptive in the long run because it prevents the diminution of fear that would normally occur when an organism or person learns that the actual trauma signaled by the conditioned stimuli is no longer occurring. Although two-factor theory does a good job of accounting for the wide range of situations that may trigger discomfort in victimized women, it does not account for the intrusions characteristic of PTSD nor does it address cognitions that play a role in altering response to trauma (Foa, Steketee, Rothbaum, & Olasov, 1989; Jones & Barlow, 1990).

Cognitive-Behavioral Models

A substantial body of evidence has demonstrated that the effect of a trauma is influenced not only by automatic forms of learning, but also by a person's ability to predict, control, or terminate the event or situation (Foa, Zinbarg, & Rothbaum, 1992; Janoff-Bulman, 1992; Peterson & Strunkard, 1992). A loss of belief in the ability to control aversive events in one's life, or learned helplessness, has been documented to occur among individuals responding to a wide variety of stressful life events and has been used to explain some posttraumatic symptoms (Peterson & Seligman, 1983). Generally, individuals interpret incoming information in ways that are consistent with their existing schemas, even when this requires distorting contradictory evidence. In the normal course of events, schemas or beliefs that the world is orderly and meaningful and that the self is worthy and invulnerable provide individuals with an intelligible and reasonably predictable universe in which to live. When an individual undergoes trauma, however, these fundamental assumptions and the familiar world they serve to maintain are severely threatened if not shattered (Janoff-Bulman & Frieze, 1983). The helplessness inherent in any victimization experience can lead to generalized beliefs about the future uncontrollability of events. These feelings can be activated across situations and across time, rendering victims numb and passive. To recover from a traumatic experience, the victim's schemas must begin to transform so that the trauma can be accommodated gradually. According to this conceptualization, symptoms of intrusion and avoidance cease only when the old schemas are updated to account for the traumatic experience.

An alternative cognitive–behavioral conceptualization of rape aftereffects is that of Foa and colleagues (Foa & Kozak, 1986; Foa, Steketee, Rothbaum, & Olasov, 1989). The central feature of their model is the fear structure, which is created through learning at the time of the actual victimization and becomes a permanent part of long-term memory. Fear structures are postulated to contain three kinds of information: (a) information about the characteristics of the feared situation, (b) programs for the verbal, physiological, and overt behavioral responses that occur when the structure is activated, and (c) cognitions about the meaning of the elements in the fear structure including the stimuli—or features that characterized the feared situation and responses—or behaviors that occurred in the feared situation. Rape-induced fear structures, as opposed to ordinary fears, are thought to be larger with a wider range of stimuli capable of activating the structure, to involve more intense verbal and physiologic responses when activated, and to have a lower threshold for activation. Because many stimuli activate the structure, frequent replays of the sensations associated with the victimization occur. These uncomfortable symptoms trigger both attempts to avoid or to escape reminders of the trauma and internal attempts to ignore or compartmentalize the discomfort (dissociation). Both behavioral avoidance and dissociation result in emotional numbing and withdrawal from an active life and prolong the changes that must occur to complete resolution, or emotional processing of the trauma. Emotional processing entails changes in the connections among the elements in the fear structure so that the stimuli are no longer linked with strong emotional responses and that the meanings ascribed to the stimuli and responses have been adaptively reformulated.

In everyday life, the stimuli that signalled the rape repeatedly reoccur but the previous outcome—rape—is absent. Therefore, one questions why habituation does not occur automatically in time. Foa and Kozak (1986) and Foa, Steketee, Rothbaum, and Olasov (1989) asserted that fear structures are rarely fully activated in daily life because no commonly occurring situations match enough of the elements to elicit full activation. Even when a victim exposes herself to a feared situation, extreme physiologic reactions may interfere with information processing. Also, because of the proactive nature of cognitive schema, contradictory evidence may not even be perceived by the victim. Recent empirical work has suggested that fear structures alone may be too narrow to account for PTSD however (Foa, Zinbarg, & Rothbaum, 1992). Women who were initially very angry and held in their anger experienced more severe PTSD at 1 month following assault (Riggs, Daneu, Gershuny, Greenberg, & Foa, 1992). To account for these findings, an anger structure was proposed that is similar in nature to the fear structure.

COMMON THEMES AND LIMITATIONS OF CURRENT MODELS

In spite of their diversity, all the theories we've reviewed here share a common set of limitations (Goodman, Koss, & Russo, 1993a, 1993b). None of them acknowledges characteristics of the victim that may shape her response, including personality, coping style, ethnicity, class, and sexual orientation. Nor does any of them address the potential that the cultural context that spawned the violence may itself present a formidable obstacle to successful recovery. Furthermore, none of these conceptual models views the victim as someone who actively participates in her recovery process. Finally, all fail to explain why some individuals exposed to trauma develop PTSD while others do not (Jones & Barlow, 1990).

A common theme across the theoretical models is the critical role of cognition in shaping the occurrence, forms, and severity of responses to violence. A promise for integrating existing conceptualizations and ameliorating some shortcomings is poised by new developments in theory and research on the links among cognition, affect, and behavior (Lazarus, 1991a, 1991b). It is now generally accepted that cognitive processes link specific aspects of the environment with emotions. A person's emotional response to an event is not determined by the actual event or by intrapsychic processes, but rather by a *cognitive appraisal* of the experience that arises out of a person–event interaction (Lazarus, 1991b). Cognitive appraisals are substantially influenced by both individual and sociocultural variables including family history, existence of prior trauma, personality, coping style, ethnicity, class, sexual orientation, community attitudes, and gender-related norms. The notion of cognitive appraisal suggests that understanding psychological responses to rape requires looking at both the trauma and the recovery process from the woman's point of view—in the context of her personal meanings. It is most important that this model acknowledges the rape victim as an active agent who vests meaning and seeks control and mastery over her environment by appraising potential benefits and harms, marshalling available resources, and choosing among options.

Critique of the PTSD Conceptualization

The PTSD conceptualization has both strengths and limitations in its applications to victims of rape. Its primary limitation is that the diagnosis of PTSD focuses on the emotions of fear and anxiety; actual reactions of rape victims are broader than this indicates. Thus, the diagnosis fails to capture the depth and complexity of response to rape. Common rape aftereffects such as suicidality, substance abuse, revictimization, physical symptoms, relational disturbances, distancing defenses, and sexual problems are missing from the criteria defining PTSD. Second, the PTSD diagnosis does not include the cognitive changes that are a central feature of postrape reactions. Janoff-Bulman and Frieze (1983) concluded that much of the psychological toll of rape on the victim derives from the shattering of basic assumptions about herself and the world, and the development of postattack perceptions characterized by threat, danger, insecurity, and self-questioning. Unfortunately, for many women such perceptions reflect their realities— they live in violent neighborhoods, continue to encounter violent men, and have few resources to avoid or stop the dangers they face. Third, the PTSD diagnosis better captures the psychiatric consequences of single traumatic events than it does chronic abusive conditions (Herman, 1992). Marital rapes, for example, may be an ongoing process more similar to familial child sexual abuse than to a one-time rape by a stranger. Finally, one can also philosophically question why the reactions of victims are considered a mental disorder, when there is no such category for rapists with the exception of those few who are exceedingly disturbed and qualify for other psychiatric diagnoses that have nothing to do with sexual assault.

Balanced against these limitations are the theoretical and practical advantages of the PTSD model of traumatic aftereffects. From a theoretical perspective, the PTSD conceptualization has the advantage of offering a parsimonious framework for describing the effects of trauma that integrates many disparate symptoms and at the same time differentiates them from other disorders (McCann & Pearlman, 1990a). By presenting a framework that establishes the relationships among previously isolated symptoms, the PTSD diagnosis encourages the development of broad and comprehensive theoretical models to explain women's reactions to rape. A practical effect of the PTSD conceptualization has been that it enabled mental health professionals to borrow from the rich body of literature on psychological trauma to aid women who have been sexually assaulted. Another practical benefit is that PTSD portrays the psychological sequelae of rape as normal responses to abnormal events, thereby lessening the pathologizing of the victim's response.

Another practical advantage of the PTSD conceptualization is in the arena of expert witness testimony. Psychologists and other mental health professionals are often called upon to testify on the typical aftereffects of rape and to provide an expert opinion that a particular complainant's behavior is consistent with having been raped. This testimony is most often used to counter defendants' claims that the sex was consensual. The courts continue to be divided on the admissibility of this testimony (Frazier & Borgida, 1985; Frazier & Borgida, in press). In earlier years, experts frequently described victims' symptoms as the "rape trauma syndrome." Many judges excluded such testimony on the grounds that it was prejudicial to the defendant and was in essence an opinion on whether rape had occurred. Although the creation of the diagnostic category of PTSD has offered a way to describe rape victims symptoms that avoids unintended prejudice, it has raised other problems. The most important one is that rape is not the only trauma that can trigger PTSD. To discredit victims, defense attorneys have attempted to link the existence of PTSD to some other trauma that occurred in the life of the victim close to the time of the rape. A sensible response to this argument is that the symptoms of PTSD are trauma-specific in that when one has been raped, one experiences intrusive memories of the sexual assault as opposed to intrusive memories of a car accident or combat (Frazier & Borgida, in press). However, future research is needed to characterize further any unique characteristics of response to rape.

11

Intervention and Treatment for Rape Survivors

R ecovery from rape is a lengthy process during which victims may require a range of different services at multiple points in time. These include the period surrounding the immediate crisis, whenever judicial procedures reactivate the incident, and when coping alone has failed to resolve persistent somatic and psychological distress. In this chapter, we review services for victims including community-based programs and formal mental health treatment. We begin with a review of characteristics that may influence response to rape.

CHARACTERISTICS THAT AFFECT RECOVERY

Experts have concluded that there are reliable predictors of the victim most likely to recover from rape (Hanson, 1990; Lurigio & Resick, 1990).

Demographic Characteristics

Men experience somewhat lower levels of postcrime distress than women, although this finding may be related to women's disproportionate risk for rape compared with other crimes against the person as well as rape's greater potentency in producing PTSD (Lurigio & Resick, 1990). Conclusions regarding demographic variables such as age and education are mixed. Several investigators have found that they have little influence on victims' responses to rape (Kilpatrick, Best, et al., 1985), and that they are not predictive of subsequent recovery (Becker, Skinner, Abel, & Treacy, 1982; Ruch & Leon, 1983). Other investigators have concluded that more educated and employed victims suffer less distress than less educated or unemployed women do (Lurigio & Resick, 1990), and that elderly victims experience a more difficult recovery than younger ones (Atkeson, Calhoun, Resick, & Ellis, 1982; Burgess & Holmstrom, 1974; Frank & Stewart, 1984; Maguire & Corbett, 1987; Ruch & Chandler, 1983; Sales, Baum, & Shore, 1984; although there is an exception to this conclusion in research by Norris & Kaniasty, 1991).

Background factors may play a role in recovery from rape. For example, greater adjustment problems have been identified among adult survivors who were sexually victimized as children, compared to those victimized only in adulthood (Burnam, Stein, Golding, Siegel, Sorenson, & Forsythe, 1988; Wyatt, Guthrie, & Notgrass, 1992). Pre-existing mental health problems also have regularly been associated with both the degree of trauma experienced and the recovery outcome (Atkeson, Calhoun, Resick, & Ellis, 1982; Frank, Turner, Stewart, Jacob, & West, 1981; Frank & Anderson, 1987; Gidycz & Koss, 1991; Lurigio & Resick, 1990; Ruch & Leon, 1983).

Culture may be an important factor in the recovery process because it may influence the way a woman perceives rape as a threat as well as the responses she expects to receive from her social network. To date, research has focused on comparing across ethnic groups the psychiatric diagnoses and symptoms of psychological distress seen in survivors of sexual assault compared to nonvictimized women (Burnam et al., 1988; Wyatt, 1992). It has failed to reveal differences among African Americans, Caucasians of European descent, and Mexican Americans in posttraumatic symptoms and diagnoses. However, this research is only a first step and should not be construed as supporting the conclusion that culture is unimportant. Even in the context of these general similarities in response, cultural influences may determine many elements of response including the meaning given to symptoms and the preferred ways of healing. Thus, our assessment and treatment efforts must be informed by medical anthropology in general as well as specific groups' cultural history with rape.

In the lives of African–American women rape has been a serious concern since their arrival on American shores. However, vulnerability and powerlessness as victims is one of the least analyzed themes in African–American women's history (Wyatt, 1992). Throughout U.S. history, the legal system has overlooked the rape of African–American women or has considered it less serious than rape of White women. Stereotypes about African–American women perpetrate negative expectations about sexual promiscuity and serve as a component of racial oppression (Wyatt, 1992). African–American women are less likely than White women to disclose their rapes either to the police or to family or friends (Wyatt, 1992). Their hesitancy anticipates the lack of community and societal support for their credibility as rape victims. African–American women are much more likely than White women to link their rape to the riskiness of their living arrangements, to believe that their risk of rape is greater than White women's, and to think that a woman's right to be protected is contingent upon the color of her skin (Wyatt, 1992).

Asian–American and Mexican–American rape victims may face a complicated recovery compared to Caucasian victims because of the shame attached to rape in these cultures (Ruch & Leon, 1983; Williams & Holmes, 1981). In the case of Mexican–American women, the two principal sources of support and identity are the family and the Church. Both may align against a rape victim. Catholicism has traditionally taught that a woman should resist rape even at the cost of her life according to the example set by Saint Maria Goretti (Williams & Holmes, 1981). Rape may be viewed by clergy as a dishonor on the victim because she did not resist enough. Equally, the rape represents dishonor for the husband because of his failure to protect his wife, who is now spoiled by "intimacy" with another.

Sexual assault also raises unique issues among lesbian victims. Lesbians may be raped by men angered by their lesbianism, or they may be raped opportunistically during the commission of another crime by a perpetrator unaware of their sexual orientation (Garnets, Herek, & Levy, 1990). Antigay violence may also include attempts by the perpetrator to degrade lesbian sexuality including forcing a couple to have sex while the perpetrator laughs or otherwise humiliates the victims. Rape can demolish a lesbian's sense of safety and shatter her self-image as someone who previously lacked feelings of dependence upon or vulnerability around men. If any physiological response other than fear is experienced by the victim during the assault or if she elects not to resist, she may later question her sexuality. Experiences that degrade their sexuality may create obstacles for lesbians in returning to positive sexuality (Garnets et al., 1990).

Prior Victimization

A substantial number of sexual assault victims have sustained previous rapes or incest. For example, in one study, women victimized as children were 2.4 times as likely to be victimized as adults (Wyatt, Guthrie, & Notgrass, 1992). Empirical comparisons of those previously victimized with first-time rape victims have found the former to be less disturbed (Ruch & Leon, 1983), more disturbed (Ruch, Amedeo, Leon, & Gartrell, 1991), and equally disturbed (Frank, Turner, & Stewart, 1980; Frank & Anderson, 1987; Marhoefer-Dvorak, Resick, Hutter, & Girelli, 1987; McCahill, Meyer, & Fischman, 1979). This inconsistency may be due to failure by some researchers to control for pre-existing life change and mental health problems. Prior-assault victims are more likely than first-assault victims to have mental health or substance abuse problems when assaulted, an eventuality that may reflect an effect of the initial assault (Ruch et al., 1991). With statistical controls for these problems, prior-assault victims emerge less traumatized than first-time victims. A second source of inconsistency is differences in the point of assessment. Although prior victims show less distress immediately following rape, their distress increases, so that by day 8 they are more distressed than first-time victims whose symptoms decrease over the same time period (Ruch & Leon, 1983; Ruch et al., 1991).

If prior victimization is conceptualized more broadly to include crimes other than rape and to include childhood as well as adult incidents, then the effect is greater and the recovery course more difficult in multiply victimized women. Follow-up interviews 4 to 6 years after assault with rape victims who sought emergency-room care revealed that 86% felt recovered among those with no prior history of victimization compared with 53% among those who had sustained past victimizations (Burgess & Holmstrom, 1979b). Elevated risk for depression among multiply victimized women has been reported in two large community studies (Kilpatrick, Saunders, Veronen, Best, & Von, 1987; Sorenson & Golding, 1990). For example, the percentage of women who had a lifetime diagnosis of depression was 46% among women who had been raped a single time and 80% among women who had been raped multiple times (Kilpatrick, Saunders, Veronen, Best, & Von, 1987). The relationship between the magnitude of other life stressors and victimization appears to be curvilinear; both women with major stress prior to rape and those with little life change prior to rape show higher levels of postrape distress (Ruch, Chandler, & Harter, 1980).

Victim–Offender Relationship

Compared with stranger rape, acquaintance assault is more likely to occur indoors, to involve drinking by both parties, and to involve less violence but more verbal threats (Bownes, O'Gorman, & Sayers, 1991). The acquaintance rapist is more likely to kiss the victim, verbally abuse her throughout the assault, commit rape repeatedly, and demand secrecy after the attack (Bownes, O'Gorman, & Sayers, 1991). In spite of these objective differences, the perception that one will be killed or seriously injured is equally common among women who were raped by husbands and dates as it is among those raped by strangers (Kilpatrick, Saunders, Amick-McMullan, Best, Veronen, & Resnick, 1989). Furthermore, contrary to stereotypes that date rape is "rapette," women raped by acquaintances are at least as affected as those raped by strangers (Katz, 1991). There has been a uniform failure to find differences in psychometrically assessed symptom severity between the two classes of victims (Atkeson et al., 1982; Frank, Turner, & Stewart, 1980; Girelli, Resick, Marhoefer-Dvorak, & Hutter, 1986; Katz, 1991; Koss, Dinero, Seibel, & Cox, 1988). Some reports have noted increased distress among acquaintance rape victims compared with stranger victims (Ellis, Atkeson, & Calhoun, 1981; Stewart, 1982). Some evidence suggests that acquaintance rape is associated with different cognitive impacts than stranger rape. For example, acquaintance rape victims, whose trust was most violated by their rape, experienced more self-blame and negative changes in self-concept than those women assaulted by strangers (Katz & Burt, 1988). The relationship also affects perceptions of the assault. The greater the intimacy, the less likely people are to judge an instance of forced sexual intercourse as rape (Koss et al., 1988). Finally, the actions taken in the aftermath of rape are different among women raped by acquaintances than among those raped by strangers. Assaults by acquaintances are less likely than those by strangers to be revealed to anyone (Koss, Dinero, Siebel, & Cox, 1988; Golding, Siegel, Sorenson, Burnam, & Stein, 1989). Likewise, women who are raped by someone they know seek help less often and are more likely to delay seeking treatment than those who knew their assailants (Stewart et al., 1987).

Severity of the Assault

Brutality scores or indices attempt to link the overall severity of an assault with the extent of the victim's reactions. Some investigators have found neither the presence nor the extent of violence per se to be strongly associated with victim reactions (Sales et al., 1984); others have reported a relationship (Cluss, Boughton, Frank, Stewart, & West, 1983; Ellis, Atkeson, & Calhoun, 1981; Gidycz & Koss, 1991). An analysis of individual assault characteristics revealed that threats against the victim's life predicted symptomatology within the first 3 months but not at the 6 month follow-up (Sales et al., 1984). Other assault variables predictive of symptoms were the number of assailants, physical threat, injury requiring medical care, and medical complications (Sales et al., 1984). The actual violence of an attack may be less crucial to the victim's reaction than the "threat felt" however (Sales et al., 1984). The victim's perception of threat predicts the extent of later fear reactions (Girelli et al., 1986) and the degree of posttraumatic symptoms (Kilpatrick, Saunders, Veronen, Best, & Von, 1987). Victims who sustained sexual penetration consistently show more psychological harm than victims of other crimes (Kilpatrick, Veronen, & Best, 1985; Kilpatrick, Saunders, Veronen, Best, & Von, 1987; Maguire & Corbett, 1987; Wirtz & Harrell, 1987).

Postassault Variables

Social support may moderate the effect of rape. Victims who receive support from friends and family show better adjustment than those who lack it (Atkeson et al., 1982; Ruch & Chandler, 1983; Sales et al., 1984). Unsupportive behavior in particular predicts poorer social adjustment (Davis, Brickman, & Baker, 1991). Postrape recovery is also influenced by experiences with the criminal justice system. Women who want to prosecute their rape cases have been shown to have greater self-esteem than those who do not want to prosecute (Cluss et al., 1983). Yet, proceeding with prosecution appears to prolong recovery (Sales et al., 1984; Wyatt et al., 1990). Women who wanted to but were unable to prosecute due to lack of an arrest or insufficient evidence showed better work adjustment and more rapid improvement in self-esteem than women who were proceeding with prosecution (Cluss et al., 1983). These studies do not allow us to determine if assaults in which prosecution was pursued had other characteristics that predicted a more difficult recovery irrespective of criminal justice involvement.

FORMAL MENTAL HEALTH TREATMENT

Relatively few victims seek mental health treatment immediately after a rape (Ageton, 1983; Brickman & Briere, 1984; Golding, Stein, Siegel, Burnam, & Sorenson, 1989, Koss, 1988a). Victims are more likely to contact physicians than mental health professionals (Koss, Woodruff, & Koss, 1991; Golding, Stein, Siegel, Burnam, & Sorenson, 1989). African-American women prefer parents and friends for assistance to the formal system (Wyatt, Newcomb, & Notgrass, 1990; Wyatt, 1992). Even when they seek emergency care, survivors of rape may hesitate to commit to a therapeutic relationship. For example, less than half of victims who were 3 months postrape and who were judged to need treatment agreed to participate in a free treatment program (Kilpatrick & Veronen, 1983). Furthermore, victims resist a patient identity (Foa, Rothbaum, Riggs, & Murdock, 1991). They are understandably upset that something which was done to them against their will has caused them to be viewed as a person with emotional problems. Many attempt to cope on their own in the immediate postrape period. However, up to 48% of one sample of nonrecent victims stated that they had to eventually seek help for rape-related concerns (Ellis, Atkeson, & Calhoun, 1981). Among the reasons given for finally seeking aid were an impending trial; persistent symptoms that did not diminish with time; the first sexual encounter after the assault; breakup or argument with a significant other; and withdrawal of support by family or friends (Stewart et al., 1987).

Crisis Intervention

Crisis intervention consists of dissemination of information, active listening, and provision of emotional support (e.g., Burgess & Holmstrom, 1976; Forman, 1980). Treatment by dynamic psychotherapy has sometimes been advocated as a supplement to crisis intervention, but formal evaluation of the effectiveness of this combination is nonexistent (Burgess & Holmstrom, 1974; Evans, 1978; Fox & Scherl, 1972). The Brief Behavioral Intervention Program (BBIP) was designed for use immediately after rape (Kilpatrick & Veronen, 1983). It is the only standard therapy for crisis intervention that has been empirically evaluated. The goal of the 4- to 6-hr treatment package is to prevent the development of phobic reactions and other PTSD symptoms. Its interventions included encouraging re-experiencing of the rape events in imagery; expression of feelings associated with the rape; education about psychological models of the development of fear; attempts to reduce feelings of guilt and responsibility for the rape by discussion of societal expectations and myths about rape; and practice in coping skills such as self-assertion, relaxation, thought stopping, and methods for resuming normal activities. The outcome of a study in which 15 women who had been recently raped were randomly assigned to one of three treatment conditions (BBIP, repeated assessment but no active treatment, or delayed assessment) indicated that repeated assessment, not the true treatment condition, had the greatest therapeutic effect (Kilpatrick, Veronen, & Resick, 1979).

Cognitive therapy and systematic desensitization (which we describe later) have also been used for crisis intervention (Frank, Anderson, Stewart,

Dancu, Hughes, & West, 1988). Participants were women who had been raped and were seeking help immediately (within 1 month of assault) or delayed (more than 2 months after assault). Both treatments were associated with significant decreases in symptoms from pretreatment to follow-up among both immediate and delayed treatment seekers. Although this study lacked an untreated comparison group, Frank and colleagues (1988) argued that treatment effectiveness is supported by comparison of symptom change with published longitudinal studies using the same assessment measures. Kilpatrick and Calhoun (1988) contended that the comparison is inappropriate and that the change observed could represent the spontaneous improvement is seen in the first weeks following rape. Thus, it remains an unanswered question whether various approaches to treating the immediate crisis of rape alter the course of recovery either by reducing symptoms or shortening recovery time.

Individual Psychotherapy

Research on psychotherapy for rape victims has focused almost exclusively on behavioral and cognitive–behavioral methods. In the following material, those techniques that have been empirically evaluated are briefly described along with the evidence supporting their effectiveness.

Exposure Techniques

The common denominator of exposure treatments is confrontation with feared situations. Exposure techniques are used when the target of treatment is excessive avoidance and the goals are both activation and modification of the fear structure (Rothbaum & Foa, 1992). Exposure techniques vary according to whether they involve imaginal or in vivo exposure, short or long exposure, and high or low arousal. *Systematic desensitization* involves low arousal to stimuli that are imagined but not actually confronted and are paired with relaxation (Frank & Stewart, 1983, 1984). Fourteen sessions of systematic desensitization resulted in a decrease in the targeted fear, as well as an increase in social adjustment. However, in the absence of a comparison group, the effects are difficult to interpret. Becker and Abel (1981) applied systematic desensitization to women suffering assault-related anxiety but concluded that it was not sufficient to reduce the distress seen in this population.

In vivo flooding represents the longest exposure and highest arousal exposure technique. Here, the victim confronts the actual setting and stimuli that occurred during the rape. Although several published case studies support the effectiveness of in vivo flooding on sexual assault victims (Haynes & Mooney, 1975), serious concerns have been expressed that the procedure is aversive for victims, results in a high dropout rate, and fails to enhance the repertoire of coping strategies (Kilpatrick, Veronen, & Resick, 1982).

Between the extremes of in vivo flooding and systematic desensitization lies imaginal flooding, a process in which the stimuli associated with the rape are confronted, but only in imagination. Foa, Rothbaum, Riggs, & Murdock (1991) developed the *prolonged exposure treatment*, an imaginal flooding approach that was administered to 45 rape victims with PTSD. The treatment consisted of seven sessions devoted to reliving the rape scene in imagination. Women were randomly assigned to prolonged exposure, stress inoculation training (described later), supportive counseling, or wait-list control. Treatment consisted of nine biweekly sessions. *None* of the active treatments was superior to the wait-list control condition in reducing anxiety, fears, or depression. At the conclusion of treatment, those patients who received stress inoculation experienced the most reduction in PTSD symptoms; however, by the follow-up assessment at 3 months, those patients who received prolonged exposure showed most improvement. The authors concluded that simple contact with a therapist was sufficient to relieve many forms of rape-induced distress, but that active treatments were necessary to reduce PTSD symptoms. However, clinicians also should be aware that case reports of negative effects of prolonged exposure with trauma victims have appeared (Pitman et al., 1991). Among the forms of deterioration noted were re-activation of chemical abuse and suicidal attempts.

Anxiety Management Techniques

These techniques teach clients to feel in control of fear, rather than activating and habituating fear as exposure techniques do (Rothbaum & Foa,

1992). Kilpatrick and colleagues developed *stress inoculation training* for victims who remained highly fearful 3 months after the assault (Kilpatrick, Veronen, & Resick, 1982). In the first phase of treatment, the victim was taught a cognitive–behavioral explanation of rape-related fear and anxiety. The second phase involved deep-muscle relaxation and breathing control, training in communication skills through role-playing and covert modeling, and thought-stopping strategies to enable the client to control intrusive thoughts. The final phase focused on internal dialogue and identified irrational, faulty, or negative self-statements that were replaced with rational and positive statements. Initial studies on the effectiveness of SIT encountered various problems including rejection of therapy by more than 50% of the pool. Subsequently SIT was shortened from 20 to eight sessions. Kilpatrick and Amick (1985) reported the successful application of the new program in a case study that included standardized assessment.

Hybrid Approaches

The newest approaches to treating rape victims are hybrid programs that combine elements of exposure and anxiety management (Foa, Rothbaum, Riggs, & Murdock, 1991; Resick, 1992; Resick & Schnicke, 1992). For example, *cognitive processing therapy* aims to elicit emotional reactions from rape victims and to train them to recognize and modify maladaptive thoughts and beliefs (Resick, in press; Resick & Schnicke, 1992). The therapy consists of 12 sessions. Interventions include an educational phase in which the therapist presents a description of PTSD and information processing (Sessions 1–3); an exposure phase during which the client writes about the incident, reads the description to the therapist, and responds to prods for more detail about sparsely elaborated sections (Sessions 4–6); and a cognitive monitoring phase in which the client tracks negative beliefs pertaining to the themes of safety, trust, power, esteem, and intimacy and is taught methods to restructure them more adaptively (Sessions 7–12). Formal evaluation of cognitive–processing therapy has been in the group format and is discussed later in this chapter.

A second hybrid approach was initially considered by many to be an exposure treatment, but is now known as *eye movement desensitization and reprocessing therapy* (EMDR); the new name emphasizes the cognitive-restructuring elements of this approach (Shapiro, 1989a, 1989b, 1991a, 1991b). Clients are instructed to focus on their incident while they fix their eyes on the therapist's finger. The therapist holds his or her finger 12 to 14 in. from the client's face and tracks the sequence of large magnitude, rhythmic saccadic eye movements. (Saccadic eye movements are "rapid involuntary small movements of both eyes simultaneously in changing the point of fixation on a visualized object, such as the series of jumps the eyes make in scanning a line of print" [Taylor, 1988, p. 1477]). Physiologic processes that could account for a relationship between saccadic eye movements and memory desensitization have been hypothesized and empirical work is under way to delineate the process of change. Published evidence has supported the effectiveness of EDMR with several groups of traumatized persons, but its success with rape victims is currently supported only by case studies (Shapiro, 1989a, 1989b; Wolpe & Abrams, 1991). EMDR may be harmful when practiced by untrained clinicians or lay persons. Negative effects may include re-traumatization, ocular problems, and suicidal reactions (Shapiro, 1991b). Rothbaum (1992) noted that EMDR appears to be ineffective with trauma victims who are recently withdrawn cocaine abusers because they are unable to track a moving finger.

Before concluding this review of individual psychotherapeutic approaches to treating rape, criticism of this entire avenue of intervention must be acknowledged. First, current treatments may not be appropriate for many of those in need. The dropout rate among those women who enter treatment is quite high across all treatments—between 20% to 30% leave before completing all sessions. Those who dropout are also more likely to be low-income, blue-collar workers (Foa, Rothbaum, Riggs, & Murdock, 1991). Second, critics have charged that individual treatments for rape represent inappropriate "medicalization," which has the effect of reducing rape from a social or political issue to an individual issue. From this perspective, psychology is viewed as an instrument that limits and personalizes women's reactions to rape, thereby obscuring political implications (Kitzinger, 1992). Psychology has been accused of encouraging women through therapy to adjust to living under heteropatriarchy by focusing energy on their own recovery, and by doing so, drains away attention from political action that could potentially force social changes that reduce rape. Although this critique is clearly important, it sets up a dicotomy that may be avoidable. It certainly would be possible to include activist components into intervention approaches and a particularly likely candidate for integration of therapy and activism is group treatment.

Group Psychotherapeutic Treatment

Many clinicians believe group settings are the intervention of choice with victims of rape. The rationale is that groups of survivors are in a unique position to counter rape-induced isolation, provide support, validate feelings, confirm the experience, counteract self-blame and promote self-esteem, share grief, provide opportunities for safe attachment, and empower survivors within an egalitarian structure (Koss & Harvey, 1991). A wide variety of group interventions are offered in community-based programs and within the formal mental health system. However, relative to the level of activity, the amount of empirical data is astonishingly meager. Although no published evaluations exist of group interventions as practiced within community-based agencies, evidence of effectiveness for several structured interventions exist. For example, Resick et al. (1989) compared three types of group therapy—stress innoculation training, assertion training, and supportive psychotherapy—with each other and with information from a naturally occurring wait-list control group. All therapy groups were conducted by a male–female team. Results indicated that all three treatments were effective in reducing symptoms, with no group differences evident. Improvement was maintained at a 6-month follow-up on rape-related fear measures, but not on depression, self-esteem, and social fears. No improvements were found in the wait-list control group. However, groups led by male–female teams are far from normative in the field, so the fact that this study used such teams was a major drawback. In a subsequent study, Resick and Schnicke (1992) compared 19 survivors treated with cognitive–processing therapy to 20 women who were put on a wait-list before receiving treatment. Assessments were made before and immediately after treatment, and at follow-up sessions at 3- and 6-months later. Treatment consisted of 12 weekly sessions of 1.5 hr duration. All therapists were women professional psychologists. The results supported the effectiveness of cognitive–processing therapy in reducing rape-related symptoms and posttreatment assessments indicated that these benefits were maintained through the 6-month follow-up.

A group-based behavioral treatment package for sexual dysfunctions among sexual assault victims was developed by Becker and Skinner (1983, 1984). Treatment consisted of 11 sessions, one for assessment and 10 for treatment. Agenda topics for these sessions included learning theory explanations of sexual problems, attention to body image, identification of satisfying sexual fantasies and activities, cognitive restructuring, anxiety reduction, communication skills, and sensate focus. Evaluation of the approach was carried out on 68 sexual-assault survivors including victims of rape, attempted rape, incest, and childhood molestation (Becker, Skinner, & Abel, 1984). Participants were randomly assigned to individual therapy or group therapy either immediately or delayed. Therapy outcome was measured by participants' self-ratings of progress on their individual goals. Improvement was reported by more than 80% of participants and was stable at the last follow-up 3 months after termination. Direct comparison of therapy formats revealed that group administration produced results that were more stable than those produced by individual treatment.

Critical Analysis of Psychotherapeutic Treatment

Review of the available literature suggests that no single therapy has demonstrated superiority for rape-related symptoms. Nor has any therapy proved effective for every client (Resick & Markaway, 1991). All efficacious therapies have common features including the avoidance of victim-blame, a supportive, nonstigmatizing view of rape as a criminal victimization, an environment to overcome cognitive and behavioral avoidance, provision of information about traumatic reactions, and the expectation that symptoms will improve (Resick & Markaway, 1991). Therapies differ in whether processing of traumatic memories is explicitly undertaken and if so, whether it is accomplished by low or high arousal methods, and in the degree of attention paid to cognitive reformulation.

Yet, there are many gaps in the clinical treatment armamentarium. An obvious shortcoming of current treatment programs has been the lack of attempts to address specific concerns about rape among various ethnic groups in the United States whose recoveries may be influenced by culture (Mollica & Son, 1989; Parson, 1985; Ruch & Leon, 1983; Williams & Holmes, 1981). Existing treatment models also have been criticized on the grounds of their race, class, and gender biases (Fine, 1984, 1989). Nor do treatment programs address the developmental implications of rape for adolescents—the group who experiences the highest rate of assault—or for lesbian victims (Wertheimer, 1990). Interventions developed and tested on conditions with some symptomatic similarity to rape are a source of ideas for successful rape treatments (Beutler & Hill, 1992). But, there are additional creative sources for interventions including knowledge accumulated from treating victims of torture, traditional rituals for healing shame, and cognitive psychology and cognitive therapy's theoretical approaches to narrative reconstruction and other memory-altering techniques.

The status quo among mental health practitioners is to ignore violence exposure in treatment planning and to focus on diagnostic categories. It is widely believed by those who specialize in work with rape victims that treatment will be more appropriate and effective if formulated to directly address traumatization by violence. However well-accepted this belief is, it has not been documented. Future research must demonstrate that treatment that attends to the specific precipitating event (rape) is more effective than treatment directed at clinical manifestations that may have a range of etiologies (depression).

Given the stage of development of treatment approaches, it is not surprising that the data base on the effectiveness of interventions also has many gaps (Beutler & Hill, 1992). Among the problems are:

1. Most evaluations of treatment have been relatively brief. Short-duration treatment may not be appropriate under all circumstances. Clearly, rape is one of the most serious human traumas, and it may take considerable time to resolve, particularly when a recent assault has compounded effects with past victimizations and is complicated

by co-existing problems. Although not all the recovery course may need to be spent in active treatment, ways must be found to allow for realistic periods of time to pass before final judgment is passed on treatment effectiveness.

2. Treatment studies to date have been limited to uncomplicated cases without other problems such as drug or alcohol abuse or history of childhood sexual victimization. Client samples should be representative of those to whom the results would be generalized. Without including women who realistically represent the victims of rape, researchers will be guilty of elitism.

3. Although assessment methods have improved considerably since early studies, no single scale assesses the full range of rape-induced specific symptoms. The measurement of the social cognitions effected by rape is particularly underdeveloped. Work on new measures must proceed with cognizance of the criticisms that current cognitive approaches to therapy are value laden and are based on the untested assumption that victims can or should reclaim sexuality (Kitzinger, 1992). Kitzinger warns, "Survivors may be right in the way they see the world. Rather than being distorted, it is free of the rose-tinted glasses of romance" (1992, p. 412).

4. Investigators must pay attention to clinical meaningfulness. The amount of symptom change deemed significant in some studies has been limited only to narrow areas. This is appropriate if the therapy is intended to have a limited impact, but it is less appropriate if the treatment aims to have significant effects across a range of recovery dimensions.

5. The number of participants who have been included in studies has been very small. Small numbers preclude examination of the interactions of treatment with symptom severity, personality characteristics, or sociodemographic variables. This information is necessary to develop a prescriptive approach to treatment that seeks indicators for the individual likely to do better in directive versus nondirective therapy or insight-oriented versus behavioral therapy.

6. Much of the data base on rape treatment is characterized by studies

done by a small number of therapists. When a therapy is administered by only one or two practitioners, it is not possible to disentangle therapist from therapy effects in the data analyses. To ensure that treatments deemed effective will also work when adopted by a range of practitioners in the real world, research studies should include multiple therapists with diverse personal characteristics.

Our picture of rape's effects is still far more complete than our ability to ameliorate those effects. There are many gaps in both the treatment armamentarium and the information base on the effectiveness of interventions. These deficits are partly attributable to lack of federal leadership in formulating and funding a research agenda on treatment of violence. A federal initiative is required to upgrade the treatment data base. Primarily needed are strategies to encourage cooperative projects involving researchers and rape-specific community resources. Indications of sustained support within this field that could assist in nurturing these relationships would be particularly helpful. The development of reliable and valid measures of key constructs should be supported, particularly measures of social cognitions that are currently unexamined in treatment outcome research. The development of new treatments also should be encouraged. Finally, funding mechanisms must support collaboration across sites, which is the only viable approach to developing a sufficient number of participants to permit examination of interactions among treatment approach, symptom profiles, and individual characteristics. Treatment research must attempt to address the range of problems experienced by rape victims, not only the subset of symptoms that are subsumed by the PTSD diagnosis. Although a large number of rape victims experience PTSD initially, the majority of victims no longer qualify for this diagnosis 3 months after their rape experience, yet they are by no means recovered.

COMMUNITY-BASED SERVICES FOR SURVIVORS AND OFFENDERS

Before 1970, no service agency or advocacy group existed to give attention to rape victims. Grass-roots rape crisis centers opened across the United

States during the 1970s and grew during the 1980s into influential settings for community action, legal advocacy, and reform of victim services (Koss & Harvey, 1991). Self-help, social support, and activism within the antirape movement were emphasized (Burt, Gornick, & Pittman, 1984; Harvey, 1985). Much of the community response to rape seen today can be traced to advocacy by crisis center personnel who emphasized the blamelessness of the rape victim, rejected commonly held beliefs concerning victims' personal culpability, and educated professionals to understand the psychological responses of rape victims as normal reactions to traumatizing events rather than as indicators of psychopathology. The adequacy of a community's response to rape is reflected by the availability, accessibility, quantity, quality, and legitimacy of rape-specific services (Koss & Harvey, 1991). The components of a comprehensive community-wide response to rape are listed in Exhibit 1.

Rape Crisis Centers

The literature on rape crisis centers reveals (a) surveys of program characteristics (Brodyaga, Gates, Singer, Tucker, & White, 1975; O'Sullivan, 1976); and (b) attempts to identify factors contributing to agency effectiveness (Burt, Gornick, & Pittman, 1984; Gornick, Burt, & Pittman, 1983; Harvey, 1985); and (c) studies of organizational affiliation and efficacy (Byington,

Exhibit 1
Components of a Comprehensive Community-Wide Response to Rape

Victim services	24-hour hot-line; crisis counseling; hospital accompaniment; hospital care; police services; liaison with district attorney's office; mental health and social services including interventions for groups with special needs, such as children, the elderly, ethnic victims, male victims, gay victims, and victims of severe, sadistic violence.
Offender services	Arrest and prosecution, the courts, and alternative treatments.
Prevention	Social action and advocacy, community education, and prevention.

Martin, DiNitto, & Maxwell, 1991; Martin & DiNitto, 1987). For example, O'Sullivan's (1976) survey of 90 representative programs revealed the following services were available in 75% or more of the sites studied: community speakers bureau, hospital and police accompaniment services to victims, court accompaniment programs, and volunteer hot lines. Short- and long-term counseling was offered by 60% of the centers. At least one third of the sites lacked rap groups, group counseling, self-defense training, court-watch programs, and training for police, court, medical, and mental health professionals. Focus groups with victims of rape within New York State revealed limited or nonexistent services available to survivors of rape and their families, especially in rural areas, and wide variation in the quality of programs (Avner, 1990). There has been a lack of collaboration between the academic community, governmental entities, and rape crisis centers. As a result, few resources exist in the form of standard training materials or treatment manuals, and evaluation of program effectiveness is virtually nonexistent.

Rape crisis centers rely on local and state funding for their existence and the amount of funds they receive is quite modest. For example, the average Department of Health grant to a rape crisis program in New York is $17,600 per year (Avner, 1990). The total annual operating budgets of centers in Florida ranged from $10,000 to $20,000 for all sites except those rape crisis centers affiliated with county health services or hospitals (Byington et al., 1991). These figures should be compared with the widely accepted figure of $35,000 in state costs to keep one offender in prison for a year. Because of a tenuous and inadequate financial base, agency staff spend much of their time preparing grants to the individual specifications of multiple funding sources. Not only does this activity drain staff energy from other functions, the precarious nature of funding precludes long-term planning (Avner, 1990). The strains of a prolonged period of fiscal conservatism and fierce competition for shrinking public resources in recent years has forced many agencies to prioritize services, a process which has usually resulted in the maintenance of crisis intervention services while other program components shrink or disappear. Other rape crisis centers have closed down entirely. To survive, many rape crisis centers have become institutionalized and are now affiliated with battered women's shelters, community mental health centers, county health or social services agencies, hospitals, colleges or universities, and legal or judicial organizations (Byington et al., 1991). As a result, many have lost the feminist fervor that originally provided energy, direction, and an interventionist philosophy (Burt et al., 1984; Byington et al., 1991).

RECOMMENDATIONS FOR IMPROVEMENTS IN VICTIM SERVICES

Recommendations to improve victim services in New York state have recently been published; these speak to issues that affect most rape crisis centers (Avner, 1990). Achieving these recommendations would require initiative at both the state and federal level. First, funding must be increased and made more predictable. Additional funding also is needed to extend rape treatment to detention centers, jails, and prisons. Second, state legislative initiatives could be helpful in several areas such as the creation of multidisciplinary victim-assistance teams to ensure sensitive and effective investigatory responses to rape, extension of the confidentiality privilege to rape crisis counselors, and expansion of the acceptable documentation of rape for victim compensation purposes to include hospital emergency room reports or statements from a victim services agency. Third, technical assistance from state and federal agencies would be helpful to develop a victim-information packet that can be available in hospitals and police stations. The information contained in such a packet must address HIV infection and the fear of AIDS among rape victims. Other areas in which technical assistance is needed include the production of training materials for staff development and therapy manuals to facilitate the teaching of empirically validated intervention methods. Fourth, strategies to foster better linkages among rape crisis centers and the formal systems of medicine, mental health, and criminal justice are needed. Lastly, state and federal leadership is needed to stimulate program evaluation of rape crisis services. Positive outcomes for them cannot be automatically assumed. One study of a peer-support group revealed increased depression among members despite reduced feelings of deviance

(Cryer & Beutler, 1980). Likewise, self-defense training under some leadership conditions has had negative effects in that participants believe they had less of a personal right to resist an assault after training than they did before (Kidder, Boell, & Moyer, 1983).

A REVIEW OF RAPE PUBLIC POLICY

The same social forces that complicate rape victims' recovery influence governmental responses to sexual assault. As the Thomas–Hill hearings or the Kennedy–Smith rape trial vividly illustrated, victims who reveal their ordeals are socially ostracized, their experiences are interpreted in light of myths that implicitly blame them, absolve the perpetrators, and make rape permissible. These myths include: "Good" women don't get raped so those that do "deserve it;" women like to be raped; women mean "yes" when they say "no;" women seduce their attackers through "provocative attire;" and women of color can't be raped (Burt, 1980; Largen, 1987). These myths have been perpetuated and reified in rape laws that highlight the behavior or reputation of the victim rather than the unlawful acts of the offender (Pinneau, 1987). Historically, rape prosecution has been subjected to (a) special rules of evidence such as stringent corroboration and proof of resistance requirements as well as procedures governing the admissability of evidence regarding women's prior sexual history, (b) special cautionary instructions to juries that entail descriptions of the difficulties faced by defendants seeking to disprove a rape change, and (c) an absolute spousal exemption from prosecution for rape in some states. These policies promote the use of information about the victim's status, character, and relationship with the defendant in making dispositions in rape cases (Berger, Searles, & Newman, 1988; Estrich, 1987; Largen, 1987). As a result, it has been extremely difficult for a rape victim to obtain a successful prosecution of her violation. Those who participate in the criminal justice process all too often find themselves subjected to harsh interrogation by dubious law enforcement officials as well as lengthy delays and a failure to notify witnesses about hearing dates. In short, rape laws and their implementation by criminal justice personnel are at least partially responsible for the low rates of arrest, prosecution, and conviction in rape cases, and for the unwillingness of victims to report rapes and to press charges (Horney & Spohn, 1991). These judicial practices are forces that silence rape victims, lead to a general invisibility of the crime of rape, and contribute to social service agencies' neglect of sexual-assault victims (Koss & Harvey, 1991).

History and Social Context of Policy Responses

In the early 1970s, the antirape movement initiated what was to become a transformation in the public policy response to violence against women. Reform efforts emerged against the backdrop of a resurgence of feminism that began in the late 1960s. By defining the "personal as political," the women's movement set the stage for activists to assert that personal acts of violence, in the home or on the street, had to be addressed as acts of oppression of all women (Burt, Gornick, & Pittman, 1984). Male violence was conceptualized as a way that men maintain power and control over women, and newly formed women's groups across the country helped women realize that they were not alone in their experiences of abuse (Schechter, 1982).

Recognizing victims' needs for emotional and legal support, women began to organize themselves into antirape groups to work on developing victim services and securing legal reforms. As a first step, these groups established emergency rape crisis hotlines (the first started in Washington, DC, in 1971) and then comprehensive crisis centers in communities across the United States (Harvey, 1985; National Center for the Prevention and Control of Rape, 1981). In 1973, the National Organization for Women (NOW) began working with local community groups to establish antirape task forces. By 1974, 61 community-based rape crisis centers had been established in 27 states and NOW-initiated local antirape projects had been developed in 39 states (Brodyaga, Gates, Singer, Tucker, & White, 1975). By 1979, a rape crisis center existed in at least one community in every state and in Puerto Rico and the District of Columbia (National Center for the Prevention and Control of Rape, 1982). Rape crisis centers soon became centers for widespread reform efforts in the arenas of community education, service delivery, and legal advocacy on behalf of victims. Community education programs were conducted in local churches, temples, schools, and in the work place. They were designed to expose and refute rape-related myths, help women learn to protect themselves, support local reform efforts, and inform citizens of available services. Service reform efforts targeted at medical and mental health personnel emphasized victims' needs for privacy, dignity, choice, and sensitivity. In addition, preference for attention to health and wellness as opposed to pathology was stressed. Advocates helped hospitals revise their emergency room protocols, establish hospital accompaniment programs, and provide follow-up crisis response services to rape victims (Koss & Harvey, 1991).

State Responses

Legal advocacy efforts aimed to increase reporting, arrest, prosecution, and conviction of rape by changing prevailing laws, law enforcement practices, and the treatment of victims in the courtroom (Berger et al., 1988). These efforts eventually resulted in a number of reforms at the state level. Although the changes were often not all that was sought because of compromises wrought by the political process, by 1987, every state in the country had enacted some measure of law reform (Largen, 1987). First, in many states, legal definitions of sexual assault were expanded to replace the single crime of rape with a series of gender-neutral graded offenses and an accompanying set of graded penalties. Advocates hoped that by developing a set of lesser charges, they would provide prosecutors with the flexibility necessary to obtain convictions through plea bargaining and provide juries with the ability to convict on a charge other than forcible rape (Horney & Spohn, 1991). Second, the need for corroborating evidence and proof of resistance were eliminated in courts throughout the country, thereby increasing the chances of prosecution and conviction (Berger et al., 1988). Third, rape shield laws, prohibiting the use in trials of certain evidence of the victim's history, were implemented (Galvin, 1986). Reformers assumed that by restricting evidence damaging to the complainant they would not only make it easier for victims to report, but would facilitate increases in arrests, prosecutions, and convictions (Horney & Spohn, 1991). Finally, marital exemptions were eliminated in many states, thereby affirming women's rights to sexual autonomy within as well as outside marriages and reconstituting the definition of coerced sex (Estrich, 1987; Goldberg-Ambrose, 1992). Complementing legal reform were progressive institutional changes in the criminal justice system, such as the development of specialized sex crime units within police departments and prosecutors' offices (Goldberg-Ambrose, 1992).

The Federal Response

Because rape, like most crimes, falls primarily under the jurisdiction of states and localities the federal government's response to violence against women has been limited. Nevertheless, several important programs have been created and supported by persevering lawmakers and dedicated advocacy groups. Although not exhaustive, the following description provides a sampling of the different types of federal programs that target violence against women.

Victims of Crime Act (VOCA)

First enacted in 1984, VOCA authorizes yearly grants to states to assist and compensate victims. Priority is given to programs serving victims of domestic violence, sexual assault, and child abuse. VOCA consists of four separate programs: The first provides funds to crime victim assistance programs, including battered women's shelters, rape crisis centers, and law enforcement-based crisis intervention. The second program provides funds for individual compensation, such as reimbursement for mental health counseling, medical expenses, lost wages, and funeral expenses. The third program provides funds to assist victims of crimes committed on federal property, such as prisons; and the fourth assists child abuse and child sexual abuse programs through the Children's Justice Act. VOCA is funded through fines collected from individuals convicted of certain federal offenses. Before VOCA, rape victims had no recourse but to pay their own medical and mental health counseling expenses. Thus, passage of this legislation represented a major step forward on the part of the federal government. Unfortunately, its implementation in many states has resulted in regulations that effectively bar those who are raped by members of their family from receiving compensation and have required documentation of rape exclusively from police reports; hospital emergency room reports or victim services agency statements are insufficient documentation (Avner, 1990).

Office for Victims of Crime

This office was established by the Justice Department in 1983 to support training programs for law enforcement officials, prosecutors, clergy, health providers, and other professionals who came into contact with victims of crime. This office sponsored the development of a model sexual assault medical examination protocol that standardized procedures for hospital personnel involved in the examination, collection, and preservation of physical evidence from victims of sexual assault. The demonstration project has been replicated in 14 states.

National Institute of Mental Health (NIMH)

By congressional mandate, the National Center for the Prevention and Control of Rape (NCPCR) was established in 1975. It was housed at the NIMH "in recognition that rape and sexual assault are serious crimes resulting in severe emotional trauma and other mental health consequences for victims, their families, and their communities (National Center for the Prevention and Control of Rape, 1982, p. 2). Its dual mandate was to support research—on the causes and mental health consequences of rape and sexual assault and the efficacy of treatment for victims and offenders—and to develop and evaluate sexual assault prevention programs. Until 1982, NCPCR operated independently with its own national advisory board and grant application review committee. Its research and program initiatives reflected the interests of feminist scholars and grass-roots rape crisis workers. In 1982, NCPCR was subsumed within the newly formed Center for the Study of Mental Health Emergencies, thereby losing much of its cherished independence (Koss & Harvey, 1991). Then in 1985, as part of an NIMH reorganization, the NCPCR was dissolved and its research agenda merged with another NIMH branch to form the Antisocial and Violent Behavior Branch. This newly created division assumed responsibility for research on antisocial and violent behavior and its mental health consequences. Sexual assault research became just one part of a much larger research program (Babich & Voit, 1992). Further, the branch did not fund treatment programs for rape victims, nor did it maintain close relationships with community-based rape crisis centers (Koss & Harvey, 1991). In 1990, the branch was further broadened to become the Violence and Traumatic Stress Research Branch; it now encompasses research on the mental health consequences of natural and civilian disasters as well as other traumatic events such as interpersonal violence (Babich & Voit, 1992). Whether or not this new reorganization will result in increased attention to research on the needs of rape victims remains to be seen.

Omnibus Crime Control Act

As part of the Omnibus Crime Control Act of 1990, Congress requires all colleges and universities receiving federal funds to disclose to students the institution's campus crime statistics on an annual basis. Required statistics must include counts of rape, murder, and robbery involving students on or near campus. A major problem with this legislation is that acquaintance rapes are dramatically underreported. In addition, colleges and universities have an inherent conflict of interest with women students over the development of a system receptive to receiving reports of sexual assaults. The institutions' commitment to itself is better served by keeping the number of rape complaints low and maintaining rape prevention education at the minimum level necessary to avoid legal liability for failure to warn (Pavela, 1992).

PROPOSED LEGISLATION AND THE STATUS OF TODAY'S ANTI-RAPE MOVEMENT

By far the broadest and most ambitious piece of legislation enacted to date is the Violence Against Women Act, introduced in 1990 by Senator Joseph Biden in the Senate and then-Congresswoman Barbara Boxer in the House of Representatives. The Senate version of the bill comprises five titles. Title 1, "Safe Streets for Women," would double penalties for federal rape offenders, creates new penalties for repeat sex offenders, and increases restitution for victims of sex crimes. Title 1 would also provide funds to increase the number of police and prosecutors working on cases involving violent crimes against women and to improve the lighting in parks and subway stations. Finally, this title would authorize new protections and services for rape victims, such as changes in federal evidentiary rules that would exclude irrelevant inquiries about clothing and past sexual history. Title 2, "Safe Homes for Women," would create the first federal laws barring spouse abuse. Title 3, "Civil Rights for Women," is probably the most controversial aspect of this legislation. It defines gender-motivated crimes as bias or hate crimes, thereby extending the same civil rights protections to women victims of violence that are currently given to persons victimized because of race or religion. Title 4, "Safe Campuses for Women," would create the first federal program for college rape education and prevention services. Finally, Title 5, "Equal Justice for Women in Courts," would create a new program for educating state and federal judges about rape, domestic violence, and gender bias.

Despite the many gains made over the last two decades in service expansion and legal reform, forces such as economic retrenchment, political conservatism, and comfort with tradition have held back and even reversed many reform efforts. It is difficult to measure exactly the success of legal reforms because the number, timing, type, and method of adoption of new laws varies widely across states (Goldberg-Ambrose, 1992). Yet, it is clear that the effect of rape reform has been limited. Criminal justice and rape crisis center personnel have indicated that victims experience less maltreatment during the criminal justice process than in years past (Marsh, Geist, & Caplan, 1982). But, reforms have had little effect on the reporting of rape or on the processing of rape cases (Horney & Spohn, 1991). Expansion of the definition of sexual assault has failed to result in an increased likelihood of convictions or plea bargains (Chappell, 1984, Marsh, Geist, & Caplan, 1982). Elimination of the corroboration and resistance requirements, although important symbolically, have had little practical effect because many prosecutors continue to require them. These prosecutors believe that juries place emphasis on these details, even when not instructed to do so (Horney & Spohn, 1991). In many jurisdictions, judges continue to have considerable discretion in deciding whether to admit evidence concerning the victim's sexual history (Berger et al., 1988; Horney & Spohn, 1991).

Many have chosen to make restrictive interpretations of such laws (Goldberg-Ambrose, 1992). Indeed, in some jurisdictions, defense attorneys have challenged the very constitutional basis of rape shield provisions (Marsh et al., 1982). Rapes perpetrated by strangers and by intimates continued to be treated differently by the criminal justice system. Simple rapes (those that are perpetrated by unarmed dates, friends, neighbors, or acquaintances) remain much more difficult to prosecute (Estrich, 1987). In contrast to the rapid adoption of laws related to nonsexual domestic violence, although nearly all states have enacted laws related to marital sexual assault, statutory provisions in approximately 30 states allow prosecutors to treat marital sexual assault less seriously than stranger assault. For example, marital rape may be prosecuted as a misdemeanor, whereas stranger rape is prosecuted as a felony (Otos, in press). This review of policy responses to rape reveals forward progress, but in very small steps. It is clear that the fight to take back the night and make the community safe for women is far from won.

PART 5

Conclusions and Recommendations

12

Common Themes and a Call for Action

S everal common themes emerge from the research findings in the areas of battering, rape, and sexual harassment. First, we see the prevalence, pervasiveness, and tenacity of violence, whatever its form. Acts of violence are everyday events in women's lives, touching even the existence of women who do not experience violence directly. Second, the forms that male violence take against women reflect the unequal power and status of the sexes: Men are predominantly the perpetrators of violent acts; women are the targets. Third, the meaning of violent acts toward women is generated in a sociocultural context that fosters, shapes, and justifies the use of violence to maintain a male-dominated status quo at home, at work, and in the community. These acts become linked to male desires for power and control and interwoven with self-definitions of manhood and male sexuality. Further, having a relationship with a man—even one of love and trust—is not protection from male violence. The majority of women who are beaten, raped, and harassed are abused by people with whom they live and work.

We also see how sociocultural context warps our understanding of the nature, extent, contexts, and consequences of violence as viewed by the women who are its victims. The prevalence of rape, battering, and sexual harassment is underestimated. Thus, many groups at high risk for intimate violence, including the very poor, nonEnglish speakers, hospitalized, homeless, institutionalized, or incarcerated women, are typically not included in national studies. The largest national survey of rape incidence—the National Crime Victims Survey (NCVS)—asks vague and ambiguous screening questions, includes interview features that undermine rapport, uses an approach that suggests only violent rapes involving strangers are of interest to the interviewer, and conducts interviews over the phone rather than in person. Studies of sexual harassment have used local or convenient samples in which minority women and women employed in nontraditional occupations have been typically underrepresented (Goodman, Koss, Fitzgerald, Russo, & Keita, 1993).

Another common theme across forms of violence against women is the victim-focused, victim-blaming character of responses to them. The consequences of violence against women continue to be trivialized, ignored, or rationalized by individuals and by social institutions. Family members, friends, teachers, religious leaders, social service workers, police, judges, physicians, and even psychologists, have all contributed to the cultural myths that perpetuate violence against women and undermine prevention and intervention efforts.

We also find commonality in the consequences of multiple forms of violence. Victimized women tend to exhibit similar cognitive and emotional aftereffects, despite some variation among individuals, across social contexts, and across different types of violent encounters (see also Coley & Beckett, 1988; Goodman, Koss, & Russo, 1993b; Koss, 1988b; Straus, Gelles, & Steinmetz, 1980). Many of these aftereffects are also observed in individuals who have survived a variety of traumatic events (Davidson & Foa, 1993; Figley, 1985; van der Kolk, 1987); accordingly, we consider post-traumatic stress disorder (PTSD) currently to be the most accurate diagnosis for many victims of violence (Burge, 1989; Davidson & Foa, 1991; Goodman, Koss, & Russo, 1993b; Herman, 1992; Koss, 1990a; van der Kolk, 1987). Using PTSD assessment instruments, researchers have documented high rates of post-traumatic stress disorder among victims of sexual assault (National Victims

Center, 1992; Rothbaum, Foa, Riggs, Murdock, & Walsch, in press) and of partner violence (Cimino & Dutton, 1991; Kemp, Rawlings, & Green, 1991). Indeed, rape victims appear to be the largest single group of PTSD sufferers (Foa, Olasev, & Steketee, 1987). Additionally, Fitzgerald (1993b) noted that the Institute for Research on Women's Health (1988) identifies sexual harassment as a severe stressor that can trigger or exacerbate mental disorders.

However, the PTSD diagnosis does not account for many of the symptoms manifested by victims of violence, and thus fails to capture the depth and complexity of women's responses to traumatic events and conditions experienced at the hands of their intimates, friends, and colleagues. Victimization is an "overwhelming assault" on the survivor's "world of meaning" (Conte, 1988, p. 325). The interpersonal dimension of male violence against women, particularly violence by people they know, makes this experience of trauma different from that of an airplane crash or an earthquake—or even military combat. A woman may cease believing that she is secure in the world, that the world has order and meaning, and that she is a worthy person (Janoff-Bulman & Frieze, 1983). Cultural myths about violence can shape the victim's beliefs and perceptions of the event and exacerbate feelings of guilt, shame, and self-blame (Roth & Lebowitz, 1988). Feelings of vulnerability, loss of control, and self-blame may persist (Burgess & Holstrom, 1979a, 1979b; Kilpatrick, Best, Veronen, Amick, Villeponteaux, & Ruff, 1985; Resick et al., 1981).

In particular, Rieker and Carmen (1986) emphasized the destructive effects on women of what they label *disconfirmatory processes*: It didn't happen; it happened but (a) it wasn't important, (b) it had no consequences,(c) she provoked it, and (d) it wasn't really abusive. On the individual level, disconfirmatory processes interfere with women's ability to cope with violence and with the process of moving from violence victim to violence survivor. They also serve to deny and rationalize the realities of violence, thus preserving current societal arrangements.

Multiple forms of violence share serious physical health consequences as well. In primary care practice, for example, women who have been raped report more symptoms of illness and more negative health behaviors, including smoking, alcohol use, and failure to use seat belts, than nonvictimized women. They also visit their physicians more than twice as often (Koss, Koss, & Woodruff, 1991). Approximately 21% of all women using emergency surgical services are suffering from the physical sequelae of partner abuse (Browne, 1993; Stark, Flitcraft, Zuckerman, Grey, Robison, & Frazier, 1981), and 52% of all women murdered in the United States during the first half of the 1980s were the victims of partner homicide (Browne & Williams, 1989).

Violence against women affects the health care, educational, and justice systems in this country, which means that such violence has direct economic as well as psychological and physical costs (Biden, 1993). There are also indirect economic costs. For example, one study found that nearly 10% of victims reported changing jobs as a result of sexual harassment (USMSPB, 1981). This figure includes those who quit as well as those who were fired, transferred, or reassigned.

Violence is self-perpetuating and will not stop without intervention. A variety of community-based services now exist for women victims of violence, many of them created by grass-roots or advocacy movements. These include shelters for battered women and their children, crisis lines, support groups, and legal aid centers (Burt, Gornick, & Pittman, 1984; Harvey, 1985; Koss & Harvey, 1991; Schechter, 1982). These vital supports are, however, seriously underfunded and cannot adequately meet the needs of a large proportion of women who seek their assistance (Avner, 1990; Browne, 1993).

Because medical and mental health professionals typically do not inquire about current or past experiences of victimization (Browne, 1993; Council on Scientific Affairs, 1992; Koss, 1988), they may not even attempt to provide appropriate services to victimized women. Additionally, research into the consequences of violence against women has yet to produce significant advances in the area of intervention. Empirical data on the effectiveness of various interventions are sparse and often insensitive to the ethnic diversity of women victimized by male violence (Fitzgerald, 1993a; Koss, 1993b).

RECOMMENDATIONS AND ROLES FOR PSYCHOLOGISTS

Psychologists have concluded that human beings are not a uniquely aggressive species, and assumptions that aggression is innate are gross oversimplifications (Lore & Schultz, 1993). In fact, human aggression is an optional strategy, sensitive to subtle social controls that can be used to reduce the frequency of individual acts of violence (Lore & Schultz, 1993). The literature reviewed in this report reveals the array of options that exist for building or strengthening social controls on violence. However, we must first recognize that male violence against women is not inevitable.

Psychologists have important roles to play as researchers, service providers, and policy advocates helping to educate and train the public, policy makers, and other health care professions to understand, identify, treat, and refer victims of violence, as well as to prevent its occurrence. In addition, organized psychology, including the American Psychological Association, divisions, state and regional associations, and other psychology-related groups have many opportunities to provide leadership, education, prevention, and intervention activities targeted against male violence. In particular, we want to emphasize the importance of cross-cutting implications and recommendations in the areas of research, education, training, and public policy initiatives.

Theory and Research

The gendered nature of violence suggests that cognitive social learning theories, applied from a feminist social–psychological perspective, have promise for bridging the structural and individual explanations of violence. Such theories can take into account multiple layers of influence, including sociocultural, interpersonal, economic, and legal levels. They can be used to examine internalization of norms of male power, domination, and entitlement and the perception of sexual access to women as an adjunct of male power and privilege. They can reveal the mechanisms by which violence becomes eroticized and intertwined with gender schemas of masculinity and expressed in relationships with women. They can help explain individual responses to violence, on the part of victims and others. But such theories need to be specifically developed and applied to the problem of understanding male violence against women in all of its manifestations.

The fact that the consequences of violence against women continue to be trivialized and ignored makes expanding the research base an urgent priority. A fuller and more accurate assessment of the nature, prevalence, and effect of multiple forms of violence, particularly as they are experienced from a woman's point of view is urgently needed. Specifically, we recommend:

1. *An enhanced federal data collection effort.* This should include the funding of an exemplary study of prevalence of multiple forms of violence in diverse populations. The Department of Health and Human Services and the Department of Justice should develop a joint strategy to conduct or contract for a national study that represents state-of-the-art sampling and face-to-face data collection. The sample must be designed so that (a) the vulnerability of high-risk groups can be determined, (b) the interrelatedness of various forms of violence can be revealed, and (c) a full portrait of women's exposure to violence can be ascertained. Groups who have been particularly neglected in current research studies include adolescents, single adult women, poor women, lesbians, physically disabled women, incarcerated women, and women from ethnically diverse backgrounds.

2. *Continued monitoring of the NCVS.* Six new questions to detect rape were introduced into the NCVS in July, 1991, although other problem-laden NCVS procedures remain unchanged. The revised questions hold no promise of rapid improvement in the validity of NCVS rape estimates because they are being phased in gradually while the bulk of respondents continue to receive the old protocol. Ongoing pressure from the professional community is needed until rape is measured with the same precision as other crimes.

3. *Ongoing collection of nationally representative data on prevalence and correlates of rape, battering, and sexual harassment in work-related and*

educational contexts. Standardized questions concerning such experiences should be routinely included in governmentally sponsored national surveys (e.g., Labor Department Surveys such as the National Longitudinal Study of Youth, the High-School and Beyond project) of both education and work-related settings. Questions should be behaviorally based and use standard terminology so that results can be compared both across and within data sets.

4. *Allowance of medical documentation of sexual violence.* Another opportunity for collecting data that will allow the magnitude of the problem of sexual violence to be evaluated exists in the standard reporting procedures that emerge from the development of a National Health Plan. The traditional practice of medicine encourages focus on illness outcomes, such as sexually transmitted disease or depression, and ignores the environmental context that created the illnesses, including rape. As reporting procedures are developed, consideration should be given to the documentation of violence against women. The information would inform treatment planning and provide another avenue for assessing the social costs of violence. Precedents already exist for collecting information on sensitive topics in ways that respect the confidentiality of the individual.

5. *Enhanced research on the origins and cultural supports for conceptions of gender and gender-related roles that promote and maintain violence.* Such research will enable the development and assessment of interventions targeted toward changing such conceptions. In particular, we need to know more about (a) what leads some men to use physical aggression as a relational tool, (b) what factors maintain aggression once abusive interactions have occurred, and (c) what factors contribute to the likelihood that aggression will escalate or desist given separation or the threat of separation from the target. Such research should include examination of protective factors that prevent high-risk men from perpetrating partner violence and evaluation of mechanisms for enhancing those factors in the lives of children and adolescents.

6. *Exploration of the social-structural context of violence.* Such an explo-

ration should include researching the gender-role constructions that promote violence against women as well as the economic, legal, religious, and other social forces that perpetuate it. We also need to know how social categories such as race, class, ethnicity, and sexual orientation shape its nature and effects. Psychological assessment and interpretation of the behaviors of victims of male violence cannot be complete unless the effects of women's differential access to power and coping resources on the dynamics of violence are understood.

7. *Increased research on the psychological sequelae of violence against women.* Research that uses nationally representative samples, recognizes women's diversity, goes beyond current diagnostic categories, and includes physiological, cognitive, affective, and behavioral components must be conducted.

8. *Increased attention to measurement issues.* Research is needed to develop reliable and valid measures of key constructs, particularly social cognitions, that will inform our understanding of women's relationships, including the dynamics of perceived rights, responsibilities, and entitlements in relationships between women and their intimates. In addition, key constructs that are currently unexamined in treatment outcome research need to be explored.

9. *Research on effective interventions.* This includes study of the effectiveness of punishment and the development of behaviors that are incompatible with violence against women. Particularly, research is needed that recognizes that the meaning of punishment is affected by the gendered nature of violence. Such research should identify under what conditions which alternatives most effectively mitigate against further harm. It should also include identification of predictors of reassault and lethal assault for women who leave violent partners or pursue legal alternatives or both.

10. *The review and evaluation of processes of diagnosis and treatment* for their effectiveness in identifying and treating women who experience various forms of male violence.

11. *Development of new research partnerships among psychological researchers, activists, and victims before research is undertaken* so that

research questions and hypotheses will reflect the priorities and issues of concern to the victims as well as to psychologists.

12. *Funding mechanisms that encourage collaboration.* Strategies are needed to encourage cooperative projects involving researchers and community groups (e.g., rape crisis centers, battered women's shelters) to ensure that the research incorporates the priorities and perspectives of victims and is designed and disseminated in ways that will serve the community.

Organized psychology has important roles to play in advocating for public and private funding for such research, helping to develop research agendas to ensure attention to critical issues, and in disseminating the research findings to professionals and to the public.

Intervention and Treatment

Because aggressive behavior, particularly when motivated by anger, is self-reinforcing, early intervention and prevention are critical. Many women believe their batterers when they express love, say they are sorry, and promise never to become violent again. Everyone, but particularly women, must be taught about the self-reinforcing properties of violence and the fact that unless there is intervention, violence escalates.

Further, many women, particularly religious women, are willing to make a personal sacrifice and suffer abuse in order to honor their commitment to their marriages and provide their children with an intact family. Traditional norms of the wife/partner role often mean that women are encouraged to tolerate the initial, less severe acts of violence in their relationships because they believe they must stand by their men and put family values over personal considerations. Ignoring the violence is often reinforced by family, friends, and religious leaders so that if the woman does seek help from these sources before the violence becomes severe, she may be encouraged to accept her situation to maintain her marriage and keep her family together. Given that such women are socialized to put the interests of their children above their own, it is important to emphasize that children are harmed by witnessing the violence. Emphasis on this fact may help empower women to seek help before the violence escalates. It may also help change the attitudes of others, so that they will be more supportive when a woman seeks help and will provide the kind of help that a woman needs to achieve her goals. Obviously, the duty of men as husbands and fathers to control their behaviors and behave in nonviolent ways must also be emphasized.

Intervention and prevention strategies must include helping to develop real options for women. For example, telling a woman to go to court and testify against a rapist, batterer, or harasser, or to leave her husband or job may entail consequences that are personally unacceptable to her. There may, for example, be basic differences in the values and attitudes between the staff of shelters and crisis centers and the women they serve (Fine, 1989). Psychologists can help identify differences between staff and clientele in such things as conceptions of the family, religion, entitlement, and the appropriate use of violence in interpersonal relationships that may undermine access to and effectiveness of services.

There needs to be an emphasis on enhancing treatment and intervention effectiveness. These efforts must recognize the sociocultural dimensions of violence against women and be designed to take them into account so that the beliefs and attitudes that reinforce male violence and domination are eliminated. Those who treat survivors must guard against allowing their focus on the individual to obscure the nature of violence as a societal problem. In particular, we recommend:

1. *The encouragement of treatment innovation.* Established methods of treatment should be adopted for use with victims of rape, battering, and sexual harassment and be tested for efficacy.
2. *The fostering of multisite studies.* Treatment outcome can be improved by matching treatment approach, symptom profile, and individual characteristics. Collaboration across sites is the only viable approach to developing a sufficient number of participants to permit examination of these interactions.
3. *The enhancment of practitioner knowledge of the history of traumatic victimization and potential posttrauma responses.* The importance of

this knowledge in designing effective supports and interventions must not be underestimated. For example, a treatment plan structured around only the manifestations of trauma cannot succeed if assaults are ongoing and post-traumatic responses continually recur or if the effects of past assaults maintain current behaviors and emotional distress (Browne, 1992). The approach to treatment must be shaped by careful and thoughtful affirmation of the client's perceptions and attention to her empowerment (McGrath et al., 1990). Attention to both emotions and cognitions must be an important aspect of the therapeutic process (Koss, 1988b).

Intervention goals for women victims of violence include the attainment of physical and psychological health and safety. To attain these goals, we recommend that mental health interventions include:

1. *Routine screening for histories of victimization.* Such screenings should take into account issues of privacy, confidentiality, and safety for women in making disclosures (e.g., potential victims should not be asked questions about physical or sexual violence within the hearing distance of a potential assailant; and disclosures of violence should not be carelessly revealed to assailants). Agency settings as well as the practitioners conducting screenings should have established links with resources for protection, shelter, legal aid, and other services that may be needed by victims or other family members.

    Practitioners in alcohol and drug treatment centers should be particularly sensitive to the possibility that their clients may have experienced violence. Victimized women may use alcohol or drugs to repress trauma, particularly childhood trauma, complicating the treatment of alcohol- and drug-abusing women. After a year of sobriety, memories of abuse may resurface and trigger depressive episodes and suicidal ideation. They may also threaten sobriety (McGrath, Keita, Strickland, & Russo, 1990). As many as three out of four chemically dependent women have been found to report incidents of sexual abuse (Wilsnack & Beckman, 1984). In one study of Native American women in drug treatment, 70% of the sample reported a history of physical or sexual abuse (Gutierres, Russo, & Urbanski, in press).

2. *Validation of the experience.* For many victimized women, such validation by a professional is a first step toward reframing abusive experiences and seeking intervention or counsel. Disclosure of victimization must be met with supportive responses, such as saying, "That was a terrible thing to happen to you" or "He had no right to do that to you" (Browne, 1992). The therapist must recognize that women who assert experiences of abuse are often met with questioning about their credibility and culpability. Accordingly, the therapist must take on a different role than that typically used in therapy. In particular, victims of interpersonal violence may perceive individuals as being "for them or against them." As such, a neutral therapeutic stance can be interpreted as adversarial (McGrath et al., 1990).

   The victim-blaming that occurs through attempts to "help" the victims understand how she "unconsciously" contributes to her victimization can impede treatment effectiveness (Hilberman, 1980). Therapists must make overt expressions of willingness to believe the victim and clearly place blame for the abuse on the perpetrator. This stance of overt advocacy and support must be combined with clear boundaries for the therapy relationship when treating survivors of violence. As APA's National Task Force on Depression pointed out, such survivors are susceptible to revictimization by therapists who are sloppy in boundary maintenance (McGrath et al., 1990).

3. *Documentation of assault histories and observed sequelae.* This is an essential component of both short- and long-term mental health interventions (Browne, 1992; Dutton, 1992a). Records should include (a) indications of trauma history, (b) specific details of assault types, threats made, and changes in patterns of assault and threat over time, (c) a description of symptomatology potentially linked to the victimization, and (d) documentation of assaults or threats made in response to victims' attempts to obtain help or terminate the relationship.

4. *Safety planning.* Some degree of safety planning should be discussed

with women who disclose abuse, whether their immediate decision is to separate from or remain with their abuser. Does the woman need immediate police protection, legal intervention, or safe shelter? Is the woman aware of resources available in her community to address these needs? Does she have a safety plan if the danger escalates or if she decides to terminate with her abuser or take legal action? What are her plans if a child is threatened with danger? These are the types of basic safety questions that must be addressed. Knowledge of societal resources for protection and aid—regardless of whether a victim makes a decision to take advantage of them—may expand a woman's perception of alternatives and mitigate against the sense of isolation and entrapment reported by so many women victims (Browne & Williams, 1989).

5. *Expanded interventions for women who are victimized by male violence.* The repertoire of interventions for rape and battering would benefit especially from further development and evaluation of multicultural approaches, programs for adolescents, and treatments for victims with multiple physical, mental, and social problems.

6. *Expanded interventions for men who rape or abuse female partners.* Priorities include the mechanisms for early identification of such men when they are seen in mental health settings; improved interventions for creating and maintaining change in violent behavior, and—potentially the most difficult—strategies for engaging a wider population of abusive men in interventions for abusers and rapists.

Although more effective measures to ensure the protection and safety of current victims are needed, greater efforts to *prevent* male violence must occur if the pool of at-risk and assaulted women is to be reduced. We recommend:

1. *Expanding interventions for children and adolescents at risk for violent behavior or involvement in violent dating or marital relationships.* Preventive interventions would include: gender equity education for children and adolescents, parenting and relationship skill training,

family planning and sex education, early identification of children and adolescents at increased risk for violent behaviors or involvement in violent relationships, and interventions geared to offset negative exposure and to strengthen protective factors and attitudes on the part of both sexes. Such interventions must specifically include individuals in unmarried (dating or living-together) relationships. We recommend that interventions include resources targeted for the thousands of individuals in dating or cohabiting relationships who are not in high school or college settings and who, thus, would not be reached through efforts structured around the educational system.

2. *Developing support groups for men in transition or crisis that include antiviolence components.* Such men include refugees, rural–urban migrants, unemployed men, alcoholics, and men in the process of separation and divorce.

Expanding the Roles of Social Institutions in Preventing Violence

The relevant "authorities" and leaders of social institutions that play a role in the development and maintenance of male violence against women—including parents, teachers, church leaders, health service providers, police officers, judges, sports figures, military personnel, and members of the media and entertainment industries—need to be educated about the consequences of such violence and made aware of their institutional roles in perpetuating and shaping it. Such authorities must help increase the social costs of gender violence, create social norms that define violence against women as unacceptable, promote concepts of male self-control, responsibility, and accountability, and foster equitable, nonviolent relationships. Although we must expand the capacity of all social institutions to prevent and intervene against violence, we emphasize strategies that focus on educational institutions, religious institutions, the workplace, and the media.

Educational Institutions

There is a particular need to include violence prevention education in the curriculum of elementary schools because this is a time in which values about men's and women's roles are still forming. This curriculum should be continued in high school. The factors that contribute to violence are so broad that a curriculum rather than an isolated lecture is needed for young people from late elementary school through college. In addition, the close links of alcohol and various forms of violence, such as rape and battering, suggest that substance abuse and violence prevention curricula might profit from integration. In the absence of curbs on media depictions of violence against women, educational curricula and public service campaigns must be developed to educate youth to be informed consumers of such images. The Center for Media and Values, which develops and disseminates materials to teach media literacy for use by educational, religious, child advocacy, and community groups, provides an example of such efforts.

Psychologists have a variety of roles to play in educational efforts designed to prevent violence against women, whether at the elementary school, secondary school, or college level. Research suggests that education can help counter an attitudinal climate that supports violence against women. For example, feminist rape education programs have been found to reduce the extent to which students blame the rape victim, accept rape myths, and define heterosexual relations as adversarial (Fonow, Richardson, & Wemmerus, 1992).

Educational systems also have critical roles to play in expanding women's life options so that they have alternatives to violent relationships. We particularly emphasize the need for elimination of gender bias in the curriculum and in educational practices, career development programs for women, and the development of re-entry programs.

APA's Committees on Precollege Psychology and Undergraduate Education should examine ways in which the association can facilitate translation of research findings into effective educational programs at all levels. The new organization, Teachers of Psychology in the Secondary Schools, provides an opportunity to develop curriculum materials and interventions at the high-school level. Such efforts should focus, in part, on examining and reconceptualizing gender roles and cultural mythologies. They should engage peer groups (including fraternities, athletic teams, and the ROTC) in developing and delivering educational interventions.

Health Care Institutions

Health service providers are a particularly important group to educate about the prevalence and consequences of violence. Victims of violence are more likely to visit a physician than a mental health professional. Psychologists have important roles to play in training physicians and working to develop a health care system that is responsive to victims' needs. We recommend that these efforts include development of a health care curriculum that incorporates information about rape, battering, sexual harassment, and other forms of male violence into the training of health practitioners at the undergraduate, graduate, and continuing education levels. Rape, battering, and other contextual influences on women's health are needed to balance extensive teaching that emphasizes reductionistic, biological explanations for disease. Health care providers must be equipped to provide victim-sensitive care. That is, they must be able to provide the treatment that emergency room protocols specify in the case of rape or other forms of violence, to offer opportunities for disclosure and validation of victimization, to educate women about the links between forms of victimization and increased illness, and to refer women in need to trauma-specific community services or to specialists within the formal mental health system.

Religious Institutions

Psychologists and other mental health professionals who deal with marriage and family issues have a particularly critical role to play in educating clergy and other religious leaders about the dynamics of violence. They should be involved in developing family-oriented prevention and intervention efforts in collaboration with religious institutions. For maximal effectiveness, we recommend that family violence prevention and intervention efforts be undertaken in the context of family authorities who are recognized as such by perpetrators and victims. For individuals who obtain their marital expectations (including expectations about male entitlements) from their church authorities, church-based prevention and intervention programs may be particularly important. There are encouraging signs that churches are beginning to recognize the role that religious values have played in promoting violence and the importance of church involvement in prevention. In

1990, the National Council of Churches, representing 32 Protestant, Orthodox, and Anglican denominations with 42 million members, urged their clergy to respond more compassionately to domestic violence. In 1992, the U. S. Roman Catholic Bishops condemned all domestic violence (physical, psychological, and verbal) as sinful (Weber, 1993). APA's Division on the Psychological Study of Religious Issues is in a particularly good position to play a leadership role in bringing psychological knowledge related to violence to bear on research, practice, and training in religious settings.

Workplace Strategies

The national strategy of the National Institute for Occupational Safety and Health (NIOSH) to prevent work-related psychological disorders provides a timely opportunity for prevention and intervention in several areas. The four cornerstones of the NIOSH initiative, which have been adopted by APA, are (a) well-designed jobs; (b) surveillance systems to detect psychological disorders and underlying risk factors; (c) education of workers and managers on the signs, causes, effects, and control of work-related psychological disorders; and (d) improved mental health service delivery for workers. We recommend that the four areas incorporate strategies to eliminate violence in the workplace and to mitigate the effects of violence at home and in the community that are reflected in the mental health of workers.

While the mission of NIOSH is, of course, to focus on the workplace, it should be recognized that the division of home and work into two separate spheres is based on traditional conceptions of male roles and is not responsive to the needs of female (and many male) workers. The gendered structures of work are undermining the productivity of the nation's workers. NIOSH will not be able to achieve its stated goals unless the issues raised by those structures are directly addressed. Thus, although the lens may be on the workplace, it will be important for strategies to conceptualize work and home relationships in a dynamic system. A "well-designed job" cannot exist unless it is in a "well-designed job environment," and a "well-designed job environment" cannot exist unless it is designed to promote a worker's ability to meet both work and family responsibilities.

In this context, a well-designed job and job environment is an important part of a national effort to prevent violence against women. In the broadest sense, providing a supportive work environment for women, promoting nonsexist attitudes in the workplace, teaching male workers to treat women with respect and to view them empathically, and in general, creating an environment that negates cultural expectations of women's subordination will all undermine male entitlement and the devaluation of women that contributes to the common character of violent acts directed toward women. In addition, strategies that directly address issues of physical abuse, rape, and sexual harassment in the workplace are needed. These are all part of designing a work place that promotes the mental health of all workers.

Education within the organizational context should include the development, implementation, and evaluation of training programs designed to prevent sexual harassment, sexual assault, and the battering of women on the part of workers. Such programs should make conceptual links among different forms of violence, mental and physical health, and work productivity.

Although we focus on NIOSH because its current initiatives promise benefits to the workplace, other critical agencies also have important roles to play in mounting a comprehensive societal effort to change the cultural supports for violence at work, whether the work place be public or private, civilian or military. Because sexual harassment is viewed as a work-related issue, its physical and mental health effects may be neglected by agencies not specifically charged with dealing with it. The NIOSH initiative is the ideal opportunity to stimulate the cross-cutting collaboration needed to promote the research, education, and intervention efforts needed in this area.

We recommend that NIOSH take a leadership role in developing interagency initiatives to fund such efforts. In particular, funds should be specifically set aside and targeted for research on potentially high-risk groups (e.g., racial and ethnic minority women and nontraditionally employed women) as well as potentially high-yield topics (e.g., prevention and intervention programs). Evaluation of the efficacy of the training programs that are rapidly proliferating is critical.

The Media

There are many things that psychologists can do to work with the media that do not engage freedom of speech issues. First, it is important to fully inform the media and the public about current research findings that document the role the media plays in shaping and contributing to violence against women as well as the response of the public to such violence. Second, psychologists have a role to play in informing the media about ways to inhibit or suppress violence. Both APA's Public Information Committee and the Division of Media Psychology should take leadership roles in these efforts. The Division of the Psychology of Women has a public information project under way that involves the development of consumer materials containing antiviolence information. Such efforts should be expanded and pursued on state and local levels.

Public Policy Initiatives

Public policy initiatives cut across research, prevention, and intervention efforts, and include legal and legislative reform. Societal implications of the research findings in this report include the need to legally proscribe all forms of violence and to carry through with prosecuting cases, especially those that involve acquaintances and intimates. The likelihood of violence may also be influenced by legislative initiatives that seek to redress gender-based power imbalances, including legislation on women's reproductive rights, pay equity, dependent care and family support, and civil rights legislation. Active efforts to help women move into jobs traditionally held by men, to eliminate discrimination in hiring and training, to move women into leadership positions, and to create a prowomen climate through policies such as family leave and child care assistance, can all be considered part of a comprehensive attack on the conditions that underlie and foster male violence against women.

Rape laws have undergone many positive modifications in recent years, although rape remains a crime for which the victim is put on trial. But many women do not even get to try for justice because prosecutors refuse to adjudicate rape cases involving acquaintances or those involving victims without pristine reputations. The rationale is that these cases cannot be won and are therefore a waste of taxpayer resources. This state of affairs fuels an illusion among American women that they are subject to legal protection that, in fact, is inoperative. Some legal scholars suggest that the laws cannot be applied successfully until public attitudes change. However, one can question how attitudes will change when the very cases that would educate the public about the range and types of rapes receive minimal exposure. The result of the status quo is a justice system that silences rape victims, promotes a general invisibility of the crime of rape, and contributes to social service agencies' neglect of sexual assault victims. Many areas of needed change are within the purview of the states not of the federal government.

The Violence Against Women Act, first introduced in 1991 by Senator Joseph Biden (Biden, 1993), is a major attempt to develop a national consensus that society will not tolerate violence against women. Such legislation signals that violence against women must be taken seriously and provides resources to states and areas most in need. Such legislative efforts are needed in a variety of areas, including better legal options and law enforcement that is more sensitive to women's issues and options. Because the contents of specific legislation change during the legislative process, we focus here on issues identified in the Violence Against Women Act and elsewhere rather than on the specific contents of the variety of bills pending in Congress. Specifically, we support:

1. *Creating special units of police, prosecutors, and victim advocates to fight crimes against women.* We would extend these efforts to include advocates to assist victims of sexual harassment through the legal process.

2. *Creating training programs for state and federal judges to raise awareness and increase sensitivity about rape, sexual assault, domestic violence, and crimes of violence motivated by the victim's gender.* Psychologists have important roles to play in developing training curricula for these programs, which should be mandated to include a number of issues, including gender stereotyping. We would extend these efforts to include health care providers, military personnel, and religious leaders,

and include explicit attention to sexual harassment as a crime motivated by the victim's gender.

3. *Confronting the problem of acquaintance rape.* Study is needed to consider options for applying more fairly and uniformly laws that already
exist. One option that might be studied is the creation of diversion
programs such as have been developed for domestic violence offenders
that acknowledge the wrong that has been done to the victim and provide assistance to men in changing their sexually violent behavior.

4. *Doubling penalties for rape and aggravated rape prosecuted in federal
courts, increasing penalties for sex offenders, and mandating restitution
for victims of sex crimes.*

5. *Extending rape shield law protection to criminal and civil cases and barring the showing of a woman's clothing at trial (which is often done in an
attempt to prove she incited or invited a sexual assault).* Such protection
should extend to victims of sexual harassment.

6. *Requiring states to pay for all forensic rape examinations.*

7. *Providing grants to model states to engage in innovative techniques to
increase arrest, prosecution, and conviction rates in domestic violence
cases.*

8. *Establishing federal penalties for crimes committed against spouses during interstate travel and crimes committed by spouse abusers who cross
state lines to continue their abuse.*

9. *Requiring a protection order of one state to be given full faith and credit
by the court of another state.*

10. *Making gender-based assaults a violation of federal civil rights laws and
allowing women to pursue a civil suit for monetary or other relief.*

11. *Changing the caps on damages for sex discrimination suits.* Although the
1991 Civil Rights Act provides harassment victims with both compensatory and punitive damages, the caps on damages that were imposed
imply that sexual discrimination is not as serious as other kinds of
legal violations. We believe that the goal of prevention would be served
better if the federal government and the states allowed for unlimited
damages. In addition, federal and state educational efforts should be
undertaken to inform judges and other legal personnel about the

extensive and serious consequences experienced by victims of sexual harassment so that damages can be awarded accordingly.

With regard to domestic violence, we support incentives to protect women from abusive partners and to encourage states to treat domestic violence as a serious crime. We specifically recommend *tripling existing levels of funding for battered women's shelters.* Funds are needed to increase the number of agencies, the number of staff within agencies, and to improve salaries so that qualified and permanent staff can be retained. It must be noted that such funding is also needed for rape crisis centers.

Violence against women cannot be prevented unless the underlying gender-based inequities that support violence are exposed and rectified. We support legislative efforts to heighten awareness about domestic violence through schools and the media. In particular, we recommend:

1. *The creation of a national media campaign against intimate violence.* Such a campaign should deal with multiple forms of violence and should not focus solely on married couples. A national effort to educate media professionals about the consequences of eroticizing violence is also critical. This educational effort must also show how the way in which the consequences of violence are portrayed can increase or decrease its probability of occurrence.
2. *The creation and funding of antiviolence programs for primary, middle, and secondary schools, as well as institutions of higher education.*

A variety of other initiatives is needed. In particular, we recommend:

1. *Putting gender-motivated bias crimes on the same footing as other bias crimes.* The creation of a civil rights remedy for gender-motivated violence is particularly important.
2. *Providing greater support for grass-roots services.* Grass-roots agencies are often the first line of response to victimized women. Support for rape education and prevention programs and battered women's shelters is an important start.

We also support *funding for rape prevention and education programs, including a grant program for the neediest colleges to fund campus rape education and prevention programs.* However, this educational effort should also include dating violence in the form of battering. Such programs should focus on the roles of athletics and fraternities in contributing to norms that foster dating violence and should work with a variety of campus groups to develop norms that are incompatible with violence.

Grass-roots agencies also need the federal government and state governments to provide *technical support for treatment programs.* Needed technical assistance includes training materials for staff development and therapy manuals to facilitate the teaching of empirically validated interventions. Attention should also be given to developing better linkages among rape crisis centers, battered women's shelters, and the formal systems of medicine, mental health, and criminal justice.

Multiple approaches must be used to reinforce the message that violence against women is illegal and will not be tolerated. This country must confront the problem of acquaintance rape. Rape myths have been perpetuated by rape laws that highlight the behavior or reputation of the victim rather than the unlawful acts of the offender. In many jurisdictions of the country, it is impossible to try acquaintance rape cases, even though the cases have been thoroughly investigated by law enforcement and the alleged perpetrator has been identified. In these jurisdictions, victims of acquaintance rape have only the illusion of legal protection.

There are a host of additional actions, legislative and executive, that could be undertaken that go beyond the actions specified in the Violence Against Women Act and other pending legislation. Issues related to custody, pornography, and sexual harassment, for example have yet to be adequately addressed. In particular, we recommend:

1. *Revisiting legal definitions of crime* so that, for example, threats of violence, stalking, and intimidation are uniformly defined as crimes in all states and are subject to swift and firm punishment.
2. *Exploring the possibility of incorporating the commission of violent acts in the presence of children into legal definitions of child abuse.* This may

help to interrupt both the intergenerational transmission of abuse and the escalation of violence in situations where children are present. Women who put their families first may be unwilling to seek help when they view it as solely for themselves. Many women tolerate abuse because the men are "good fathers." If women understand the negative consequences witnessing abuse has on children, their commitment to the mother role may help empower them to seek help for the sake of their children when the abuse first starts.

3. *Reviewing policies that provide for involuntary joint custody to ensure that it is not mandated for couples who are in conflict.* Many states have placed women and children in danger of their lives through involuntary joint custody legislation that does not recognize the prevalence and tenacity of violence against women. Psychological research that is based on parents who actively want to share custody of children (Wallerstein & Kelly, 1980) or that has not adequately taken into account the potential effect of male violence (Braver et al., in press) is being used inappropriately to advocate for joint custody. Yet there is evidence that joint custody is no better than sole custody, and that it can be harmful in some situations (Wallerstein & Blakeslee, 1989).

4. *Expanding access to low-income housing.* It is well known that many women lack access to economic resources. If they also lack access to low-income housing, these women (particularly those with children) may have to choose between staying in violent homes or living on violent streets.

5. *Requiring employers by law to develop a clear policy against harassment as well as clear and accessible grievance procedures.* Employers should be further required to notify employees of the policy, post it prominently in the work place, and provide employees with education and training about harassment. This will both save employers money and reduce or eliminate their liability.

6. *Strengthening enforcement agencies and providing them with sufficient resources to carry out responsibilities.* The Violence Against Women Act, which creates special units of police, prosecutors, and victim advocates to fight crimes against women, is a beginning. But it is important to strengthen agencies that deal with sexual harassment as well. The

EEOC has a large backlog of cases and many state agencies routinely fail to meet their own regulatory deadlines.

7. *Extending the statute of limitations for filing sexual harassment charges with the EEOC beyond the current 180 days.* As Bravo and Cassedy (1992) have pointed out, "No justification exists for such a short statute of limitations, especially since it often takes harassment victims a long time to sort through their experience and decide on a course of action" (p. 141).

8. *Reforming unemployment compensation statutes to ensure that women who quit their jobs because of harassment can receive unemployment compensation.* In every state, quitting a job because of sexual harassment should be defined as a "constructive discharge," the equivalent of an involuntary dismissal without cause, for which the victim is entitled to compensation.

Psychological Training and Practice

APA's Educational Affairs Directorate should examine how violence information may be best incorporated into the training and continuing education experiences of psychologists. Continuing education institutes might be developed in tandem with graduate training programs, state psychological associations, and the relevant divisions. Curriculum materials to facilitate incorporation of up-to-date scientific knowledge about violence against women should be developed and disseminated.

Ultimately, psychologists as individuals have the responsibility to educate themselves about male violence against women: its nature and effects, the multiple and complex factors that cause and perpetuate it, and potential avenues toward reducing its prevalence, whether through personal change, professional endeavor, or social action. The true understanding of the prevalence, severity, and tenacity of male violence against women that such an education provides would have many benefits. It could, in fact, lead to:

- Different bases for initial and long-term responses by mental health and legal practitioners and other professionals;
- A different understanding of the legitimacy of women's reactions to trauma and life-threat;

- Expansion of society's remedies of choice: There is a desperate need for the development of long-term resources for the stabilization of women and children apart from violent mates;
- Stronger emphasis on new remedies for rape, battering, and sexual harassment, given the resilience of such behaviors in the face of current levels of awareness, interventions, and sanctions; and
- New emphasis on preventive strategies for children and adolescents to avoid the regeneration of violence and sexual coercion and harassment in adult relationships.

In offering these recommendations, we emphasize urgency in addressing issues of male violence against women. So long as the multiple forms, effects, and costs of such violence are ignored and condoned, the health and well-being of women, children, and society will be undermined. As Senator Joseph Biden (1993) has so eloquently stated, "If the leading newspapers were to announce tomorrow a new disease that, over the past year, had afflicted from 3 to 4 million citizens, few would fail to appreciate the seriousness of the illness. Yet, when it comes to the 3 to 4 million women who are victimized by violence each year, the alarms ring softly" (p. 1059). Psychologists must take on leadership roles—as individual professionals and as concerned citizens—in sounding the alarms and marshalling constructive action. We all have a crucial part to play in eradicating this destructive, tragic phenomenon from our country and from the world. The violence must be stopped.

Task Force on Violence Against Women Advisory Committee Members

Hortensia Amaro, PhD
School of Public Health
Boston University
Boston, MA

Laura Brown, PhD
Private Practice
Seattle, WA

Mary Pat Brygger
National Women Abuse
   Prevention Project
Washington, DC

Christine A. Courtois, PhD
Center for Abuse Recovery and
   Empowerment
Washington, DC

Irene H. Frieze, PhD
Department of Psychology
University of Pittsburgh
Pittsburgh, PA

Barbara Gutek, PhD
College of Business and Public
   Administration
University of Arizona
Tucson, AZ

Mary R. Harvey, PhD
Cambridge Associates
Cambridge, MA

Dean G. Kilpatrick, PhD
Department of Psychiatry and
   Behavioral Science
Medical University of South
   Carolina
Charleston, SC

Robin A. LaDue, PhD
Department of Psychiatry and
   Behavioral Science
University of Washington
Seattle, WA

Michele Paludi, PhD
Michele Paludi & Associates
Schenectady, NY

Lenore E. Walker, PhD
Walker & Associates
Denver, CO

Jacquelyn W. White, PhD
Department of Psychology
University of North Carolina
Greensboro, NC

Gail E. Wyatt, EdD
Neuropsychiatric Institute
University of California
Los Angeles, CA

References

Abbey, A. (1982). Sex differences in attributions for friendly behavior: Do males misperceive females' friendliness? *Journal of Personality and Social Psychology, 42,* 830–838.

Abbey A. (1987a). Misperceptions of friendly behavior as sexual interest: A survey of naturally occurring incidents. *Psychology of Women Quarterly, 11,* 173–194.

Abbey, A. (1987b). Perceptions of personal avoidability versus responsibility: How do they differ? *Basic and Applied Social Psychology, 8,* 3–19.

Abbey, A. (1991). Misperception as an antcedent of acquaintance rape: A consequence of ambiguity in communication between women and men. In A. Parrot & L. Bechhofer (Eds.), *Acquaintance rape: The hidden crime* (pp. 96–112). New York: Wiley.

Abbey, A., & Thomson, L. (1992). *Psychosocial explanations of alcohol's role in forced sexual experiences.* Paper prepared for the U.S. Department of Education, Fund for the Improvement of Secondary Education.

Adams, D. (1988). Treatment models of men who batter: A profeminist analysis. In K. Yllö & M. Bograd (Eds.), *Feminist perspectives on wife abuse* (pp. 176–200). Beverly Hills, CA: Sage.

Adams, J. W., Kottke, J. L., & Padgitt, J. S. (1983). Sexual harassment of university students. *Journal of College Student Personnel, 24,* 484–490.

Ageton, S. S. (1983). *Sexual assault among adolescents.* Lexington, MA: D.C. Heath.

Allen, P. G. (1990). Violence and the American Indian Woman. *The speaking profits us: Violence in the lives of women of color.* Seattle: SAFECO Insurance Company.

Allen, D., & Erickson, J. (1989). *Sexual harassment of faculty at the University of Illinois.* Champaign, IL: Union of Professional Employees, University of Illinois at Urbana-Champaign.

Alliance Against Sexual Coercion (1981). *Fighting against sexual harassment: An advocacy handbook.* Boston: Alyson Publishers.

Alsdurf, J. (1985). Wife abuse and the church: The response of pastors. *Response,* Winter, 9–11.

American Psychiatric Association. (1987). *Diagnostic and statistical manual of mental disorders* (3rd ed., rev.). Washington, DC: Author.

American Psychiatric Association. (1994). Diagnostic and statistical manual of mental disorders (4th ed.). Washington, DC: Author.

American Psychological Association. (1992). *Myths and facts about sexual harassment.* Washington, DC: Author.

Anderson, M. L. (1993). *Thinking about women: Sociological perspectives on sex and gender* (3rd ed.). New York: Macmillan.

Arendt, H. (1951). *The origins of totalitarianism.* New York: Harcourt-Brace.

Arnold, M. B. (1967). Stress and emotion. In M. H. Appley & R. Trumbull (Eds.), *Psychological Stress* (pp. 123–150). New York: Appleton-Century-Crofts.

Atkeson, B. M., Calhoun, K. S., Resick, P. A., & Ellis, E. M. (1982). Victims of rape: Repeated assessment of depressive symptoms. *Journal of Consulting and Clinical Psychology, 50,* 96–102.

Avner, J. I. (1990). *Rape, sexual assault, and child sexual abuse: Working toward a more responsive society.* Albany, NY: New York State Division for Women.

Babich, K. S., & Voit, E. S. (1992). The research base for treatment of sexually abused women. In C. M. Sampselle (Ed.), *Violence against women: Nursing research, education, and practice issues* (pp. 91–113). New York: Hemisphere.

Bahnson, C. B. (1964). Emotional reactions to internally and externally derived threats of annihilation. In G. H. Grosser, H. Wechsler, & M. Greenblatt (Eds.), *The threat of impending disaster* (pp. 251–280). Cambridge, MA: M.I.T. Press.

Baker, N. L. (1989). *Sexual harassment and job satisfaction in traditional and nontraditional industrial occupations.* Unpublished doctoral dissertation, California School of Professional Psychology, Los Angeles.

Baker, T. C., Burgess, A. W., Brickman, E., & Davis, R. C. (1990). Rape victims' concerns about possible exposure to HIV infection. *Journal of Interpersonal Violence, 5,* 49–60.

Bandura, A., Underwood, B., & Fromson, M. E. (1975). Disinhibition of aggression through diffusion of responsibility and dehumanization. *Journal of Research in Personality, 9,* 253–269.

Bandy, N. (1989). *Relationships between male and female employees at Southern Illinois University.* Unpublished doctoral dissertation, College of Education, Southern Illinois University, Chicago.

Barbaree, H. E., & Marshall, W. L. (1991). The role of male sexual arousal in rape: Six models. *Journal of Consulting and Clinical Psychology, 59,* 621–630.

Bard, L. A., Carter, D. L., Cerce, D. D., Knight, R. A., Rosenberg, R., & Schneider, B.

(1987). A descriptive study of rapists and child molesters: Developmental, clinical, and criminal characteristics. *Behavioral Sciences and the Law, 5*, 203–220.

Bard, M., & Sangrey, D. (1986). *The crime victims' book* (2nd ed.). New York: Brunner/Mazel.

Bard, M., & Zacker, J. (1971). The prevention of family violence: Dilemmas of community intervention. *Journal of Marriage and the Family, 33*, 677–682.

Bargh, J., & Raymond, P. (1992). *An automatic power–sex association in men likely to be sexual harassers.* Paper presented at the meeting of the Society for Experimental Social Psychology, San Antonio, TX.

Barnard, G. W., Vera, M., & Newman, G. (1982). "Till death do us part": A study of spouse murder. *Bulletin of the American Academy of Psychiatry and Law, 10,* 271–280.

Barnett, O., & Hamberger, L. K. (1992). The assessment of maritally violent men on the California Psychological Inventory. *Violence and Victims, 7,* 15–22.

Baron, L., & Straus, M. A. (1989). *Four theories of rape in American society.* New Haven, CT: Yale University Press.

Bart, P. B. (1981). A study of women who both were raped and avoided rape. *Journal of Social Issues, 37,* 123–136.

Bassuk, E. L., Rubin, L., & Lauriat, A. (1986). Characteristics of sheltered homeless families. *American Journal of Public Health, 76,* 1097–1101.

Baum, A. (1990). Stress, intrusive imagery, and chronic distress. *Health Psychology, 9,* 653–675.

Becker, J. V., & Abel, G. G. (1981). Behavioral treatment of victims of sexual assault. In S. M. Turner, K. S. Calhoun, & H. E. Adams (Eds.), *Handbook of clinical behavior therapy* (pp. 347–379). New York: Wiley.

Becker, J. V., Abel, G. G., & Skinner, L. J. (1979). The impact of a sexual assault on the victim's sexual life. *Victimology: An International Journal, 4,* 229–235.

Becker, J. V., & Skinner, L. J. (1983). Assessment and treatment of rape-related sexual dysfunctions. *The Clinical Psychologist, 36,* 102–105.

Becker, J. V., & Skinner, L. J. (1984). Behavioral treatment of sexual dysfunctions in sexual assault survivors. In I. Stuart & J. Greer (Eds.), *Victims of sexual aggression* (pp. 211–234). New York: Van Nostrand Reinhold.

Becker, J. V., Skinner, L. J., & Abel, G. G. (1984). Time-limited therapy with sexually dysfunctional sexually assaulted women. *Journal of Social Work and Human Sexuality, 3,* 97–115.

Becker, J. V., Skinner, L. J., Abel, G. G., & Cichon, J. (1986). Level of postassault sexual functioning in rape and incest victims. *Archives of Sexual Behavior, 15,* 37–49.

Becker, J. V., Skinner, L. J., Abel, G. G., & Treacy, E. C. (1982). Incidence and types of sexual dysfunction in rape and incest victims. *Journal of Sex and Marital Therapy, 8,* 65–74.

Beebe, D. K. (1991). Emergency management of the adult female rape victim. *American Family Physician, 43,* 2041–2046.

Belle, D. (1990). Poverty and women's mental health. *American Psychologist, 45,* 385–389.

Belnap, J. (1989). The sexual victimization of unmarried women by nonrelative acquaintances. In M. A. Pirog-Good & J. E. Stets (Eds.), *Violence in dating relationships: Emerging issues* (pp. 205–218). New York: Praeger.

Bem, S. (1993). *The lenses of gender: Transforming the debate on sexual inequality.* New Haven, CN: Yale University Press.

Beneke, T. (1982). *Men who rape.* New York: St. Martin's Press.

Benson, D. J., & Thomson, G. E. (1982). Sexual harassment on a university campus: The confluence of authority relations, sexual interest and gender stratification. *Social Problems, 29,* 236–251.

Berger, R., Searles, P., & Newman, W. (1988). The dimensions of rape reform legislation. *Law and Society Review, 22,* 329–349.

Berkowitz, A. (1992). College men as perpetrators of acquaintance rape and sexual assault: A review of recent research. *Journal of the American College Health Association, 40,* 175–181.

Berkowitz, L. (1973). Simple views of aggression: An essay review. In L. S. Wrightsman & J. C. Brigham (Eds.), *Contemporary issues in social psychology* (2nd ed., pp. 194–201). Monterey, CA: Brooks/Cole.

Berkowitz, L. (1974). Some determinants of impulsive aggression: Role of mediated associations with reinforcements for aggression. *Psychological Review, 82,* 165–176.

Berrill, K. T. (1990). Anti-gay violence and victimization in the United States: An overview. *Journal of Interpersonal Violence, 5,* 274–294.

Betts, N. D., & Newman, G. C. (1982). Defining the issue: Sexual harassment in college and university life. *Contemporary Education, 54,* 48–52.

Beutler, L. E., & Hill, C. E. (1992). Process and outcome research in the treatment of adult victims of childhood sexual abuse: Methodological issues. *Journal of Consulting and Clinical Psychology, 60,* 204–212.

Biaggio, M. K., Watts, D., & Brownell, A. (1990). Addressing sexual harassment: Strategies for prevention and change. In M. Paludi (Ed.), *Ivory power: Sexual harassment on campus.* Albany: State University of New York Press.

Biden, J. R. (1993). Violence against women: The congressional response. *American Psychologist, 48*, 1059–1061.

Biderman, A. D. (1967). Life and death in extreme captivity situations. In M. H. Appley & R. Trumball (Eds.), *Psychological Stress: Issues in Research* (pp. 242–264). New York: Appleton-Century-Crofts.

Biderman, A. D., & Lynch, J. P. (1991). *Understanding crime incidence statistics.* Secaucus, NJ: Springer-Verlag.

Bienen, L. B. (1980). Rape III—National developments in rape reform legislation. *Women's Rights Law Reporter, 6,* 171–213.

Blackman, J. (1989). *Intimate violence: A study of injustice.* New York: Columbia University Press.

Bograd, M. (1984). Family systems approaches to wife battering: A feminist critique. *American Journal of Orthopsychiatry, 54,* 558–568.

Bologna, M. J., Waterman, C. K., & Dawson, L. J. (1987, July). *Violence in gay male and lesbian relationships: Implications for practitioners and policy makers.* Paper presented at the Third National Conference for Family Violence Researchers, Durham, NH.

Bond, M. E. (1988). Division 27 sexual harassment survey: Definition, impact and environmental context. *The Community Psychologist, 21,* 7–10.

Bowker, L. (1979). The criminal victimization of women. *Victimology: An International Journal, 4,* 371–384.

Bowker, L. (1983). *Beating wife-beating.* Lexington, MA: D.C. Heath.

Bowker, L. (1986). *Ending the violence.* Holmes Beach, FL: Learning Publications.

Bownes, I. T., O'Gorman, E. C., & Sayers, A. (1991). Rape—A comparison of stranger and acquaintance assaults. *Medical Science and Law, 31,* 102–107.

Bramel, D., Taub, B., & Blum, B. (1968). An observer's reaction to the suffering of his enemy. *Journal of Personality and Social Psychology, 8,* 384–392.

Braver, S. L., Wolchik, S. A., Sandler, I. N., Sheets, V. L., Fogas, B., & Bay, R. C. (in press). A longitudinal study of non-custodial parents: Parents without children. *Journal of Family Psychology.*

Bravo, E., & Cassedy, E. (1992). *The 9 to 5 guide to combating sexual harassment.* New York: Wiley.

Breslau, N., Davis, G., Andreski, P., & Peterson, E. (1991). Traumatic events and post-traumatic stress disorder in an urban population of young adults. *Archives of General Psychiatry, 48,* 216–222.

Brickman, J., & Briere, J. (1984). Incidence of rape and sexual assault in an urban Canadian population. *International Journal of Women's Studies, 7,* 195–206.

Brief for *amicus curiae*: American Psychological Association in Harris v. Forklift Systems, Inc., 114 S. Ct. 367 (1993).

Briere, J. (1988). Long-term clinical correlates of childhood sexual victimization. *Annals of the New York Academy of Sciences, 528,* 327–334.

Briere, J. (1989). *Therapy for adults molested as children: Beyond survival.* New York: Springer.

Briere, J. (1992). Methodological issues in the study of sexual abuse effects. *Journal of Consulting and Clinical Psychology, 60,* 196–203.

Briere, J., & Malamuth, N. (1983). Self-reported likelihood of sexually aggressive behavior: Attitudinal versus sexual explanations. *Journal of Research in Personality, 17,* 315–323.

Brodyaga, L., Gates, M., Singer, S., Tucker, M., & White, R. (1975). *Rape and its victims: A report for citizens, health facilities and criminal justice agencies.* Washington, DC: National Institute of Law Enforcement and Criminal Justice.

Brooks, L., & Perot, A. R. (1991). Reporting sexual harassment: Exploring a predictive model. *Psychology of Women Quarterly, 15,* 31–47.

Brown, S. E. (1984). Police responses to wife beating: Neglect of a crime of violence. *Journal of Criminal Justice, 12,* 277–288.

Browne, A. (1980, April). *Comparison of victim's reactions across traumas.* Paper presented at the meeting of the Rocky Mountain Psychological Association, Tucson, AZ.

Browne, A. (1987). *When battered women kill.* New York: Macmillan/Free Press.

Browne, A. (1991). The victim's experience: Pathways to disclosure. *Psychotherapy, 28,* 150–156.

Browne, A. (1992). Violence against women: Relevance for medical practitioners. *Journal of the American Medical Association, 267,* 3184–3189.

Browne, A. (1993). Violence against women by male partners: Prevalence, outcomes, and policy implications. *American Psychologist, 48,* 1077–1087.

Browne, A., & Dutton, D. G. (1990). Escape from violence: Risks and alternatives for abused women—What do we currently know? In R. Roesch, D. G. Dutton, & V. F. Sacco (Eds.), *Family violence: Perspectives on treatment, research, and policy* (pp. 65–91). Burnaby, British Columbia, Canada: British Columbia Institute on Family Violence.

Browne, A., & Finkelhor, D. (1986). The impact of child sexual abuse: A review of the research. *Psychological Bulletin, 99,* 66–77.

Browne, A., & Williams, K. R. (1989). Exploring the effect of resource availability and the likelihood of female-perpetrated homicides. *Law and Society Review, 23,* 75–94.

Browne, A., & Williams, K. R. (1993). Gender, intimacy, and lethal violence: Trends from 1976 through 1987. *Gender and Society, 7,* 78–98.

Brush, L. (1990). Violent acts and injurious outcomes in married couples: Methodological issues in the National Survey of Families and Households. *Gender and Society, 4,* 56–67.

Bryer, J. B., Nelson, B. A., Miller, J. B., & Krol, P. A. (1987). Childhood sexual and physical abuse as factors in adult psychiatric illness. *American Journal of Nursing,* 1,153–1,155.

Bullock, L., & McFarlane, J. (1989). The birth weight/battering connection. *American Journal of Nursing, 89,* 1153–1155.

Bunch, C. (1991). *Women's rights as human rights: Toward a re-vision of human rights.* Unpublished manuscript, Rutgers University, Center for Women's Global Leadership.

Bureau of Justice Statistics. (1985, March). *The crime of rape* (NCJ-96777). Washington, DC: U.S. Department of Justice.

Bureau of Justice Statistics. (1989). *Criminal victimization in the United States. 1987.* Washington, DC: U.S. Department of Justice.

Bureau of Justice Statistics. (1992). *Criminal victimization in the United States. 1990.* Washington, DC: U.S. Department of Justice.

Burge, S. K. (1989). Violence against women as a health care issue. *Family Medicine, 21,* 368–373.

Burgess, A. W., & Holmstrom, L. L. (1974). Rape trauma syndrome. *American Journal of Psychiatry, 131,* 981–986.

Burgess, A. W., & Holmstrom, L. L. (1976). Coping behavior of the rape victim. *American Journal of Psychiatry, 133,* 413–418.

Burgess, A. W., & Holmstrom, L. L. (1979a). *Rape: Crisis and recovery.* Bowie, MD: Bardy.

Burgess, A. W., & Holmstrom, L. L. (1979b). Rape: Sexual disruption and recovery. *American Journal of Orthopsychiatry, 49,* 648–657.

Burgess, A. W., & Holmstrom, L. L. (1988). Treating the adult rape victim. *Medical Aspects of Human Sexuality, January,* 36, 38, 42–43.

Burnam, M. A., Stein, J. A., Golding, J. M., Siegel, J. M., Sorenson, S. B., Forsythe,

A. B., & Telles, C. A. (1988). Sexual assault and mental disorders in a community population. *Journal of Consulting and Clinical Psychology, 56*, 843–850.

Burt, M. R. (1979). *Attitudes supportive of rape in American culture*. Rockville, MD: U.S. Department of Health and Human Services.

Burt, M. R. (1980). Cultural myths and supports for rape. *Journal of Personality and Social Psychology, 38*, 217–230.

Burt, M. R. (1991). Rape myths and acquaintance rape. In A. Parrot & L. Bechhofer, (Eds.), *Acquaintance rape: The hidden crime* (pp. 26–40). New York: Wiley.

Burt, M. R., Gornick, J., & Pittman, K. (1984). *Feminism and rape crisis centers*. Washington, DC: Urban Institute.

Burt, M. R., & Katz, B. (1987). Dimensions of recovery from rape: Focus on growth outcomes. *Journal of Interpersonal Violence, 2*, 57–81.

Byington, D. B., Martin, P. Y., DiNitto, D. M., & Maxwell, M. S. (1991). Organizational affiliation and effectiveness: The case of rape crisis centers. *Administration in Social Work, 15*, 83–103.

Caesar, P. L. (1988). Exposure to violence in the families-of-origin among wife abusers and maritally nonviolent men. *Violence and Victims, 2*, 145–156.

Calhoun, K. S., Atkeson, B. M., & Ellis, E. M. (1981). Social adjustment in victims of sexual assault. *Journal of Consulting and Clinical Psychology, 49*, 705–712.

Caputi, J. (1989). The sexual politics of murder. *Gender and Society, 3*, 437–456.

Carmen, E. H., Rieker, P. P., & Mills, T. (1984). Victims of violence and psychiatric illness. *American Journal of Psychiatry, 141*, 378–383.

Caruthers, C., & Crull, P. (1984). Contrasting sexual harassment in female and male-dominated occupations. In K. Brodkin-Sachs & D. Remy (Eds.), *My troubles are going to have trouble with me* (pp. 219–228). New Brunswick, NJ: Rutgers University Press.

Cascardi, M., & O'Leary, K. D. (1992). Depressive symptomatology, self-esteem and self-blame in battered women. *Journal of Family Violence, 7*, 249–259.

Castellow, W. A., Wuenisch, K. L., & Moore, C. H. (1990). Effects of physical attractiveness of the plaintiff and defendant in sexual harassment judgments. *Journal of Social Behavior and Personality, 6*, 547–562.

Cate, R. M., Henton, J. M., Koval, J. F., Christopher, F. S., & Lloyd, S. (1982). Premarital abuse: A social psychological perspective. *Journal of Family Issues, 3*, 79–90.

Cazenave, N. A., & Straus, M. A. (1979). Race, class, network embeddedness and family violence: A search for potent support systems. *Journal of Comparative Family Studies, 10*, 280–300.

Cazenave, N.A., & Straus, M. A. (1990). Race, class network embeddedness, and family violence: A search for potent suppport systems. In M. A. Straus & R. J. Gelles (Eds.), *Physical violence in American families: Risk factors and adaption to violence in 8,145 families.* (pp. 321–339) New Brunswick, NJ: Transaction Publishers.

Centers for Disease Control. (1989). Education about adult violence in U.S. and Canadian medical schools: 1987–1988. *Morbidity and Mortality Weekly Report, 38*, 17–19.

Chapman, D. W. (1962). A brief introduction to contemporary disaster research. In G. W. Baker & D. W. Chapman (Eds.), *Man and society in disaster* (pp. 3–22). New York: Basic.

Chappell, D. (1984). The impact of rape legislation: Some comparative trends. *International Journal of Women's Studies, 7*, 70–80.

Check, J. V. P., & Malamuth, N. M. (1983). Sex role stereotyping and reactions to depictions of stranger versus acquaintance rape. *Journal of Personality and Social Psychology, 45*, 344–356.

Chesler, P. (1986). *Mothers on trial.* Seattle: Seal Press.

Chimbos, P. D. (1978). *Marital violence: A study of interspousal homicide.* San Francisco: R & E Research Associates.

Cimino, J. J., & Dutton, M. A. (1991, August). *Factors influencing the development of PTSD in battered women.* Poster presented at the 99th Annual Convention of the American Psychological Association, San Francisco.

Clayton, E., Murphy, S., Osborne, E. M., Kitchen, V., Smith, J. R., Harris, J. R. W. (1991). Rape and HIV. *International Journal of STD and AIDS, 2*, 200–201.

Cleveland, J., & Kerst, M. W. (1993). Sexual harassment and perceptions of power: An under-articulated relationship. *Journal of Vocational Behavior, 42*, 49–67.

Cluss, P. A., Boughton, J., Frank, E., Stewart, B. D., & West, D. (1983). The rape victims: Psychological correlates of participation in the legal process. *Criminal Justice and Behavior, 10*, 342–357.

Cohen S., & Williamson, G. M. (1991). Stress and infectious disease in humans. *Psychological Bulletin, 109*, 5–24.

Coles, F. S. (1986). Forced to quit: Sexual harassment complaints and agency response. *Sex Roles, 14*, 81–95.

Coley, S. A., & Beckett, J. O. (1988). Black battered women: A review of empirical literature. *Journal of Counseling and Development, 66*, 266–70.

Collins, E. G. C., & Blodgett, T. B. (1981). Sexual harassment: Some see it...some won't. *Harvard Business Review, 59*, 76–95.

Congressional Caucus for Women's Issues. (1991). *Preventing domestic violence against women, 1986. (Report on violence against women).* Washington, DC: U. S. Department of Justice.

Conte, J. (1988). The effects of sexual abuse on children: Results of a research project. *Annals of the New York Academy of Sciences, 528*, 311–326.

Costin, F. (1985). Beliefs about rape and women's social roles. *Archives of Sexual Behavior, 14*, 319–325.

Council on Scientific Affairs (1992). Violence against women: Relevance for medical practitioners. *Journal of the American Medical Association, 267*, 3184–3189.

Court, J. H. (1976). Pornography and sex crimes: A re-evaluation in light of recent trends around the world. *International Journal of Criminology and Penology, 5*, 129–157.

Craig, M. E. (1990). Coercive sexuality in dating relationships: A situational model. *Clinical Psychology Review, 10*, 395–423.

Crull, P. (1982). Stress effects of sexual harassment on the job: Implications for counseling. *American Journal of Orthopsychiatry, 52*, 539–544.

Crull, P. (1984). Sexual harassment and women's health. In W. Chavkin (Ed.), *Double exposure* (pp. 100–120). New York: Monthly Review Press.

Cryer, L., & Beutler, L. (1980). Group therapy: An alternative treatment approach for rape victims. *Journal of Sex and Marital Therapy, 6*, 40–46.

Culbertson, A. L., Rosenfeld, P., Booth-Kewley, S., & Magnusson, P. (1992). *Assessment of sexual harassment in the Navy: Results of the 1989 Navy-wide survey* (Tech. Rep. No. 92-11). San Diego: Naval Personnel Research and Development Center.

Curtis, L. A. (1976). Present and future measures of victimization in forcible rape. In M. J. Walker & S. L. Brodsky (Eds.), *Sexual assault* (pp. 61–68). Lexington, MA: D.C. Heath.

Daly, M., & Wilson, M. (1988). *Homicide.* New York: Aldine de Gruyter.

Daniel, A. E., & Harris, P. W. (1982). Female homicide offenders referred for pre-trial psychiatric examination: A descriptive study. *Bulletin of the American Academy of Psychiatry and Law, 10*, 261.

Darke, J. L. (1990). Sexual aggression. In W. L. Marshall, D. R. Laws, & H. E. Barbaree

(Eds.), *Handbook of sexual assault: Issues, theories, and treatment of the offender* (pp. 55–72). New York: Plenum.

Davidson, L. M., & Baum, A. (1990). Posttraumatic stress in children following natural and human-made trauma. In L. M. Davison & A. Baum (Eds.), *Handbook of developmental psychopathology* (pp. 251–259). New York: Plenum.

Davidson, J. R., & Fairbank, J. A. (1993). The epidemiology of posttraumatic stress disorder. In J. R. Davidson & E. B. Foa (Eds.), *Posttraumatic stress disorder: DSM-IV and beyond* (pp. 147–169). Washington, DC: American Psychiatric Press.

Davidson, J. R., & Foa, E. B. (1991). Diagnostic issues in posttraumatic stress disorder: Considerations for the *DSM-IV*. *Journal of Abnormal Psychology, 100,* 346–355.

Davidson, J. R., & Foa, E. B. (1993). *Posttraumatic Stress Disorder: DSM-IV and beyond*. Washington, D.C.: American Psychiatric Press.

Davis, R. C., Brickman, E., & Baker, T. (1991). Supportive and unsupportive responses of others to rape victims: Effects on concurrent victim adjustment. *American Journal of Community Psychology, 19,* 443–451.

DeFour, D. C. (1989, August). Intersection of racism and sexism in the academy. In M. Paludi (Chair), *Sexual harassment in the academy: Women, sex, and power*. Workshop presented to the 97th Annual Convention of the American Psychological Association, New Orleans.

DeFour, D. C. (1990). The interface of racism and sexism on college campuses. In M. Paludi (Ed.), *Ivory power: Sexual harassment of campus* (pp. 45–52). Albany: State University of New York Press.

D'Ercole, A., & Struening, E. (1990). Victimization among homeless women: Implications for service delivery. *Journal of Community Psychology, 18,* 141–152.

Dietz, P. E. (1978). Social factors in rapist behavior. In R. J. Rada (Ed.), *Clinical aspects of the rapist*. New York: Grune & Stratton.

Dietz, S. R., Blackwell, K. T., Daley, P. C., & Bentley, B. J. (1982). Measurement of empathy toward rape victims and rapists. *Journal of Personality and Social Psychology, 43,* 372–384.

DiTomaso, N. (1989). Sexuality in the workplace: Discrimination and harassment. In J. Hearn, D. L. Sheppard, P. Tancred-Sheriff, & G. Burrell (Eds.), *The sexuality of organizations* (pp. 71–90). London: Sage.

Dobash, R. E., & Dobash, R. (1978). Wives: The "appropriate" victims of marital violence. *Victimology, 2,* 426–442.

Dobash, R. E., & Dobash, R. (1979). *Violence against wives.* New York: Free Press.

Dolkart, J. L. (1992, March). *Working paper on legal reform in the area of sexual harassment: Procedural and evidentiary reform.* Paper presented at the First National Conference on Sex and Power Issues in the Workplace, Bellevue, WA.

Domino, J. V., & Haber, J. D. (1987). Prior physical and sexual abuse in women with chronic headache: Clinical correlates. *Headache, 27,* 310–314.

Doyle, R. (1993, June). No-phone homes. *The Atlantic Monthly,* p. 77.

Draucker, C. B. (1989). Cognitive adaptation of female incest survivors. *Journal of Consulting and Clinical Psychology, 57,* 668–670.

Drossman, D. A., Lesserman, J., Nachman, G., Li, Z., Gluck, H., Toomey, T. C., & Mitchell, M. (1990). Sexual and physical abuse in women with functional or organic gastrointestinal disorders. *Annals of Internal Medicine, 113,* 828–833.

Dunwoody-Miller, V., & Gutek, B. A. (1985). *S.H.E. Project Report: Sexual harassment in the state workforce: Results of a survey.* Sacramento: Sexual Harassment in Employment Project of the California Commission on the Status of Women.

Duran, E., Guillory, B., & Tingley, P. *Domestic violence in Native American communities: The effects of intergenerational posttraumatic stress.* Unpublished manuscript.

Dutton, D. G. (1987). The criminal justice response to wife assault. *Law and Human Behavior, 2,* 189–206.

Dutton, D. G. (1988a). Profiling of wife assaulters: Preliminary evidence for a trimodal analysis. *Violence and Victims, 3,* 5–29.

Dutton, D. G. (1988b). *The domestic assault of women: Psychological and criminal justice perspectives.* Boston, MA: Allyn and Bacon.

Dutton, D. G., & Browning, J. J. (1987). Power struggles and intimacy anxieties as causative factors of violence in intimate relationships. In G. Russell (Ed.), *Violence in intimate relationships* (pp. 163–175). New York: Sage.

Dutton, D. G., & Browning, J. J. (1988). Concern for power, fear of intimacy, and aversive stimuli for wife assault. In G. T. Hotaling, D. Finkelhor, J. T. Kirkpatrick, & M. Straus (Eds.), *Family abuse and its consequences: New directions in family violence research* (pp. 163–175). Beverly Hills, CA: Sage.

Dutton, M. A. (1992a). *Empowering and healing the battered woman: A model for assessment and intervention.* New York: Springer.

Dutton, M. A. (1992b). Assessment and treatment of PTSD among battered women. In D. Foy (Ed.), *Treating PTSD: Cognitive and behavioral strategies* (pp. 69–98). New York: Guilford.

Dutton, M. A. (1994). *Understanding women's response to domestic violence: A redefinition of Battered Woman's Syndrome.* Hempstead, NY: Hofstra Law Review.

Dziech, B. W., & Weiner, L. (1990). *The lecherous professor: A study in power relations* (2nd ed.). Champaign, IL: University of Illinois Press.

Ehrhart, J., & Sandler, B. (1985). *Campus gang rape: Party games?* Washington, DC: Association of American Colleges.

Eichler, A., & Parron, D. L. (1987). *Women's mental health agenda for research.* Rockville, MD: National Institute of Mental Health.

Eigenberg, H. M. (1990). The National Crime Survey and Rape: The case of the missing question. *Justice Quarterly, 7,* 655–671.

Elbow, M. (1977). Theoretical considerations of violent marriages. *Social Casework, 58,* 515–526.

Elliott, D. S., Huizinga, D., & Morse, B. J. (1986). Self-reported violent offending: A descriptive analysis of juvenile offenders and their offending careers. *Journal of Interpersonal Violence, 1,* 472–514.

Ellis, E. M. (1983). A review of empirical rape research: Victim reactions and response to treatment. *Clinical Psychology Review, 3,* 473–490.

Ellis, E. M., Atkeson, B. M., & Calhoun, K. S. (1981). An assessment of long-term reactions to rape. *Journal of Abnormal Psychology, 90,* 263–266.

Ellis, E. M., Calhoun, K. S., & Atkeson, B. M. (1980). Sexual dysfunctions in victims of rape: Victims may experience a loss of sexual arousal and frightening flashbacks even one year after the assault. *Women and Health, 5,* 39–47.

Ellis, L. (1989). *Theories of rape: Inquiries into the causes of sexual aggression.* New York: Hemisphere.

Ellis, L. (1991). A synthesized (biosocial) theory of rape. *Journal of Consulting and Clinical Psychology, 59,* 631–642.

Ellison v. Brady, 924 F.2d 872 (9th Cir. 1991).

Essock-Vitale, S. M., & McGuire, M. T. (1985). Women's lives viewed from an evolutionary perspective: Part I. Sexual histories, reproductive success, and demographic characteristics of a random sample of American women. *Ethology and Sociobiology, 6,* 137–154.

Estrich, S. (1987). *Real rape.* Cambridge, MA: Harvard University Press.

Evans, H. I. (1978). Psychotherapy for the rape victim: Some treatment models. *Hospital and Community Psychiatry, 29,* 309–312.

Fagan, J., & Browne, A. (in press). Marital violence: Physical aggression between women and men in intimate relationships. In A. Reiss, Jr. & J. Roth (Eds.), *Understanding and preventing violence: Vol. 3. Social influences*. Washington, DC: National Academy of Sciences.

Fagan, J., Friedman, E., Wexler, S., & Lewis, V. (1984). *The national family violence evaluation: Final report, Vol. 1. Analytical findings*. San Francisco: URSA Institute.

Fagan, J. A., Stewart, D. K., & Hansen, K. V. (1983). Violent men or violent husbands? Background factors and situational correlates. In D. Finkelhor, R. J. Gelles, G. T. Hotaling, & M. A. Straus (Eds.), *The dark side of families* (pp. 49–67). Beverly Hills, CA: Sage.

Fain, T. C., & Anderson, D. L. (1987). Organizational context and diffuse status. *Sex Roles, 17*, 291–311.

Fairbanks, J. A., & Nicholson, R. A. (1987). Theoretical and empirical issues in the treatment of posttraumatic stress disorder. *Journal of Clinical Psychology, 43*, 44–45.

Family Violence Project (1990). *Family violence: Improving court practice*. Reno, NV: Recommendations from the National Council of Juvenile and Family Court Judges.

Farley, L. (1978). *Sexual shakedown: The sexual harassment of women on the job*. New York: McGraw-Hill.

Federal Bureau of Investigation (1982). *Uniform crime reports*. Washington, DC: U.S. Department of Justice.

Federal Bureau of Investigation (1991). *Uniform crime reports*. Washington, DC: U.S. Department of Justice.

Feldman-Summers, S., Gordon, P. E., & Meagher, J. F. (1979). The impact of rape on sexual satisfaction. *Journal of Abnormal Psychology, 88*, 101–105.

Fellitti, V. J. (1991). Long-term medical consequences of incest, rape, and molestation. *Southern Medical Journal, 84*, 328–331.

Field, H. S. (1978). Attitudes toward rape: A comparative analysis of police, rapists, crisis counselors, and citizens. *Journal of Personality and Social Psychology, 36*, 156–179.

Field, M. H., & Field, H. F. (1973). Marital violence and the criminal process: Neither justice nor peace. *Social Service Review, 47*, 221–240.

Figley, C. R. (Ed.). (1985). *Trauma and its wake: The study and treatment of post-traumatic stress disorder*. New York: Brunner/Mazel.

Fine, M. (1984). Coping with rape: Critical perspectives on consciousness. *Imagination, Cognition, and Personality, 3*, 249–267.

Fine, M. (1989). The politics of research and activism. *Gender and Society, 3*, 549–558.

Finkelhor, D., & Browne, A. (1985). The traumatic impact of child sexual abuse: A conceptualization. *American Journal of Orthopsychiatry, 55*, 530–541.

Finkelhor, D., & Yllö, K. (1983). Rape in marriage: A sociological view. In D. Finkelhor, R. J. Gelles, G. T. Hotaling, & M. A. Straus (Eds.), *The dark side of families*. Beverly Hills, CA: Sage.

Finkelhor, D., & Yllö, K. (1985). *License to rape: Sexual abuse of wives*. New York: Holt, Rinehart, & Winston.

Finn, P., & Colson, S. (1990). *Civil protection orders: Legislation current court practice, and enforcement, 33*, National Institute of Justice.

Fiora-Gormally, N. (1978). Battered wives who kill: Double standard out of court, single standard in? *Law and Behavior, 2*, 133–165.

Fischer, C. T., & Wertz, F. J. (1979). Empirical phenomenological analyses of being criminally victimized. In A. Giorgi, R. Knowles, & D. L. Smith (Eds.), *Duquesne studies in phenomenological psychology* (Vol. 3, pp. 135–158). Pittsburgh: Duquesne University Press.

Fiske, S. T., & Borgida, E. (in press). Sexual harassment. *Journal of Social Issues*.

Fitzgerald, L. F. (1990). Sexual harassment: The definition and measurement of a construct. In M. Paludi (Ed.), *Ivory power: Sexual harassment on campus* (pp. 21–44). Albany, NY: State University of New York Press.

Fitzgerald, L. F. (1992). *Sexual harassment in higher education: Concepts and issues*. Washington, DC: National Education Association.

Fitzgerald, L. F. (1993a). *The last great open secret: The sexual harassment of women in the workplace and academia*. Washington, DC: Federation of Behavioral, Psychological and Cognitive Sciences.

Fitzgerald, L. F. (1993b). *Sexual harassment in organizations*. Washington, DC: American Society of Association Executives.

Fitzgerald, L. F. (1993c). Sexual harassment: Violence against women in the workplace. *American Psychologist, 48*, 1070–1076.

Fitzgerald, L. F. (1994, April). *Measuring sexual harassment: Theoretical and psychometric advances*. Paper presented at the Ninth Annual Conference of the Society for Industrial/Organizational Psychology, Nashville, TN.

Fitzgerald, L. F., Gold, Y., Brock, K., & Gelfand, M. (1993). *Women's responses to victimization: Validation of an objective inventory for assessing strategies for responding to sexual harassment*. Unpublished manuscript.

Fitzgerald, L. F., & Hesson-McInnis, M. (1989). The dimensions of sexual harassment: A structural analysis. *Journal of Vocational Behavior, 35*, 309–326.

Fitzgerald, L. F., Hulin, C., & Drasgow, F. (1992, November). *Predicting outcomes of sexual harassment: An integrated process model.* Paper presented at the 2nd APA/NIOSH Conference of Stress and the Workplace. Washington, DC.

Fitzgerald, L. F., & Ormerod, A. J. (1991). Perceptions of sexual harassment: The influence of gender and context. *Psychology of Women Quarterly, 15*, 281–294.

Fitzgerald, L. F., & Ormerod, A. J. (1993). Breaking silence: The sexual harassment of women in academia and the workplace. In F. I. Denmark & M. A. Paludi (Eds.), *Psychology of Women: A handbook of issues and theories* (pp. 553–582). Westport, CT: Greenwood Press.

Fitzgerald, L. F., & Shullman, S. L. (1993). Sexual harassment: A research analysis and agenda for the 1990's. *Journal of Vocational Behavior, 42*, 5–27.

Fitzgerald, L. F., Shullman, S. L., Bailey, N., Richards, M., Swecker, J., Gold, A., Ormerod, A. J., & Weitzman, L. (1988). The incidence and dimensions of sexual harassment in academia and the workplace. *Journal of Vocational Behavior, 32*, 152–175.

Fitzgerald, L. F., Swan, S., & Fisher, K. (in press). The illusion of the appropriate response: The psychological and legal context of women's strategies for responding to sexual harassment. *Journal of Social Issues.*

Fitzgerald, L. F., Weitzman, L., Gold, Y., & Ormerod, A. J. (1988). Academic harassment: Sex and denial in scholarly garb. *Psychology of Women Quarterly, 12*, 329–340.

Flannery, R. B., & Harvey, M. R. (1991). Psychological trauma and learned helplessness: Seligman's paradigm reconsidered. *Psychotherapy, 28*, 374–378.

Fleming, J. B. (1979). *Stopping wife abuse: A guide to the emotional, psychological, and legal implications for the abused woman and those helping her.* Garden City, NY: Anchor Press.

Foa, E. B., & Kozak, M. J. (1986). Emotional processing of fear: Exposure to corrective information. *Psychological Bulletin, 99*, 20–35.

Foa, E. B., Rothbaum, B. O., & Kozak, M. J. (1989). Behavioral treatments for anxiety and depression. In P. Kendall & D. Watson (Eds.), *Anxiety and depression: Distinctive and operlapping features* (pp. 413–454). New York: Academic Press.

Foa, E. B., Rothbaum, B. O., & Steketee, G. (1987). Treatment of rape victims. *Journal of Interpersonal Violence, 8*, 256–276.

Foa, E. B., Rothbaum, B. O., Riggs, D. S., & Murdock, T. B. (1991). Treatment of post-traumatic stress disorder in rape victims: A comparison between cognitive–behavioral procedures and counseling. *Journal of Consulting and Clinical Psychology, 59*, 715–723.

Foa, E. B., Steketee, G., Rothbaum, B., & Olasov, B. (1989). Behavioral–cognitive conceptualization of posttraumatic stress disorder. *Behavior Therapy, 20*, 155–176.

Foa, F. B., Zinbarg, R., & Rothbaum, B. O. (1992). Uncontrollability and unpredictability in posttraumatic stress disorder: Experimental evidence. *Psychological Bulletin, 112*, 218–238.

Follingstad, D. R., Brennan, A. F., Hause, E. S., Polek, D. S., & Rutledge, L. L. (1991). Factors moderating physical and psychological symptoms of battered women. *Journal of Family Violence, 6*, 81–95.

Fonow, M. M., Richardson, L., & Wemmerus, V. A. (1992). Feminist rape education: Does it work?, *Gender and Society, 6*, 109–21.

Forman, B. (1980). Psychotherapy with rape victims. *Psychoterapy: Theory, Research, and Practice, 17*, 304–311.

Forster, G. E., Estrich, S., & Hooi, Y. S. (1991). Screening for STDs [Letter to the editor]. *Annals of Emergency Medicine, 324*, 161–162.

Fortune, M. M. (1983). *Sexual violence: The unmentionable sin.* New York: Pilgrim Press.

Fox, S. S., & Scherl, D. J. (1972). Crisis intervention with victims of rape. *Social Work, 17*, 37–42.

Frank, E., & Anderson, B. P. (1987). Psychiatric disorders in rape victims: Past history and current symptomatology. *Comprehensive Psychiatry, 28*, 77–82.

Frank, E., & Stewart, B. D. (1983). Treating depression in victims of rape. *The Clinical Psychologist, 36*, 95–98.

Frank, E., & Stewart, B. D. (1984). Depressive symptoms in rape victims: A revisit. *Journal of Affective Disorders, 7*, 77–85.

Frank, E., Turner, S. M., & Duffy, B. (1979). Depressive symptoms in rape victims. *Journal of Affective Disorders, 1*, 269–277.

Frank, E., Turner, S. M., & Stewart, B. D. (1980). Initial response to rape: The impact of factors within the rape situation. *Journal of Behavioral Assessment, 2*, 39–53.

Frank, E., Turner, S. M., Stewart, B. D., Jacob, J., & West, D. (1981). Past psychiatric symptoms and the response to sexual assault. *Comprehensive Psychiatry, 22*, 479–487.

Frank, E., Anderson, B., Stewart, B. D., Dancu, C., Hughes, C., & West, D. (1988). Efficacy of cognitive behavior therapy and systematic desensitization in the treatment of rape trauma. *Behavior Therapy, 19,* 403–420.

Franklin v. Gwinnett County School District, 112 S.Ct. 1028 (1992).

Frazier, P. A. (1990). Victim attributions and post-rape trauma. *Journal of Personality and Social Psychology, 59,* 298–304.

Frazier, P. A., & Borgida, E. (1985). Rape trauma syndrome evidence in court. *American Psychologist, 40,* 984–993.

Frazier, P. A., & Borgida, E. (in press). Rape trauma syndrome: A review of case law and psychological research. *Law and Human Behavior.*

Frazier, P. A., & Schauben, L. (in press). Causal attributions and recovery from rape and other stressful life events. *Journal of Social and Clinical Psychology.*

Freud, S. (1955). Beyond the pleasure principle. In J. Strachey (Ed. and Trans.), *The standard edition of the complete psychological works: Vol. 18.* London: Hogarth Press. (Original work published 1922)

Friedrich, W. N., Beilke, R. L., & Urquiza, A. J. (1988). Behavior problems in young sexually abused boys. *Journal of Interpersonal Violence, 3,* 1–12.

Frieze, I. H. (1983). Investigating the causes and consequences of marital rape. *Signs, 8,* 532–553.

Frieze, I. H., & Browne, A. (1989). The incidence and prevalence of violence in marriage. In L. Ohlin & M. H. Tonry (Eds.), *Crime and justice—A review of research: Vol. 11. Family Violence* (pp. 163–218). Chicago: University of Chicago Press.

Frieze, I. H., Hymer, S., & Greenberg, M. S. (1987). Describing the crime victim. Psychological reactions to victimization. *Professional Psychology, 18,* 299–315.

Frieze, I. H., Knoble, J., Washburn, C., & Zomnir, G. (1980, March). *Types of Battered Women.* Paper presented at the meeting of the Annual Research Conference of the Association for Women in Psychology, Santa Monica, CA.

Fritz, N. R. (1989). Sexual harassment and the working woman. *Personnel, 66,* 4–8.

Galvin, H. (1986). Shielding rape victims in the state and federal courts: A proposal for the second decade. *Minnesota Law Review, 70,* 763–916.

Garnets, L., Herek, G. M., & Levy, B. (1990). Violence and victimizations of lesbians and gay men: Mental health consequences. *Journal of Interpersonal Violence, 5,* 366–383.

Gaquin, D. A. (1977–1978). Spouse abuse: Data from the National Crime Survey. *Victimology, 2,* 632–643.

Geen, R. G., Stonner, D., & Shope, G. L. (1975). The facilitation of aggression by aggression. Evidence against the catharsis hypothesis. *Journal of Personality and Social Psychology, 31*, 721–726.

Geist, R. F. (1988). Sexually related trauma. *Emergency Medical Clinics of North America, 6*, 439–466.

Gelfand, M., Fitzgerald, L. F., & Drasgrow, F. (1993). *The latent structure of sexual harassment: A cross-cultural confirmatory analysis.* Unpublished manuscript, Department of Psychology, University of Illinois, Champaign.

Gelinas, D. (1983). The persisting negative effects of incest. *Psychiatry, 46*, 312–332.

Gellen, M. I., Hoffman, R. A., Jones, M., & Stone, M. (1984). Abused and nonabused women: MMPI profile differences. *Personnel and Guidance Journal, 62*, 601–604.

Gelles, R. J. (1976). Abused wives: Why do they stay? *Journal of Marriage and the Family, 38*, 659–668.

Gelles, R. J. (1980). Violence in the family: A review of research in the seventies. *Journal of Marriage and the Family, 42*, 873–885.

Gelles, R. J. (1988). Violence and pregnancy: Are pregnant women at greater risk of abuse? *Journal of Marriage and the Family, 50*, 841–847.

Gelles, R. J., & Harrop, J. W. (1989). Violence, battering, and psychological distress among women. *Journal of Interpersonal Violence, 4*, 400–420.

Gelles, R. J., & Straus, M. A. (1988). *Intimate violence.* New York: Simon and Schuster.

George, L. K., & Winfield-Laird, I. (1986). *Sexual assault: Prevalence and mental health consequences.* A final report to the National Institute of Mental Health for supplemental funding to the Duke University Epidemiologic Catchment Area Program.

George, L. K., Winfield, I., & Blazer, D. G. (1992). Sociocultural factors in sexual assault: Comparison of two representative samples of women. *Journal of Social Issues, 48*, 105–126.

George, W. H., & Marlatt, G. A. (1986). The effects of alcohol and anger on interest in violence, erotica, and deviance. *Journal of Abnormal Psychology, 95*, 150–158.

Gershman, L. (1991). Enhancement of physicians treatment of illness by behavior therapy. *Journal of Behavioral Therapy and Experimental Psychiatry, 22*, 103–112.

Gidycz, C. A., & Koss, M. A. (1991). Predictors of long-term sexual assault trauma among a national sample of victimized college women. *Violence and Victims, 6*, 175–190.

Gilbert, B. J., Heesacker, M., & Gannon, L. J. (1991). Changing the sexual aggression–supportive attitudes of men: A psychoeducational intervention. *Journal of Counseling Psychology, 38*, 197–203.

Gillespie, C. (1989). *Justifiable homicide: Battered women, self-defense, and the law.* Columbus: Ohio State University Press.

Girelli, S. A, Resick, P. A., Marhoefer-Dvorak, S., & Hutter, C. K. (1986). Subjective distress and violence during rape: Their effects on long-term fear. *Violence and Victims, 1*, 35–45.

Glaser, R. D., & Thorpe, J. S. (1986). Unethical intimacy: A survey of contact and advances between psychology educators and female graduate students. *American Psychologist, 41*, 43–51.

Gold, Y. (1987, August). *The sexualization of the workplace: Sexual harassment of pink, white and blue collar workers.* Paper presented to the 95th Annual Conference of the American Psychological Association, New York.

Goldberg-Ambrose, C. (1992). Unfinished business in rape law reform. *Journal of Social Issues, 48*, 173–186.

Golding, J. M., Siegel, J. M., Sorenson, S. B., Burnam, M. A., & Stein, J. A. (1989). Social support sources following sexual assault. *Journal of Community Psychology, 17*, 92–107.

Golding, J. M., Stein, J. A., Siegal, J. M., Burnam, M. A., & Sorenson, S. B. (1988). Sexual assault history and use of health and mental health services. *American Journal of Community Psychology, 16*, 625–644.

Goldsmith, H. T. (1990). Men who abuse their spouses: An approach to assessing future risk. In N. J. Pallone & S. Chaneles (Eds.), *Clinical treatment of the clinical offender* (pp. 45–46). New York: Haworth Press.

Goldstein, J. H., Davis, R. W., & Herman, D. (1975). Escalation of aggression: Experimental studies. *Journal of Personality and Social Psychology, 31*, 162–170.

Goldstein, J. H., Davis, R. W., Kerns, M., & Cohn, E. S. (1981). Retarding the escalation of agression. *Social Behavior and Personality, 9*, 65–70.

Gondolf, E. W. (1988). Who are these guys? Toward a behavioral typology of batterers. *Violence and Victims, 3*, 187–203.

Gondolf, E. W. (1990). *Psychiatric responses to family violence: Identifying and confronting neglected danger.* Lexington, MA: Lexington Books.

Gondolf, E. W., Fisher, E., & McFerron, J. R. (1988). Racial differences among shelter residents: A comparison of Anglo, Black, and Hispanic battered women. *Journal of Family Violence, 3*, 39–51.

Goodchilds, J., & Zellman, G. (1984). Sexual signaling and sexual aggression in adolescent relationships. In N. Malamuth & E. Donnerstein (Eds.), *Pornography and sexual aggression* (pp. 233–243). New York: Academic Press.

Goodchilds, J., Zellman, G., Johnson, P. B., & Giarrusso, R. (1988). Adolescents and their perceptions of sexual interactions. In A. W. Burgess (Ed.), *Rape and sexual assault* (Vol. 2, pp. 245–270). New York: Garland.

Goodman, L. A.(1991). The prevalence of abuse among homeless and housed poor mothers: A comparison study. *American Journal of Orthopsychiatry, 61,* 163–169.

Goodman, L. A., Koss, M. P., Fitzgerald, L. F., Russo, N. F., & Keita, G. P. (1993). Male violence against women: Current research and future directions. *American Psychologist, 48,* 1054–1058.

Goodman, L. A., Koss, M. P., & Russo, N. F. (1993a). Violence against women: Physical and mental health effects: Part 1. Research findings. *Applied and Preventive Psychology, 2,* 79–89.

Goodman, L. A., Koss, M. P., & Russo, N. F. (1993b). Violence against women: Mental health effects: Part 2. Conceptualizations of posttraumatic stress. *Applied and Preventive Psychology, 2,* 123–130.

Gordon, M. T., & Riger, S. (1989). *The female fear.* New York: Free Press.

Gornick, J., Burt, M., & Pittman, K. (1983). *Structure and activities of rape crisis centers in the early 1980s.* Washington, D.C.: The Urban Institute.

Grauerholz, E., & Koralewski, M. A. (1991). *Sexual coercion: A sourcebook on its nature, causes, and prevention.* Lexington, MA: D. C. Heath.

Greenblatt, C. S. (1985). Don't hit your wife. . . unless: Preliminary findings on normative support for the use of physical force by husbands. *Victimology, 10,* 221–241.

Greendlinger, V., & Byrne, D. (1987). Coercive sexual fantasies of college men as predictors of self-reported likelihood to rape and overt sexual aggression. *Journal of Sex Research, 23,* 1–11.

Grieco, A. (1987). Scope and nature of sexual harassment in nursing. *Journal of Sex Research, 23,* 261–266.

Groth, A. N., & Birnbaum, A. H. (1979). *Men who rape: The psychology of the offender.* New York: Plenum.

Gruber, J. E. (1992, March). *The sexual harassment experiences of women in nontraditional jobs: Results from cross-national research.* Paper presented at the First National Conference on Sex and Power Issues in the Workplace, Bellevue, WA.

Gruber, J. E., & Bjorn, L. (1982). Blue-collar blues: The sexual harassment of women autoworkers. *Work and Occupations, 9,* 271–298.

Gruber, J. E., & Bjorn, L. (1986). Women's responses to sexual harassment: An analysis of sociocultural, organizational, and personal resource models. *Social Science Quarterly, 67*, 814–826.

Guralnik, D. B. (Ed.). (1984). *Webster's New World Dictionary of the American Language*. New York: New American Library.

Gutek, B. (1985). *Sex and the workplace*. San Francisco: Jossey-Bass.

Gutek, B., & Cohen, A. G. (1987). Sex ratios, sex role spillover, and sex at work: A comparison of men's and women's experiences. *Human Relations, 40*, 97–115.

Gutek, B., & Dunwoody, V. (1988). Understanding sex and the workplace. In A. H. Stromberg, L. Larwood, & B. A. Gutek (Eds.), *Women and work: An annual review* (Vol. 2, pp. 249–269). Newbury Park, CA: Sage.

Gutek, B., & Koss, M. P. (1993). Changed women and changed organizations: Consequences of and coping with sexual harassment. *Journal of Vocational Behavior, 42*, 28–48.

Gutek, B., & Morasch, B. (1982). Sex ratios, sex role spillover, and sexual harassment of women at work. *Journal of Social Issues, 38*, 55–74.

Gutek, B., Morasch, B., & Cohen, A. (1983). Interpreting social–sexual behavior in a work setting. *Journal of Vocational Behavior, 22*, 30–48.

Gutierres, S. E., Russo, N. F., & Urbanski, L. (in press). Sociocultural and psychological factors in American Indian drug use: Implications for treatment. *International Journal of the Addictions*.

Gutierres, S. E., Urbanski, L., & Russo, N. F. (1992, April). Gender differences in Native American Drug Treatment Populations. Paper presented at the annual meeting of the Rocky Mountain Psychological Association, Boise, ID.

Haber, J. D., & Roos, C. (1985a). Traumatic events in chronic pain patients. *Western Journal of Nursing Research, 7*, 1–2.

Haber, J. D., & Roos, C. (1985b). Effects of spouse and/or sexual abuse in the development and maintenance of chronic pain in women. In H. L. Fields, R. Dubner, & F. Cervero (Eds.), *Advances in pain research and therapy* (Vol. 9, pp. 889–895). New York: Raven Press.

Hall, E. R., & Flannery, P. J. (1984). Prevalence and correlates of sexual assault experiences in adolescents. *Victimology, 9*, 398–406.

Hall, E. R., Howard, J. A., & Boezio, S. L. (1986). Tolerance of rape: A sexist or antisocial attitude? *Psychology of Women Quarterly, 10*, 101–108.

Hall, G. C. N. (1990). Prediction of sexual aggression. *Clinical Psychology Review, 10*, 229–245.

Hall, G. C. N., & Hirschman, R. (1991). Toward a theory of sexual aggression: A quadripartite model. *Journal of Consulting and Clinical Psychology, 59*, 662–669.

Hamberger, L. K., & Hastings, J. E. (1986). Personality correlates of men who abuse their partners: A cross-validation study. *Journal of Family Violence, 1*, 323–341.

Hamberger, L. K., & Hastings, J. E. (1991). Personality correlates of men who batter and nonviolent men: Some continuities and discontinuities. *Journal of Family Violence, 6*, 131–147.

Hamberger, L. K., Saunders, D. G., & Hovey, M. (1992). The prevalence of domestic violence in community practice and rate of physician inquiry. *Family Medicine, 24*, 283–287.

Hamilton, J. A., Alagna, S. W., King, L. S., & Lloyd, C. (1987). The emotional consequences of gender-based abuse in the workplace: New counseling programs for sex discrimination. In M. Braude (Ed.), *Women, power and therapy.* New York: Haworth Press.

Hamilton, J. A., & Dolkart, J. (1992, March). *Working paper on legal reform in the area of sexual harassment: Contributions from social science.* Paper presented at the First National Conference on Sex and Power Issues in the Workplace, Bellevue, WA.

Hanson, R. K. (1990). The psychological impact of sexual assault on women and children: A review. *Annals of Sex Research, 3*, 187–232.

Harris v. Forklift Systems, Inc., 114 S. Ct. 367 (1993).

Harrop-Griffiths, J., Katon, W., Walker, E., Holm, L., Russo, J., & Hickok, L. (1988). The association between chronic pelvic pain, psychiatric diagnosis, and childhood sexual abuse. *Obstetrics and Gynecology, 71*, 589–596.

Hart, B. (1986). Lesbian battering: An examination. In K. Lorbel (Ed.), *Naming the violence: Speaking out about lesbian battering* (pp. 173–189). Seattle: Seal Press.

Hartnett, J. J., Robinson, D., & Singh, B. (1989). Perceptions of males and females toward sexual harassment and acquiesence. *Journal of Social Behavior and Personality, 4*, 291–298.

Harvey, M. R. (1985). *Exemplary rape crisis program: Cross-site analysis and case studies.* Washington, DC: National Center for the Prevention and Control of Rape.

Harvey, M. R., & Herman, J. (1992). The trauma of sexual victimization: Feminist contributions to theory, research and practice. *PTSD Research Quarterly, 3*, 1–7.

Harvey, W. B. (1986). Homicide among young black adults: Life in the subculture of exasperation. In D. F. Hawkins (Ed.), *Homicide among Black Americans* (pp. 153–171). Lanham, MD: University Press of America.

Hasanovich, E. (1918). *One of them.* Boston: Houghton Press.

Hastings, J. E., & Hamberger, L. K. (1986). Personality characteristics of spouse abusers: A controlled comparison. *Violence and Victims, 3*(3), 31–48.

Hawkins, D. F. (1986). *Homicide among Black Americans.* Lanham, MD: University Press of America.

Hawkins, D. F. (1987). Devalued lives and racial stereotypes: Ideological barriers to the prevention of family violence among blacks. In R. L. Hampton (Ed.), *Violence in the Black Family: Correlates and Consequences* (pp. 189–205). Lexington, MA: Lexington Books.

Haynes, S. N., & Mooney, D. K. (1975). Nightmares: Etiological, theoretical and behavioral treatment considerations. *Psychological Record, 25,* 225–236.

Health Care Systems Committee of Tulsa, Oklahoma. (1984). *Adult abuse and neglect: Handbook for medical personnel.* Tulsa, OK: Health Care Systems Committee.

Heise, L., & Chapman, J. R. (1992). Reflections on a movement: The U.S. battle against women abuse. In M. Schuler (Ed.), *Freedom from violence: Women's strategies around the world* (pp. 259–296). Washington, DC: OEF International.

Helton, A., McFarlane, J., & Anderson, E. (1987a). Battered and pregnant: A prevalence study. *American Journal of Public Health, 77,* 1337–1339.

Helton, A., McFarlane, J., & Anderson, E. (1987b). Prevention of battering during pregnancy: Focus on behavioral change. *Public Health Nursing, 4,* 166–174.

Hendricks-Matthews, M. K. (1991). The importance of assessing a woman's history of sexual abuse before hysterectomy. *Journal of Family Practice, 32,* 631–632.

Henton, J. M., Cate, R. M., Koval, J. F., Lloyd, S., & Christopher, F. S. (1983). Romance and violence in dating relationships. *Journal of Family Issues, 4,* 467–482.

Herek, G. M. (1986). On heterosexual masculinity: Some psychical consequences of the social construction of gender and sexuality. *American Behavioral Scientist, 29,* 563–577.

Herman, J. L. (1986). Histories of violence in an outpatient population: An exploratory study. *American Journal of Orthopsychiatry, 56,* 137–141.

Herman, J. L. (1992). *Trauma and recovery.* New York: Basic Books.

Herman, J. L. (1993). Sequelae of prolonged and repeated trauma: Evidence for a complex posttraumatic syndrome. In R. T. Davidson & E. B. Foa (Eds.), *Posttraumatic stress disorder: DSM-IV and beyond* (pp. 213–229). Washington, DC: American Psychiatric Press.

Hesson-McInnis, M., & Fitzgerald, L. F. (1992). *Sexual harassment: A preliminary test of an integrative model.* Manuscript submitted for publication.

Hicks, D. J. (1988, November). The patient who's been raped. *Emergency Medicine,* pp. 106–122.

Hicks, D. J. (1990). Sexual battery: Management of the patient who has been raped. In J. J. Sierra (Ed.), *Gynecology and Obstetrics* (Vol. 6, pp. 1–11).

Hilberman, E. (1980). Overview: The "wife-beater's wife" reconsidered. *American Journal of Psychiatry, 137,* 1336–1347.

Hilberman, E., & Munson, K. (1978). Sixty battered women. *Victimology: An International Journal, 2,* 460–470.

Hill, H. (1992, March). *Working with an emotionally distressed client.* Paper presented at the First National Conference on Sex and Power Issues in the Workplace, Bellevue, WA.

Hindelang, M. J., & Davis, B. J. (1977). Forcible rape in the United States: A statistical profile. In D. Chappel, R. Geis, & G. Geis (Eds.), *Forcible rape: The crime, the victim, and the offender* (pp. 87–114). New York: Columbia University Press.

Ho, C. K. (1990). An analysis of domestic violence in Asian–American communities: A multicultural approach to counseling. In L. S. Brown & M. P. P. Root (Eds.), *Diversity and complexity in feminist therapy* (pp. 129–150). New York: Haworth Press.

Hochbaum, S. R. (1987). The evaluation and treatment of the sexually assaulted patient. *Obstetric and Gynecologic Emergencies, 5,* 601–621.

Hoffman, F. (1986). Sexual harassment in academia: Feminist theory and institutional practice. *Harvard Educational Review, 56,* 105–121.

Hogbacka, R., Kandolin, I., Haavio-Mannila, E., & Kauppinen-Toropainen, K. (1987). *Sexual harassment in the workplace: Result of a survey of Finns* (Ministry of Social Affairs and Health, *Equality Publications, Series E: Abstracts, 1*). Helsinki: Valtion Painatuskeskus.

Hokanson, J. E., & Burgess, M. (1962a). The effects of three types of aggression on vascular processes. *Journal of Abnormal and Social Psychology, 64,* 446–449.

Hokanson, J. E., & Burgess, M. (1962b). The effects of status, type of frustration, and aggression on vascular processes. *Journal of Abnormal and Social Psychology, 65,* 232–237.

Hokanson, J. E., Burgess, M., & Cohen, M. F. (1963). Effects of displaced aggression on systolic blood pressure. *Journal of Abnormal and Social Psychology, 67,* 214–218.

Holgate, A. (1989). Sexual harassment as a determinant of women's fear of rape. *Australian Journal of Sex, Marriage and the Family, 10,* 21–28.

Holmes, M. R., & St. Lawrence, J. S. (1983). Treatment of rape induced trauma: Proposed behavioral conceptualization and review of the literature. *Clinical Psychology Review, 3,* 417–433.

Horney, J., & Spohn, C. (1991). Rape law reform and instrumental change in six urban jurisdictions. *Law and Society Review, 25,* 117–153.

Horowitz, M. J. (1975). Intrusive and repetitive thoughts after experimental stress: a summary. *Archives of General Psychiatry, 32,* 1457–1463.

Horowitz, M. J. (1976a). *States of mind.* New York: Plenum Medical.

Horowitz, M. (1976b). *Stress response syndromes.* New York: Jason Aronson.

Horowitz, M. (1979). Psychological responses to serious life events. In V. Hamilton & D. Warburton (Eds.), *Human stress and cognition* (pp. 237–264). New York: Wiley.

Hotaling, G. T., & Sugarman, D. B. (1986). An analysis of risk markers in husband to wife violence: The current state of knowledge. *Violence and Victims, 1,* 101–124.

Hulin, C. L. (1993, May). *A framework for the study of sexual harassment in organizations: Climate, stressors, and patterned responses.* Paper presented at a meeting of the Society of Industrial and Organizational Psychology, San Francisco.

Hunter, C., & McClelland, K. (1991). Honoring accounts for sexual harassment: A factorial survey analysis. *Sex Roles, 24,* 725–751.

Independent Commission of the Los Angeles Police Department (1991). *Report of the Independent Commission.* Los Angeles: Author.

Institute for Research on Women's Health (1988). *Sexual harassment and employment discrimination against women: A consumer handbook for women who are harmed, and those who care.* Bethesda, MD: Feminist Institute Clearinghouse.

Jackson, J. (1990). Testimony before the Senate Subcommittee on Children, Families, Drugs, and Alcoholism.

Jacobson, A., & Richardson, B. (1987). Assault experiences of 100 psychiatric inpatients: Evidence of the need for routine inquiry. *American Journal of Psychiatry, 144,* 908–913.

Jaffee, D., & Strauss, M. A. (1987). Sexual climate and reported rape: A state-level analysis. *Archives of Sexual Behavior, 16,* 107–124.

Janoff-Bulman, R. (1985a). Criminal vs. non-criminal victimization: Victim's reactions. *Victimology: An International Journal, 10,* 498–511.

Janoff-Bulman, R. (1985b). The aftermath of victimization: Rebuilding shattered assumptions. In C. R. Figley (Ed.), *Trauma and its wake* (Vol. 1, pp. 15–35). New York: Brunner/Mazel.

Janoff-Bulman, R. (1992). *Shattered assumptions: Towards a new psychology of trauma.* New York: Free Press.

Janoff-Bulman, R., & Frieze, I. H. (1983). A theoretical perspective for understanding reactions to victimization. *Journal of Social Issues, 39,* 1–17.

Javorek, F. J. (1979). When rape is not inevitable: Discriminating between completed and attempted rape cases for nonsleeping targets. *Research Bulletin,* 75–82.

Jenkins, M. J., & Dambrot, F. H. (1985). The attribution of date rape: Observer's attitudes and sexual experiences and the dating situation. *Journal of Applied Social Psychology, 17,* 875–895.

Jenny, C., Hooton, T. M., Bowers, A., Copass, M. K., Krieger, J. N., Hiller, S. L., Kiviat, N., & Corey, L. (1990). Sexually transmitted diseases in victims of rape. *The New England Journal of Medicine, 322,* 713–716.

Jensen, G. F., & Karpos, M. (1993). Managing rape: Exploratory research on the behavior of rape statistics. *Criminology, 31,* 363–385.

Jensen, I., & Gutek, B. A. (1982). Attributions and assignment of responsibility for sexual harassment. *Journal of Social Issues, 38,* 121–136.

Johnson, J. D., & Jackson, L. A. (1988). Assessing the effects of factors that might underlie the differential perception of acquaintance and stranger rape. *Sex Roles, 19,* 37–44.

Jones, A. (1994). *Next time she'll be dead: Battering and how to stop it.* Boston: Beacon Press.

Jones, A., & Schechter, S. (1992). *When love goes wrong: What to do when you can't do anything right.* New York: Harper Collins.

Jones, C. J., & Barlow, D. H. (1990). The etiology of posttraumatic stress disorder. *Clinical Psychology Review, 10,* 229–328.

Jones, T. S., & Remland, M. S. (1992). Sources of variability in perceptions of and responses to sexual harassment. *Sex Roles, 27,* 121–142.

Junger, M. (1987). Women's experiences of sexual harassment. *British Journal of Criminology, 27,* 358–383.

Kahn, A. S. (1984). *Victims of crime and violence.* Washington, DC: American Psychological Association.

Kalmuss, D. S. (1984). The intergenerational transmission of marital aggression. *Journal of Marriage and the Family, 46,* 11–19.

Kalmuss, D. S., & Straus, M. A. (1983). Feminist, political, and economic determinants of wife abuse services. In D. Finkelhor, R. J. Gelles, G. T. Hotaling, & M. A. Straus (Eds.), *The dark side of families* (pp. 363–376). Beverly Hills, CA: Sage.

Kanin, E. J. (1967). Reference groups and sex conduct norm violations. *Sociological Quarterly, 8,* 495–504.

Kanin, E. J. (1985). Date rapists: Differential sexual socialization and relative deprivation. *Archives of Sexual Behavior, 14,* 219–231.

Kanuha, V. (1990). Compounding the triple jeopardy: Battering in lesbian of color
relationships. *Women and Therapy, 9,* 169–184.

Katon, W., Ries, R. K., & Kleinman, A. (1984). The prevalence of somatization in primary care. *Comprehensive Psychiatry, 25,* 208–215.

Katz, B. (1991). The psychological impact of stranger versus nonstranger rape on victims' recovery. In A. Parrot & L. Bechhofer (Eds.), *Acquaintance rape: The hidden
crime* (pp. 251–269). New York: Wiley.

Katz, B., & Burt, M. R. (1988). Self-blame in recovery from rape: Help or hindrance?
In A. Burgess (Ed.), *Rape and Sexual Assault* (Vol. 2, pp. 151–169). New York:
Garland.

Kelly, L. (1988). *Surviving sexual violence.* Minneapolis: University of Minnesota Press.

Kemp, A., Rawlings, E. I., & Green, B. L. (1991). Posttraumatic stress disorder (PTSD)
in battered women: A shelter example. *Journal of Traumatic Stress Studies, 4,*
137–148.

Kenig, S., & Ryan, J. (1986). Sex differences in levels of tolerance and attributions of
blame for sexual harassment on a university campus. *Sex Roles, 15,* 535–549.

Kerouac, S., & Lescop, J. (1986). Dimensions of health in violent families. *Health Care
for Women International, 7,* 413–426.

Kidder, L. H., Boell, J. L., & Moyer, M. M. (1983). Rights consciousness and victimization prevention: Personal defense and assertiveness training. *Journal of Social
Issues, 39,* 155–170.

Kiecolt-Glaser, J. K., & Glaser, R. (1987). Psychosocial moderators of immune function. *Annals of Behavioral Medicine, 9,* 16–20.

Kilpatrick, D. G., & Amick, A. E. (1985). Rape trauma. In M. Hersen & C. G. Last
(Eds.), *Behavior Therapy Casebook* (pp. 86–103). New York: Springer.

Kilpatrick, D. G., Best, C. L., Veronen, L. J., Amick, A. E., Villeponteaux, L. A., and
Ruff, G. A. (1985). Mental health correlates of criminal victimization: A random
community survey. *Journal of Consulting and Clinical Psychology, 53,* 866–873.

Kilpatrick, D. G., & Calhoun, K. S. (1988). Early behavioral treatment for rape trauma:
Efficacy or artifact? *Behavior Therapy, 19,* 421–427.

Kilpatrick, D. G., Saunders, B. E., Amick-McMullan, A., Best, C. L., Veronen, L. J., &
Resnick, H. S. (1989). Victim and crime factors associated with the development
of crime-related posttraumatic stress disorders. *Behavior Therapy, 20,* 199–214.

Kilpatrick, D. G., Saunders, B. E., Veronen, L. J., Best, C. L., & Von, J. M. (1987).

Criminal victimization: Lifetime prevalence, reporting to police, and psychological impact. *Crime and Delinquency, 33,* 479–489.

Kilpatrick, D. G., & Veronen, L. J. (1983). Treatment for rape-related problems: Crisis intervention is not enough. In L. H. Cohen, W. Claiborn, & G. Specter (Eds.), *Crisis intervention* (pp. 165–185). New York: Human Sciences Press.

Kilpatrick, D. G., Veronen, L. J., & Best, V. L. (1985). Factors predicting psychological distress among rape victims. In C. R. Figley (Ed.), *Trauma and its wake* (Vol. 1, pp. 113–141). New York: Brunner/Mazel.

Kilpatrick, D. G., Veronen, L. J., & Resick, P. A. (1979). *The rape victim: Issues in treatment failure.* Paper presented at the Eighth Annual Conference of the American Psychological Association, New York.

Kilpatrick, D. G., Veronen, L. J., & Resick, P. A. (1982). Psychological sequelae to rape. In D. M. Doleys, R. L. Meredith, & A. R. Ciminero (Eds.), *Behavioral medicine: Assessment and treatment strategies* (pp. 473–497). New York: Plenum.

Kirkpatrick, C., & Kanin, F. J. (1957). Male sexual aggression on a university campus. *American Sociological Review, 22,* 52–58.

Kitzinger, J. (1992) Sexual violence and compulsory heterosexuality. *Feminism and Psychology, 2,* 399–418.

Klecka, W. R., & Tuchfarber, A. J. (1978). Random digit dialing: A comparison to personal surveys. *Public Opinion Quarterly, 42,* 105–114.

Kleckner, J. H. (1978). Wife beaters and beaten wives: Co-conspirators in crimes and violence. *Psychology, 15,* 54–56.

Kleinbaum, D. G., Kupper, L. L., & Morgenstern, H. (1982). *Epidemiologic research: Principles and quantitative methods.* Belmont, CA: Lifetime Learning.

Koenig, S., & Ryan, J. (1986). Sex differences in levels of tolerance and attribution of blame for sexual harassment on a university campus. *Sex Roles, 15,* 535–549.

Koss, M. P. (1985). The hidden rape victim: Personality, attitudinal, and situational characteristics. *Psychology of Women Quarterly, 9,* 193–212.

Koss, M. P. (1988a). Hidden rape: Sexual aggression and victimization in a national sample of students in higher education. In A. W. Burgess (Ed.), *Rape and sexual assault* (Vol. 2, pp. 3–25). New York: Garland.

Koss, M. P. (1988b). Women's mental health research agenda: Violence against women. *Women's Mental Health Occasional Paper Series.* Washington, DC: National Institute of Mental Health.

Koss, M. P. (1990a). The women's mental health research agenda: Violence against women. *American Psychologist, 45,* 374–80.

Koss, M. P. (1990b). Changed lives: The psychological impact of sexual harassment. In M. Paludi (Ed.), *Ivory power: Sex and gender harassment in the academy* (pp. 73–92). New York: State University of New York Press.

Koss, M. P. (1992). The underdetection of rape. *Journal of Social Issues, 48,* 63–75.

Koss, M. P. (1993a). Detecting the scope of rape: A review of prevalence research methods. *Journal of Interpersonal Violence, 8,* 198–222.

Koss, M. P. (1993b). Rape: Scope, impact, interventions, and public policy responses. *American Psychologist, 48,* 1062–1069.

Koss, M. P., & Dinero, T. E. (1989a). Predictors of sexual aggression among a national sample of male college students. *Human sexual aggression: Current perspectives, Annals of the New York Academy of Science, 528,* 113–146.

Koss, M. P., & Dinero, T. E. (1989b). Discriminant analysis of risk factors for sexual victimization among a national sample of college women. *Journal of Consulting and Clinical Psychology, 57,* 242–250.

Koss, M. P., Dinero, T. E., Siebel, C., & Cox, S. (1988). Stranger, acquaintance, and date rape: Is there a difference in the victim's experience? *Psychology of Women Quarterly, 12,* 1–24.

Koss, M. P., & Gaines, J. A. (1993). The prediction of sexual aggression by alcohol use, athletic participation, and fraternity affiliation. *Journal of Interpersonal Violence, 8,* 94–106.

Koss, M. P., Gidycz, C. A., & Wisniewski, N. (1987). The scope of rape: Incidence and prevalence of sexual aggression and victimization in a national sample of higher education students. *Journal of Consulting and Clinical Psychology, 55,* 162–170.

Koss, M. P., & Harvey, M. R. (1991). *The rape victim: Clinical and community interventions.* Newbury Park, CA: Sage.

Koss, M. P., & Heslet, L. (1992). Somatic consequences of violence against women. *Archives of Family Medicine, 1,* 53–59.

Koss, M. P., Koss, P., & Woodruff, W. (1991). Deleterious effects of criminal victimization on women's health and medical utilization. *Archives of Internal Medicine, 151,* 342–357.

Koss, M. P., Leonard, K. E., Beezley, D. A., & Oros, C. (1985). Nonstranger sexual aggression: A discriminant analysis of the psychological characteristics of undetected offenders. *Sex Roles, 12,* 981–992.

Koss, M. P., & Oros, C. (1982). The sexual experiences survey: A research instrument investigating sexual aggression and victimization. *Journal of Consulting and Clinical Psychology, 50,* 455–457.

Koss, M. P., Woodruff, W. J., & Koss, P. (1991). Criminal victimization among primary care medical patients: Prevalence, incidence, and physician usage. *Behavioral Sciences and the Law, 9*, 85–96.

Kottak, C. P. (1991). *Anthropology: The exploration of human diversity.* New York: McGraw-Hill.

Kurz, D. (1987). Responses to Battered Women: Resistance to Medicalization. *Social Problems, 34*, 501–13.

Kushner, M. G., Riggs, D. S., Foa, E. B., & Miller, S. M. (1993). Perceived controllability and the development of posttraumatic stress disorder in crime victims. *Behavior Research and Therapy, 31*, 105–110.

Lacey, H. B. (1990). Sexually transmitted diseases and rape: The experience of a sexual assault centre. *International Journal of STD and AIDS, 1*, 405–409.

Lach, D. H., & Gwartney-Gibbs, P. A. (1993). Sociological perspectives on sexual harassment and workplace resolution. *Journal of Vocational Behavior, 42*, 102–115.

LaFree, G. (1989). *Rape and criminal justice: The social construction of sexual assault.* Belmont, CA: Wadsworth.

LaFontaine, E., & Tredeau, L. (1986). The frequency, sources and correlates of sexual harassment among women in traditional male occupations. *Sex Roles, 15*, 423–432.

Laner, M. R., & Thompson, J. (1982). Abuse and aggression in courting couples. *Deviant Behavior: An Interdisciplinary Journal, 3*, 229–244.

Langan, P. A., & Innes, C. A. (1986). *Preventing domestic violence against women.* Washington, DC: U.S. Department of Justice, Bureau of Justice Statistics.

Largen, M. A. (1987). A decade of change in the rape reform movement. *Response, 10*, 4–9.

LaVite, C. M. (1992). *The interactions between situational factors and individual predispositions in the likelihood to sexually harass.* Unpublished master's thesis, Illinois State University, Chicago.

Lazarus, R. S. (1967). Cognitive and personality factors underlying threat and coping. In M. H. Appley & R. Trumbull (Eds.), *Psychological stress* (pp. 151–181). New York: Appleton-Century-Crofts.

Lazarus, R. S. (1991a). Cognition and motivation in emotion. *American Psychologist, 46*, 352–367.

Lazarus, R. S. (1991b). Progress on a cognitive–motivational–relational theory of emotion. *American Psychologist, 46*, 819–834.

Leibowitz, L., Harvey, M. R., & Herman, J. L. (1993). A stage by dimension model of recovery from sexual trauma. *Journal of Interpersonal Violence, 8,* 378–391.

Leidig, M. (1981). Violence against women: A feminist psychological analysis. In S. Cox (Ed.). *Female Psychology: The Emerging Self* (pp. 190–205). New York: St. Martin's Press.

Lentzner, H. R., & DeBerry, M. M. (1980). *Intimate victims: A study of violence among friends and relatives.* Washington, DC: U.S. Department of Justice, Bureau of Justice Statistics.

Lerman, L. G. (1980). State legislation on domestic violence. *Response to Violence in the Family, 3,* 1.

Lerman, L. G. (1981). *Prosecution of spouse abuse: Innovations in criminal justice response.* Washington, DC: Center for Women Policy Studies.

Lerman, L. G., & Livingston, F. (1983). State legislation on domestic violence. *Response to Violence in the Family, 6,* 1.

Lerner, G. (1986). *The creation of patriarchy.* New York: Oxford University Press.

Lerner, M. J. (1980). *The belief in a just world.* New York: Plenum Press.

Lester, D., Banta, B., Barton, J., Elian, N., Mackiewicz, L., & Winkelried, J. (1986). Judgements about sexual harassment: Effects of the power of the harasser. *Perceptual and Motor Skills, 63,* 990.

Levenson, H. (1972). Distinctions within the concept of internal-external control: Development of a new scale. *Proceedings of the 80th Annual Convention of the American Psychological Association, 7,* 261–262.

Levine-MacCombie, J., & Koss, M. P. (1986). Acquaintance rape: Effective avoidance strategies. *Psychology of Women Quarterly, 10,* 311–320.

Levy, B. (Ed.). (1991). *Dating violence: Young women in danger.* Seattle, WA: The Seal Press.

Liese, B. S., Larson, M. W., Johnson, C. A., & Hourigan, R. J. (1989). An experimental study of two methods for teaching sexual history taking skills. *Family Medicine, 21,* 21–24.

Lindsey, K. (1977, November). Sexual harassment on the job and how to stop it. *Ms.,* 47–51, 74–78.

Linz, D., Wilson, B. J., & Donnerstein, E. (1992). Sexual violence in the mass media: Legal solutions, warnings, and mitigation through education. *Journal of Social Issues, 48,* 145–172.

Lisak, D., & Roth, S. (1988). Motivational factors in nonincarcerated sexually aggressive men. *Journal of Personality and Social Psychology, 55,* 795–802.

Livingston, J. A. (1982). Responses to sexual harassment on the job: Legal, organizational and individual actions. *Journal of Social Issues, 38,* 5–22.

Lobel, K. (Ed.). (1986). *Naming the violence: Speaking out about lesbian battering.* Seattle: Seal Press.

Lobel, S. A. (1993). Sexuality at work: Where do we go from here? *Journal of Vocational Behavior, 42,* 136–152.

Lockhart, L. (1985). Methodological issues in comparative racial analyses: The case of wife abuse. *Social Work Research and Abstracts, 21,* (2), 35–41.

Lockhart, L., & White, B. (1989). Understanding marital violence in the Black community. *Journal of Interpersonal Violence, 4,* 421–436.

Loftin, C., & Parker, R. N. (1985). An errors-in-variable model of the effect of poverty on urban homicide rates. *Criminology, 23,* 269–285.

Lonsway, K. (1992). *Rape myths: A theoretical and empirical revision.* Unpublished master's thesis, University of Illinois at Urbana-Champaign, Department of Psychology.

Lonsway, K., & Fitzgerald, L. F. (in press). Rape myths: In review. *Psychology of Women Quarterly.*

Lore, R. K., & Schultz, L. A. (1993). Control of human aggression. *American Psychologist, 48,* 16–26.

Lott, B., Reilly, M. E., & Howard, D. (1982). Sexual assault and harassment: A campus community case study. *Signs, 8,* 296–319.

Loy, P. H., & Stewart, L. P. (1984). The extent and effects of sexual harassment of working women. *Sociological Focus, 17,* 31–43.

Lurigio, A. J., & Resick, P. A. (1990). Healing the psychological wounds of criminal victimization: Predicting postcrime distress and recovery. In A. J. Lurigio, W. G. Skogan, & R. C. Davis (Eds.), *Victims of crime: Problems, policies, and programs* (pp. 51–67). Newbury Park, CA: Sage.

Lyons, J. (1987). Posttraumatic stress disorder in children and adolescents: A review of the literature. *Developmental and Behavioral Pediatrics, 8,* 349–356.

MacKinnon, C. A. (1979). *Sexual harassment of working women.* New Haven: Yale University Press.

Maguigan, H. (1991). Battered women and self-defense: Myths and misconceptions in current reform proposals. *University of Pennsylvania Law Review, 140,* 379–486.

Maguire, M., & Corbett, C. (1987). *The effects of crime and the work of victims' support schemes.* Hants, England: Gower.

Mahoney, E. R., Shively, M. D., & Traw, M. (1986). Sexual coercion and assault: Male socialization and female risk. *Sexual Coercion and Assault, 1*, 2–8.

Mahoney, M. R. (1991). Legal images of battered women: Redefining the issue of separation. *Michigan Law Review, 1*, 43–49.

Maihoff, N., & Forrest, L. (1983). Sexual harassment in higher education: An assessment study. *Journal of the NAWDAC, 46*, 3–8.

Makepeace, J. M. (1989). Dating, living together, and courtship violence. In M. A. Pirog-Good & J. Sets (Eds.), *Violence in dating relationships: Emerging social issues* (pp. 94–107). New York: Praeger.

Makepeace, J. M. (1981). Courtship violence among college students. *Family Relations, 30*, 97–102.

Malamuth, N. M. (1981). Rape proclivity among males. *Journal of Social Issues, 37*, 520–547.

Malamuth, N. M. (1983). Factors associated with rape as predictors of laboratory aggression against women. *Journal of Personaltiy and Social Psychology, 45*, 432–442.

Malamuth, N. M. (1986). Predictors of naturalistic aggression. *Journal of Personality and Social Psychology, 50*, 953–962.

Malamuth, N. M. (1988). A multidimensional approach to sexual aggression: Combining measures of past behavior and present likelihood. *Human Sexual Aggression: Current Perspectives, Annals of the New York Academy of Science, 528*, 113–146.

Malamuth, N. M. (1989a). The attraction to sexual aggression scale: Part 1. *The Journal of Sex Research, 26*, 26–49.

Malamuth, N. M. (1989b). The attraction to sexual aggression scale: Part 2. *The Journal of Sex Research, 26*, 324–354.

Malamuth, N. M., & Ceniti, J. (1986). Repeated exposure to violent and nonviolent pornography: Likelihood of raping ratings and laboratory aggression against women. *Aggressive Behavior, 12*, 129–137.

Malamuth, N. M., Check, J. V. P., & Briere, J. (1986). Sexual arousal in response to aggression: Ideological, aggressive, and sexual correlates. *Journal of Personality and Social Psychology, 50*, 330–340.

Malamuth, N. M., & Dean, K. (1991). Attraction to sexual aggression. In A. Parrot (Ed.), *Acquaintance rape: The hidden crime* (pp. 229–248). New York: Wiley.

Malamuth, N. M., Sockloskie, R., Koss, M. P., & Tanaka, J. (1991). The characteristics of aggressors against women: Testing a model using a national sample of college students. *Journal of Consulting and Clinical Psychology, 59,* 670–681.

Malovich, N. J., & Stake, J. E. (1990). Sexual harassment on campus: Individual differences in attitudes and beliefs. *Psychology of Women Quarterly, 14,* 63–81.

Man cleared of marital rape. (1992, April 18) *Washington Post,* p. A2.

March, J. S. (1990). The nosology of postttraumatic stress disorder. *Journal of Anxiety Disorders, 4,* 61–82.

Margolin, G. (1988). Interpersonal and intrapersonal factors associated with marital violence. In G. T. Hotaling, D. Finkelhor, J. T. Kirkpatrick, & M. A. Straus (Eds.), *Family abuse and its consequences: New directions for research* (pp. 203–217). Newbury Park, CA: Sage.

Marhoefer-Dvorak, S., Resick, P. A., Hutter, C. K., & Girelli, S. A. (1987). Single versus multiple incident rape victims: A comparison of psychological reactions to rape. *Journal of Interpersonal Violence, 3,* 145–160.

Marks, M. A., & Nelson, E. S. (1993). Sexual harassment on campus: Effects of professor gender on perception of sexually harassing behaviors. *Sex Roles, 28,* 207–217.

Marsh, J., Geist, A., & Caplan, N. (1982). *Rape and the limits of law reform.* Boston: Auburn House.

Marshall, W. L. (1989). Pornography and sex offenders. In D. Zillmann & J. Bryant (Eds.), *Pornography: Research advances and policy considerations* (pp. 185–214). Hillsdale, NJ: Erlbaum.

Martin, D. (1976). *Battered wives.* San Francisco, CA: Glide.

Martin, P. Y., & DiNitto, D. M. (1987). The rape exam: Beyond the emergency room. *Women and Health, 12,* 5–28.

Martin, P. Y., & Hummer, R. A. (1989). Fraternities and rape on campus. *Gender and Society, 3,* 457–473.

Martin, S. (1978). Sexual politics in the workplace: The interactional world of policewomen. *Symbolic Interaction, 1,* 55–60.

Martin, S. (1980). *Breaking and entering: Policewomen on patrol.* Berkeley, CA: University of California Press.

Martin, S. E. (1984). Sexual harassment: The link between gender stratification, sexuality and women's economic status. In J. Freeman (Ed.), *Women: A feminist perspective* (pp. 54–69). Palo Alto, CA: Mayfield.

Martindale, M. (1990). *Sexual harassment in the military: 1988.* Arlington, VA: Defense Manpower Data Center.

Mason, A., & Blankenship, V. (1987). Power and affiliation, motivation, stress, and abuse in intimate relationships. *Journal of Personality and Social Psychology, 52,* 203–210.

Mazer, D. B., & Percival, E. F. (1989). Ideology or experience? The relationships among perceptions, attitudes and experiences of sexual harassment in university students. *Sex Roles, 20,* 135–170.

Maypole, D. E., & Skaine, R. (1983). Sexual harassment in the workplace. *Social work, 28,* 385–390.

McCahill, T. W., Meyer, L. C., & Fischman, A. M. (1979). *The aftermath of rape.* Lexington, MA: D.C. Heath.

McCambridge, R. (1989). Domestic violence. In *Injury prevention: Meeting the challenge.* Oxford: Oxford University Press.

McCann, I. L., & Pearlman, L. A. (1990a). *Psychological trauma and the adult survivor: Theory, therapy, and transformation.* New York: Brunner/Mazel.

McCann, I. L., & Perlman, L. A. (1990b). Vicarious traumatization: A framework for understanding the psychological effects of working with victims. *Journal of Traumatic Stress, 3,* 131–149.

McCann, I. L. Sakheim, D. K., & Abrahamson, D. J. (1988). Trauma and victimization: A model of psychological adaptation. *The Counseling Psychologist, 6,* 531–594.

McCarthy, C. (1991, July 23). Countering violence at home. *Washington Post,* p. D13.

McFarlane, J., Parker, B., Soeken, K., & Bullock, L. (1992). Assessing for abuse during pregnancy: Severity and frequency of injuries associated with entry into prenatal care. *Journal of the American Medical Association, 267,* 3176–3178.

McGrath, E., Keita, G. P., Strickland, B. R., & Russo, N. F. (Eds.). (1990). *Women and depression: Risk factors and treatment issues.* Washington, DC: American Psychological Association.

McHugh, M. C., Frieze, I. H., & Browne, A. (1993). Research on battered women and their assailants. In M. Paludi & F. Denmark (Eds.), *Handbook on the psychology of women* (pp. 513–552). New York: Greenwood Press.

McKinney, K. (1990). Sexual harassment of university faculty by colleagues and students. *Sex Roles, 23,* 421–438.

McKinney, K. (1992). Contrapower sexual harassment: The effects of student sex and type of behavior on faculty perceptions. *Sex Roles, 27,* 627–643.

Meritor Savings Bank v. Vinson, 477 U.S. 57 (1986).

Merry, S. (1981). *Urban danger.* Philadelphia: Temple University Press.

Meyer, C. B., & Taylor, S. E. (1986). Adjustment of rape. *Journal of Personality and Social Psychology, 50,* 1226–1234.

Michigan Stat. Ann. §§28.788 (1) (h) (Callaghan) (Cum. Supp.) (1980).

Mileti, D. S., Drabek, T. E., & Hass, J. E. (1975). *Human systems in extreme environments*. Boulder: University of Colorado, Institute of Behavioral Science.

Miletich, E. (1990). Testimony before the Senate Labor and Human Resources Subcommittee on Children, Family, Drugs, and Alcoholism. Cited in the Congressional Caucus for Women's Issues Report on Violence Against Women, 1991.

Miller, B., & Marshall, J. C. (1987, January). Coercive sex on the university campus. *Journal of College Student Personnel*, 38–47.

Miller, J. G. (1964). A theoretical review of individual and group psychological reactions to stress. In G.H. Grosser, H. Wechsler, & M. Greenblatt (Eds.), *The threat of impending disaster* (pp. 11–33). Cambridge, MA: MIT. Press.

Miller, S. L., & Simpson, S. S. (1991). Courtship violence and social control: Does gender matter? *Law and Society Review, 25*, 335–357.

Mills, C. W. (1959). *The sociological imagination*. New York: Grove Press.

Mollica, R. F., & Son, L. (1989). Cultural dimensions in the evaluation and treatment of sexual trauma: An overview. *The Psychiatric Clinics of North America, 12*, 363–381.

Moore, K. A., Nord, C. W., & Peterson, J. L. (1989). Nonvoluntary sexual activity among adolescents. *Family Planning Perspectives, 21*, 110–114.

Moorman, M. A., & Mankin, D. (1992, March). *Selecting out sexual harassers: A video-based approach*. Paper presented at First National Conference on Sex and Power Issues in the Workplace, Bellevue, WA.

Mosher, D. L., & Anderson, R. D. (1986). Macho personality, sexual aggression, and reactions to guided imagery of realistic rape. *Journal of Research in Personality, 20*, 77–94.

Mosher, D. L., & Sirkin, M. (1984). Measuring a macho personality constellation. *Journal of Research in Personality, 18*, 150–163.

Muehlenhard, C. L., Friedman, D. E., & Thomas, C. M. (1985). Is date rape justifiable? The effects of dating activity, who initiated, who paid, and men's attitudes toward women. *Psychology of Women Quarterly, 9*, 297–310.

Muehlenhard, C. L., & Hollabaugh, L. (1988). Do women sometimes say no when they mean yes? The prevalence and correlates of women's token resistance to sex. *Journal of Personality and Social Psychology, 54*, 872–879.

Muehlenhard, C. L., & Linton, M. A. (1987). Date rape and sexual aggression in dating situations: Incidence and risk factors. *Journal of Counseling and Psychology, 34*, 186–196.

Muehlenhard, C. L., Powch, I. G., Phelps, J. L., & Giusti, L. M. (1992). Definitions of rape: Scientific and political implications. *Journal of Social Issues, 48,* 23–44.

Muram, D., Miller, K., & Cutler, A. (1992). Sexual assault of the elderly victim. *Journal of Interpersonal Violence, 7,* 70–77.

Murphy, C. M., Meyer, S., & O'Leary, K. D. (1991). Emotional vulnerability, psychopathology, and family of origin violence in men who assault female partners. Unpublished manuscript, State University of New York, Stony Brook.

Murphy, S. M. (1990). Rape, sexually transmitted diseases and human immunodeficiency virus infection. *International Journal of STD and AIDS, 1,* 79–82.

Murphy, S. M., Amick-McMullan, A., Kilpatrick, D. G., Haskett, M. E., Veronen, L. J., Best, C. L., & Saunders, B. E. (1988). Rape victims' self-esteem: A longitudinal analysis. *Journal of Interpersonal Violence, 3,* 355–370.

Murphy, S. M., Kitchen, V., Harris, J. R. W., & Forster, S. M. (1989). Rape and subsequent seroconversion to HIV. *British Medical Journal, 10,* 699–718.

Myers, M. P., Templar, D. L., & Brown, R. (1984). Coping ability of women who become rape victims. *Journal of Consulting and Clinical Psychology, 52,* 73–78.

National Center for the Prevention and Control of Rape. (1981). *National directory: Rape prevention and treatment resources.* Washington, DC: U.S. Government Printing Office.

National Center for the Prevention and Control of Rape. (1982). *Research program notice.* Rockville, MD: National Institute of Mental Health.

National Council for Research on Women. (1991). *Sexual harassment: Research and resources.* New York: Author.

National Victims Center. (1992). *Rape in America: A report to the nation.* Arlington, VA: Author.

National Women's Health Resource Center. (1991). *Violence against women: Report of a conference sponsored by the National Women's Health Resource Center.* Washington, DC: Author.

Newberger, E. H., Lieberman, E. S., McCormick, M. C., Yllö, K., Gary, L. T., & Schechter, S. (1990). *Pregnant woman abuse and adverse birth outcomes: Current knowledge and implications for practice.* New York: McGraw-Hill.

NiCarthy, G. (1982). *Getting free.* Seattle: Seal Press.

Norris, F. H. (1992). Epidemiology of trauma: Frequency and impact of different potentially traumatic events on different demographic groups. *Journal of Consulting and Clinical Psychology, 60,* 409–418.

Norris, F. H., & Kaniasty, K. (1991). The psychological experience of crime: A test of the mediating role of beliefs in explaining the distress of victims. *Journal of Social and Clinical Psychology, 10,* 239–261.

Novaco, R. W. (1976). The functions and regulation of the arousal of anger. *American Journal of Psychiatry, 133,* 1,124–1,128.

O'Carroll, P. W., & Mercy, J. A. (1986). Patterns and recent trends in Black homicide. In D. F. Hawkins (Ed.), *Homicide among Black Americans* (pp. 29–42). Lanham, MD: University Press of America.

Ochberg, F. M. (1988). *Posttraumatic therapy and victims of violence.* New York: Brunner/Mazel.

O'Farrell, B., & Harlan, S. L. (1982). Craftworkers and clerks: The effects of male coworker hostility on women's satisfaction with nontraditional jobs. *Social Problems, 29,* 252–264.

Okun, L. (1986). *Women abuse: Facts replacing myths.* Albany, NY: State University of New York Press.

O'Leary, K. D. (1988). Physical aggression between spouses: A social learning theory perspective. In V. B. Van Hasselt, R. L. Morrison, A. S. Bellak, & M. Herson (Eds.), *Handbook of family violence* (pp. 31–55). New York: Plenum.

O'Leary, K. D., & Jacobson, N. S. (1992). *Partner relational problems with physical abuse: DSM-IV Literature Summary.* Unpublished manuscript, State University of New York, Stony Brook.

Ormerod, A. J. (1991). *The effect of self-efficacy and outcome expectations on responses to sexual harassment.* Unpublished master's equivalency project, University of Illinois, Department of Educational Psychology, Champaign.

Osipow, S. H., & Fitzgerald, L. F. (in press). *Theories of career development* (4th ed.). Needham Heights, MA: Allyn & Bacon.

O'Sullivan, E. (1976). What has happened to the rape crisis center? A look at their structures, members and funding. *Victimology: An International Journal, 3,* (1-2), 45–62.

Otos, S. (in press). Marital rape: Unfinished reform. *Columbia Journal of Gender and Law.*

Otterbein, K. F. (1979). A cross-cultural study of rape. *Aggressive Behavior, 5,* 425–435.

Paddison, P. L., Gise, L. H., Lebovits, A., Strain, J. J., Cirasole, D. M., & Levine, J. P. (1990). Sexual abuse and premenstrual syndrome. *Psychosomatics, 3,* 265–272.

Padgitt, S. C., & Padgitt, J. S. (1986). Cognitive structure of sexual harassment: Implications for university policy. *Journal of College Student Personnel, 27,* 34–39.

297

Pagelow, M. D. (1981). *Woman-battering: Victims and their experiences.* Beverly Hills, CA: Sage.

Pagelow, M. D. (1984). *Family violence.* New York: Prager.

Palau, N. (1981). *Battered women: A homogenous group? Theoretical considerations and MMPI data interpretation.* Paper presented at the annual meeting of the American Psychological Association, Los Angeles, CA.

Paludi, M. A. (Ed.) (1990). *Ivory power: Sexual harassment on campus.* Albany, NY: State University of New York Press.

Paludi, M. A., & Barickman, R. B. (1991). *Academic and workplace sexual harassment: A manual of resources.* New York: State University of New York Press.

Paone, D., Chavkin, W., Willets, I., Friedman, P., & Des Jarlais, D. (1992). The impact of sexual abuse: Implications for drug treatment. *Journal of Women's Health, 1,* 149–153.

Parker, R. N., & Toth, A. M. (1990). Family, intimacy, and homicide: A macrosocial approach. *Violence and Victims, 5,* 195–210.

Parmerlee, M. A., Near, J. P., & Jensen, T. C. (1982). Correlates of whistleblowers' perceptions of organizational retaliation. *Administrative Science Quarterly, 27,* 17–34.

Parson, E. R. (1985). Ethnicity and traumatic stress: The intersecting point in psychotherapy. In C. R. Figley (Ed.), *Trauma and its wake: The study and treatment of posttraumatic stress disorder* (pp. 314–337). New York: Brunner/Mazel.

Patterson, G. (1982). *Coercive family processes.* Eugene, OR: Cataglia.

Pavela, G. (1992). Should colleges resolve sexual assault cases? *Synthesis: Law and Policy in Higher Education, 4,* 276–278.

Pence, E., & Shephard, M. (1988). Integrating feminist theory and practice: The challenge of the battered women's movement. In K. Yllo & M. Bograd (Eds.), *Feminist approaches on wife abuse* (pp. 282–298). Newbury Park, CA: Sage Publications.

Pendergrass, V. E., Kimmel, E., Joesling, J., Petersen, J., & Bush, E. (1976). Sex discrimination counseling. *American Psychologist, 31, 36–46.*

Pennebaker J. W., Kiecolt-Glaser, J. K., & Glaser, R. (1988). Disclosure of traumas and immune function: Health implications for psychotherapy. *Journal of Consulting and Clinical Psychology, 56,* 239–245.

Perry, P. A. (1983, March 26). Sexual harassment on the campuses: Deciding where to draw the line. *Chronicle of Higher Education,* 21–22.

Peters, J. J. (1973). The Philadelphia rape victim study. In I. Drapkin & E. Viano (Eds.), *Victimology: A New Focus* (Vol. 3, pp. 181–199). Lexington, MA: Lexington.

Peterson, C., & Seligman, M. (1983). Learned helplessness and victimization. *Journal of Social Issues, 2,* 103–116.

Peterson, C., & Strunkard, A. J. (1992). Cognates of personal control: Locus of control, self-efficacy, and explanatory style. *Applied and Preventive Psychology, 1,* 111–117.

Petty, R. E., & Cacioppo, J. T. (1986). *Communication and persuasion: Central and peripheral routes to attitude change.* New York: Springer-Verlag.

Pinneau, L. (1987). Date rape: A feminist analysis. *Law and Philosophy, 8,* 217–243.

Pirog-Good, M. A., & Stets, J. E. (1989). *Violence in dating relationships: Emerging social issues.* New York: Praeger.

Pitman, R. K. (1993). Biological findings in posttraumatic stress disorder: Implications for *DSM-IV* Classification. In J. R. Davidson & E. B. Foa (Eds.), *Posttraumatic stress disorder: DSM-IV and beyond* (pp. 173–189). Washington, DC: American Psychiatric Press.

Pitman, R. K., Altman, B., Greenwald E., Longpre, R. W., Macklin, M. L., Poire, R. E., & Steketee, G. (1991). Psychiatric complications during flooding therapy for posttraumatic stress disorder. *Journal of Clinical Psychiatry, 52,* 17–20.

Pizzey, E. (1974). *Scream quietly or the neighbors will hear.* London, Penguin.

Pleck, E. (1987). *Domestic tyranny: The making of American social policy against family violence from colonial times to the present.* New York: Oxford University Press.

Pontara, G. (1978). The concept of violence. *Journal of Peace Research, 15,* 19–32.

Pope, K. S., Levenson, H., & Schover, L. R. (1979). Sexual intimacy in psychology training: Results and implications of a national survey. *American Psychologist, 34,* 682–689.

Popovich, P. M., Gehlauf, D. N., Jolton, J. A., Somers, J. M., & Godinho, R. M. (1992). Perceptions of sexual harassment as a function of sex of rater and incident form and consequences. *Sex Roles, 27,* 609–625.

Powell, G. N. (1986). Effects of sex-role identity and sex on definitions of sexual harassment. *Sex Roles, 14,* 9–19.

Prentky, R. A., Burgess, A. W., & Carter, D. L. (1986). Victim response by rapist type: An empirical and clinical analysis. *Journal of Interpersonal Violence, 1,* 73–98.

Prentky, R. A., & Knight, R. A. (1991). Identifying critical dimensions for discriminating among rapists. *Journal of Consulting and Clinical Psychology, 59,* 643–661.

President's Task Force on Victims of Crime (1982). *President's task force on victims of crime final report.* Washington, DC: U.S. Government Printing Office.

Project on the Education and Status of Women (1978). *Sexual harassment: A hidden issue.* Washington, DC: Association of American Colleges.

Pryor, J. B. (1985). The layperson's understanding of sexual harassment. *Sex Roles, 13,* 273–286.

Pryor, J. B. (1987). Sexual harassment proclivities in men. *Sex Roles, 17,* 269–290.

Pryor, J. B. (1992, March). *The social psychology of sexual harassment: Person and situation factors which give rise to sexual harassment.* Proceedings of the First National Conference on Sex and Power Issues in the Workplace, Bellevue, WA.

Pryor, J. B., & Day, J. D. (1988). Interpretations of sexual harassment: An attributional analysis. *Sex Roles, 18,* 405–417.

Pryor, J. B., & McKinney, K. (in press). Sexual harassment. *Basic and Applied Social Psychology.*

Pryor, J. B., LaVite, C. M., & Stoller, L. M. (1993). A social psychological analysis of sexual harassment: The person/situation interaction. *Journal of Vocational Behavior, 42,* 68–83.

Pryor, J. B., & Stoller, L. M. (1992). *Sexual cognition processes in men who are high in the likelihood to sexually harass.* Unpublished manuscript, Illinois State University, Chicago.

Ptacek, J. (1988). Why do men batter their wives? In K. Yllo and M. Bograd (Eds.), *Feminist perspectives on wife abuse* (pp. 133–157). Beverly Hills, CA: Sage.

Public Health Service. (1985). *Women's health: Vol. 1, Report of the Public Health Service Task Force on Women's Health Issues* (DHHS Publication No. PHS 85-50206). Washington, DC: U.S. Department of Health and Human Services.

Quackenbush, R. L. (1989). A comparison of androgynous, masculine sex-typed, and undifferentiated males in dimensions of attitudes toward rape. *Journal of Research in Personality, 23,* 318–342.

Quina, K. (1990). The victimizations of women. In M. Paludi (Ed.), *Ivory power: Sexual harassment on campus.* Albany: State University of New York Press.

Quinsey, V. L. (1984). Sexual aggression: Studies of offenders against women. In D. Weistub (Ed.), *Law and Mental Health: International Perspectives* (Vol. 1, pp. 84–121). New York: Pergamon.

Quinsey, V. L., & Chaplin, T. C. (1984). Stimulus control of rapists' and non-sex offenders' sexual arousal. *Behavioral Assessment, 6,* 169–176.

Quinsey, V. L., & Upfold, D. (1985). Rape completion and victim injury as a function of female resistance strategy. *Canadian Journal of Behavioral Science, 17,* 40–50.

Radloff, L. S. (1977). The CES-D Scale: A self-report depression scale for research in the general population. *Applied Psychological Measurement, 1,* 385–401.

Randall, T. (1990). Domestic violence intervention calls for more than treating injuries. *Journal of the American Medical Association, 264,* 939–944.

Rapkin, A. J., Kames, L. D., Darke, L. L., Stampler, F. M., & Naliboff, B. D. (1990).

History of physical and sexual abuse in women with chronic pelvic pain. *Obstetrics and Gynecology, 76,* 92–96.

Rapaport, K. R., & Burkhart, B. R. (1984). Personality and attitudinal characteristics of sexually coercive college males. *Journal of Abnormal Psychology, 93,* 216–221.

Rapaport, K. R., & Posey, D. D. (1991). Sexually coercive college males. In A. Parrot & L. Bechhofer (Eds.), *Acquaintance rape: The hidden crime* (pp. 217–228). New York: Wiley.

Reid, J. B., Taplin, P. S., & Lorber, R. (1981). A social interactional approach to the treatment of abusive families. In R. B. Stuart (Ed.), *Violent behavior: Social learning approaches to prediction, management, and treatment* (pp. 3–19). New York: Brunner/Mazel.

Reilly, M. E., Caldwell, D., & DeLuca, L. (1992). Tolerance for sexual harassment related to self-reported sexual victimization. *Gender and Society, 6,* 122–138.

Reilly, M. E., Lott, B., & Gallogly, S. M. (1986). Sexual harassment of university students. *Sex Roles, 15,* 333–358.

Reilly, T., Carpenter, S., Dull, V., & Bartlett, K. (1982). The factorial survey technique: An approach to defining sexual harassment on campus. *Journal of Social Issues, 38,* 99–110.

Reiter, R. C. (1990). A profile of women with chronic pelvic pain. *Clinical Obstetrics and Gynecology, 33,* 131–136.

Reiter, R. C., & Gambone J. C. (1990). Demographic and historic variables in women with idiopathic chronic pelvic pain. *Obstetrics and Gynecology, 75,* 428–432.

Reiter, R. C., Sharkerin, L. R., Gambone, J. C., & Milburn, A. K. (1991). Correlation between sexual abuse and somatization in women with somatic and nonsomatic chronic pelvic pain. *American Journal of Obstetrics and Gynecology, 165,* 104–109.

Rendall, J. (1985). *The origins of modern feminism.* London: Macmillan.

Renzetti, C. (1992). *Violent betrayal: Partner abuse in lesbian relationships.* Newbury Park, CA: Sage.

Resick, P. A. (1983). Sex-role stereotypes and violence against women. In V. Franks & E. D. Rothblum (Eds.), *The stereotyping of women: Its effects on mental health* (pp. 230–256). New York: Springer.

Resick, P. A. (1987). Psychological effects of victimization: Implications for the criminal justice system. *Crime and Delinquency, 33,* 468–478.

Resick, P. A. (1990). Victims of sexual assault. In A. J. Lurigio, W. G. Skogan, & R. C. Davis (Eds.) *Victims of crime: Problems, policies, and programs* (pp. 69–85). Newbury Park, CA: Sage.

Resick, P. A. (1992). Cognitive treatment of crime-related PTSD. In R. Peters, R. McMahon, & V. Quinsey (Eds.), *Aggression and violence throughout the lifespan* (pp. 171–191). Newbury Park, CA: Sage.

Resick, P. A., Calhoun, K. S., Atkeson, B. M., & Ellis, E. M. (1981). Social adjustment in victims of sexual assault. *Journal of Consulting and Clinical Psychology, 49,* 705–712.

Resick, P. A., Jordan, C. G., Girelli, S. A., Hutter, C. K., & Marhoefer-Dvorak, S. (1989). A comparative outcome study of behavioral group therapy for sexual assault victims. *Behavior Therapy, 19,* 385–401.

Resick, P. A., & Markaway, B. K. (1991). Clinical treatment of adult female victims of sexual assault. In C. R. Hollin & K. Howells (Eds.), *Clinical approaches to sex offenders and their victims* (pp. 261–284). New York: Wiley.

Resick, P. A., & Schnicke, M. K. (1991). Treating symptoms in adult victims of sexual assault. *Journal of Interpersonal Violence, 5,* 488–506.

Resick, P. A., & Schnicke, M. K. (1992). Cognitive processing therapy for sexual assault victims. *Journal of Consulting and Clinical Psychology, 60,* 748–756.

Richardson, D., & Hammock, G. (1991). Alcohol and acquaintance rape. In A. Parrot & L. Bechhofer (Eds.), *Acquaintance rape: The hidden crime* (pp. 83–95). New York: Wiley.

Rieker, P. P., & Carmen, E. H. (1986). The victim-to-patient process: The disconfirmation and transformation of abuse. *American Journal of Orthopsychiatry, 56,* 360–370.

Riger, S., & Gordon, M. T. (1988). The impact of crime on urban women. In A. W. Burgess (Ed.), *Rape and sexual assault* (Vol. 2, pp. 139–156). New York: Garland.

Riger, S., LeBailly, R. K., & Gordon, M. T. (1981). Community ties and urbanites fear of crime: An ecological investigation. *American Journal of Community Psychology, 9,* 653–665.

Riggs, D. S., Dancu, D. V., Gershuny, B. S., Greenberg, D., & Foa, E. B. (1992). Anger and posttraumatic stress disorder in female crime victims. *Journal of Traumatic Stress, 5,* 613–625.

Robinson v. Jacksonville Shipyards, Inc., Fla. 760 F. Supp. 1486 (M. D. 1991).

Romero, M. (1985). A comparison between strategies used on prisoners of war and battered wives. *Sex Roles, 13,* 537–547.

Root, M. P., & Fallon, P. (1988). The incidence of victimization experiences in a bulimic sample. *Journal of Interpersonal Violence, 3,* 161–173.

Root, M. P., Fallon, P., Friedrich, W. N. (1986). *Bulimia: A systems approach to treatment.* New York: Norton.

Roscoe, B., Goodwin, M. P., Repp, S. E., & Rose, M. (1987). Sexual harassment of university students and student employers: Findings and implications. *College Student Journal, 21,* 254–273.

Rose, H. M. (1978). The geography of despair. *Annals of the Association of American Geographers, 68,* 453–464.

Rosenbaum, A., & O'Leary, K. D. (1981). Marital violence: Characteristics of abusive couples. *Journal of Clinical and Consulting Psychology, 49,* 63–71.

Rosewater, L. B. (1985a). Schizophrenic, borderline, or battered? In L. B. Rosewater & L. E. Walker (Eds.), *Handbook of feminist therapy: Women's issues in psychotherapy* (pp. 215–225). New York: Springer.

Rosewater, L. B. (1985b). Feminist interpretation of traditional testing. In L. B. Rosewater & L. E. Walker (Eds.), *Handbook of feminist therapy: Women's issues in psychotherapy* (pp. 266–273). New York: Springer.

Rosewater, L. B. (1988). Battered or schizophrenic? Psychological tests can't tell. In K. Yllö & M. Bograd (Eds.), *Feminist perspectives on wife abuse.* Newbury Park, CA: Sage.

Ross, L. (1977). The intuitive psychologist and his shortcomings: Distortions in the attribution process. In L. Berkowitz (Ed.), *Advances in Experimental Social Psychology, 35,* 485–494. New York: Academic Press.

Ross, V. M. (1977). Rape as a social problem: A byproduct of the feminist movement. *Social Problems, 25,* 75–89.

Rossi, P. H., & Weber-Burdin, E. (1983). Sexual harassment on the campus. *Social Science Research, 12,* 131–158.

Roth, S., & Lebowitz, L. (1988). The experience of sexual trauma. *Journal of Traumatic Stress, 1,* 79–107.

Rothbaum, B. O. (1992). How does EMDR work? *The Behavior Therapist, 15,* 46.

Rothbaum, B. O., & Foa, E. B. (1992). Cognitive–behavioral treatment of posttraumatic stress disorder. In P. A. Saigh (Ed.), *Posttraumatic stress disorder: A behavioral approach to assessment and treatment* (pp. 85–110). New York: Pergamon.

Rothbaum, B. O., Foa, E. B., Riggs, D. S., Murdock, T., & Walsh, W. (in press). A prospective examination of posttraumatic stress disorder in rape victims. *Journal of Traumatic Stress.*

Rouse, L. P. (1988). Abuse in dating relationships: A comparison of Blacks, Whites, and Hispanics. *Journal of College Student Development, 29,* 312–319.

Ruback, R. B., & Ivie, D. L. (1988). Prior relationship, resistance, and injury in rapes: An analysis of crisis center records. *Violence and Victims, 3*, 99–111.

Rubin, L. J., & Borgers, S. B. (1990). Sexual harassment in universities during the 1980s. *Sex Roles, 23*, 397–411.

Ruch, L. O., Amedeo, S. R., Leon, J. J., & Gartrell, J. W. (1991). Repeated sexual victimization and trauma change during the acute phase of the sexual assault trauma syndrome. *Women and Health, 17*, 1–19.

Ruch, L. O., & Chandler, S. M. (1983). Sexual assault trauma during the acute phase: An exploratory model and multivariate analysis. *Journal of Health and Social Behavior, 24*, 174–185.

Ruch, L. O., Chandler, S. M., & Harter, R. A. (1980). Life change and rape impact. *Journal of Health and Social Behavior, 21*, 248–260.

Ruch, L. O., Gartrell, J. W., Amedeo, S., & Coyne, B. J. (1991). The sexual assault symptom scale: Measuring self-reported sexual assault trauma in the emergency room. *Psychological Assessment, 3*, 3–8.

Ruch, L. O., Gartrell, J. W., Ramelli, A., & Coyne, B. J. (1991). The clinical trauma assessment: Evaluating sexual assault victims in the emergency room. *Psychological Assessment, 3*, 405–411.

Ruch, L. O., & Leon, J. J. (1983). Sexual assault trauma and trauma change. *Women and Health, 8*, 5–21.

Russell, D. E. H. (1982a). *Rape in marriage*. New York: Macmillan.

Russell, D. E. H. (1982b). The prevalence and incidence of forcible rape and attempted rape of females. *Victimology: An International Journal, 7*, 81–93.

Russell, D. E. H. (1984). *Sexual exploitation: Rape, child sexual abuse, and work*. Beverly Hills, CA: Sage.

Russell, D. E. H. (1986). *The secret trauma: Incest in the lives of girls and women*. New York: Basic.

Russell, D. E. H. (1989). Sexism, violence, and the nuclear mentality. In *Exposing Nuclear Phallacies* (1st ed., pp. 63–73). New York: Pergamon.

Russell, D. E. H. (1990). *Rape in marriage* (rev. ed.). Bloomington: Indiana University Press.

Russo, N. F. (Ed.). (1985). *A women's mental health agenda*. Washington, DC: American Psychological Association.

Russo, N. F., & Green, B. L. (1993). Women and mental health: Selected issues. In F. L. Denmark & M. Paludi (Eds.), *Handbook on the psychology of women* (pp. 379–436). Westport, CN: Greenwood Press.

Saakvitne, K. W., & Pearlman, L. A. (1993). The impact of internalized misogyny and violence against women on feminine identity. In E. P. Cook (Ed.), *Women, relationships, and power: Implications for counseling* (pp. 247–274). Alexandria, VA: American Counseling Association.

Safran, C. (1976, November). What men do to women on the job: A shocking look at sexual harassment. *Redbook*, 217–224.

Sales, E., Baum, M., & Shore, B. (1984). Victim readjustment following assault. *Journal of Social Issues, 37*, 5–27.

Salisbury, J., Ginorio, A. B., Remick, H., & Stringer, D. M. (1986). Counseling victims of sexual harassment. *Psychotherapy, 23*, 316–324.

Saltzman, L. E. (1990). Battering during pregnancy: A role for physicians. *Atlanta Medicine, 64*, 45–48.

Sanday, P. R. (1981). The socio-cultural context of rape: A cross-cultural study. *The Journal of Social Issues, 37*, 5–27.

Sanday, P. R. (1990). *Sex and brotherhood on campus.* New York: New York University Press.

Saunders, B. E. (1992, Oct. 23). *Sexual harassment on women in the workplace: Results from the National Women's Study.* Paper presented at the Eighth Annual North Carolina–South Carolina Labor Law Seminar, Ashville, NC.

Saunders, D. G. (1987). *Are there different types of men who batter?* Paper presented at the Third Annual Conference of Family Violence Researchers, Durham, NH.

Saunders, D. G. (1992). A typology of men who batter: Three types derived from cluster analysis. *American Journal of Orthopsychiatry, 62*, 264–275.

Saunders, D. G., & Size, P. (1986). Attitudes about woman abuse among police officers, victims, and victim advocates. *Journal of Interpersonal Violence, 1*, 25–42.

Schechter, S. (1982). *Women and male violence: The visions and struggles of the battered women's movement.* Boston: South End Press.

Schepple, K. L., & Bart, P. B. (1983). Through women's eyes: Defining danger in the wake of sexual assault. *Journal of Social Issues, 39*, 63–81.

Schneider, B. E. (1982). Consciousness about sexual harassment among heterosexual and lesbian women workers. *Journal of Social Issues, 38*, 75–98.

Schneider, B. E. (1991). Put up and shut up: Workplace sexual assaults. *Gender and Society, 5*, 533–548.

Schneider, E. M. (1986). Describing and changing: Women's self-defense work and the problem of expert testimony on battering. *Women's Rights Law Reporter, 9*, 195–222.

Schneider, K., & Swan, S. (1994, April). *Job-related, psychological and health-related outcomes of sexual harassment.* Paper presented at the 9th Annual Conference for Industrial Organizational Psychology, Nashville, TN.

Schultz, L. G. (1960). The wife assaulter. *Journal of Social Therapy, 6,* 103–112.

Scott, R. G. (1992, March). *Long term emotional reactions to and workplace impact of sexual harassment.* Paper presented at the First National Conference on Sex and Power Issues in the Workplace. Bellevue, WA.

Scully, D., & Marolla, J. (1984). Convicted rapists' vocabulary of motive: Excuses and justifications. *Social Problems, 31,* 530–544.

Searles, P. & Berger, R. (1987). The current status of rape reform legislation: An examination of state statutes. *Women's Rights Law Reporter,* 25–43.

Seligman, M. (1975). *Helplessness: On depression, development, and death.* San Francisco: Freeman Press.

Selkin, J. (1978). Protecting personal space: Victim and resister reactions to assaultive rape. *Journal of Community Psychology, 6,* 263–268.

Shainess, N. (1977). *Psychological aspects of wife-battering.* In M. Roy (Ed.), *Battered Women* (pp. 111–119). New York: Van Nostrand Reinhold.

Shapiro, F. (1989a). Efficacy of the eye movement desensitization procedure in the treatment of traumatic memories. *Journal of Traumatic Stress, 2,* 199–223.

Shapiro, F. (1989b). Eye movement desensitization: A new treatment for posttraumatic stress disorder. *Journal of Behavior Therapy and Experimental Psychiatry, 20,* 211–217.

Shapiro, F. (1991a). Eye movement desensitization and reprocessing procedure: From EMD to EMD/R: A new treatment model for anxiety and related trauma. *The Behavior Therapist, 14,* 133–135.

Shapiro, F. (1991b). Eye movement desensitization and reprocessing: A cautionary note. *The Behavior Therapist, 14,* 188.

Shen, W., Bowman, E. S., & Markland, O. N. (1990). Presenting the diagnosis of pseudoseizure. *Neurology, 40,* 756–759.

Shepard, J. M. (1987). *Sociology* (3rd ed.). St. Paul, MN: West.

Sheppard, D. (1989). Organizations, power and sexuality: The image and self-image of women managers. In J. Hearn, D. L. Sheppard, P. Tancred-Sheriff, & G. Burrell (Eds.), *The sexuality of organization* (pp. 139–157). Newbury Park, CA: Sage.

Sherman, L. W., & Cohen, E. G. (1989). The impact of research on legal policy: The Minneapolis domestic violence experiment. *Law and Society Review, 23,* 117–144.

Shields, N. M., & Hanneke, C. R. (1983). Battered wives' reactions to marital rape. In D. Finkelhor, R. J. Gelles, G. T. Hotaling, & M. A. Straus (Eds.), *The dark side of families: Current family violence research* (pp. 131–148). Beverly Hills, CA: Sage.

Shields, N. M., McCall, G. J., & Hanneke, C. R. (1988). Patterns of family and non-family violence: Violent husbands and violent men. *Violence and Victims, 3,* (2), 83–87.

Shotland, R. L. (1992). A theory of the causes of courtship rape: Part 2. *Journal of Social Issues, 48,* 127–145.

Shullman, S. L. (1991, August). *Counseling psychologists working with sexual harassment situations: Parallel victimization processes.* Paper presented at the 99th Annual Convention of the American Psychological Association, San Francisco.

Siegel, J. M., Sorenson, S. B., Golding, J. M., Burnam, M. A., & Stein, J. A. (1989). Resistance of sexual assault: Who resists and what happens? *American Journal of Public Health, 79,* 27–31.

Silverman, D. (1976–1977). Sexual harassment: Working women's dilemma. *Quest: A Feminist Quarterly, 3,* 15–24.

Snell, J., Rosenwald, R., & Robey, A. (1964). The wife beater's wife: A study of family interaction. *Archives of General Psychiatry, 11,* 107–113.

Solomon, S. D., Gerrity, E. T., & Muff, A. M. (1992). Efficacy of treatments for post-traumatic stress disorder: An empirical review. *Journal of the American Medical Association, 268,* 633–638.

Sonkin, D. J., & Durphy, M. (1982). *Learning to live without violence: A handbook for men.* San Francisco: Volcano Press.

Sonkin, D. J., & Dutton, D. G. (Eds.). (1988). Wife assaulters [Special issue]. *Violence and Victims, 3.*

Sonkin, D. J., Martin, D., & Walker, L. E. (Eds.). (1985). *The male batterer: A treatment approach.* New York: Springer.

Sorenson, S. B., & Golding, J. M. (1990). Depressive sequelae of recent criminal victimization. *Journal of Traumatic Stress, 3,* 337–350.

Sorenson, S. B., & Siegel, J. M. (1992). Gender, ethnicity, and sexual assault: Findings from a Los Angeles study. *Journal of Social Issues, 48,* 93–104.

Sorenson, S. B., Stein, J. A., Siegel, J. M., Golding, J. M., & Burnam, M. A. (1987). Prevalence of adult sexual assault: The Los Angeles Epidemiologic Catchment Area Study. *American Journal of Epidemiology, 126,* 1154–1164.

Sorenson, S. B., & Telles, C. A. (1991). Self-reports of spousal violence in a

Mexican–American and non-Hispanic White population. *Violence and Victims,* 6, 3–15.

Stanko, E. (1985). *Intimate intrusions.* London: Routledge & Kegan Paul.

Stark, E., & Flitcraft, A. (1983). Social knowledge, social policy, and the abuse of women: The case against patriarchal benevolence. In D. Finkelhor, R. Gelles, G. T. Hotaling, & M. A. Straus (Eds.), *The dark side of families: Current family violence research* (pp. 330–348). Beverly Hills, CA: Sage.

Stark, E., & Flitcraft, A. (1988). Violence among intimates: An epidemiological review. In V. B. Van Hasselt, R. L. Morrison, A. S. Bellack, & M. Hersen (Eds.), *Handbook of family violence* (pp. 293–317). New York: Plenum.

Stark, E., Flitcraft, A., & Frazier, W. (1979). Medicine and patriarchal violence: The social construction of a "private" event. *International Journal of Health Services, 9,* 461–493.

Stark, E., Flitcraft, A., Zuckerman, D., Grey, A., Robison, J., & Frazier, W. (1981). *Wife abuse in the medical setting: An introduction for health personnel* (Monograph No. 7). Washington, DC: Office of Domestic Violence.

Steele, E., Mitchell, J., Graywolf, E., Belle, D., Chang, W., & Schuller, R. B. (1982). The human cost of discrimination. In D. Belle (Ed.), *Lives in stress: Women and depression* (pp. 109–119). Beverly Hills, CA: Sage.

Steiger, H., & Zanko, M. (1990). Sexual traumata among eating-disordered, psychiatric, and normal female groups. *Journal of Interpersonal Violence, 5,* 74–86.

Stets, J. E., & Pirog-Good, M. A. (1989). Patterns of physical and sexual abuse for men and women in dating relationships: A descriptive analysis. *Journal of Family Violence, 4,* 63–76.

Stets, J. E., & Straus, M. A. (1990a). The marriage license as a hitting license: A comparison of assaults in dating, cohabiting, and married couples. In M. A. Straus & R. J. Gelles (Eds.), *Physical violence in American families: Risk factors and adaptation to violence in 8,145 families* (pp. 227–244). New Brunswick, NJ: Transaction.

Stets, J. E., & Straus, M. A. (1990b). Gender differences in reporting of marital violence and its medical and psychological consequences. In M. A. Straus & R. J. Gelles (Eds.), *Physical violence in American families: Risk factors and adaptation to violence in 8,145 families* (pp. 151–165). New Brunswick, NJ: Transaction.

Stewart, A. (1982). The course of individual adaptation to life changes. *Journal of Personality and Social Psychology, 42,* 1100–1113.

Stewart, B. D., Hughes, C., Frank, E., Anderson, B., Kendall, K., & West, D. (1987).

The aftermath of rape: Profiles of immediate and delayed treatment seekers. *Journal of Nervous and Mental Disease, 175*, 90–94.

Stockdale, M. S. (1993). The role of sexual misperceptions of women's friendliness in an emerging theory of sexual harassment. *Journal of Vocational Behavior, 42*, 84–101.

Stout, A. L., Steege, J. F., Blazer, D. G., & George, L. K. (1986). Comparisons of lifetime psychiatric diagnosis in premenstrual syndrome and community samples. *Journal of Nervous and Mental Disease, 174*, 517–522.

Straus, M. A. (1976). Sexual inequality, cultural norm, and wife beating. *Victimology: An International Journal, 1*, 54–76.

Straus, M. A. (1983). Ordinary violence, child abuse, and wife-beating: What do they have in common and why? In D. Finkelhor, R. J. Gelles, G. T. Hotaling, & M. A. Straus (Eds.), *The dark side of families*. Beverly Hills, CA: Sage.

Straus, M. A. (1989, November). *Assaults by wives on husbands: Implications for primary prevention of marital violence*. Debate at the annual meeting of the American Society of Criminology, Reno, NV.

Straus, M. A. (1990a). The conflict tactics scales and its critics: An evaluation and new data on validity and reliability. In M. A. Straus & R. J. Gelles (Eds.), *Physical violence in American families: Risk factors and adaptation to violence in 8,145 families* (pp. 49–73). New Brunswick, NJ: Transaction.

Straus, M. A. (1990b). The national family violence surveys. In M. A. Straus & R. J. Gelles (Eds.), *Physical violence in American families: Risk factors and adaptation to violence in 8,145 families* (pp. 3–16). New Brunswick, NJ: Transaction.

Straus, M. A., & Gelles, R. J. (1990). *Physical violence in American families: Risk factors and adaptation to violence in 8,145 families*. New Brunswick, NJ: Transaction.

Straus, M. A., Gelles, R. J., & Steinmetz, S. (1980). *Behind closed doors: Violence in the American family*. Garden City, NY: Anchor Press.

Strube, M. J., & Barbour, L. S. (1983). The decision to leave an abusive relationship: Economic dependence and psychological commitment. *Journal of Marriage and the Family, 45*, 785–793.

Studd, M. V., & Gattiker, U. E. (1991). The evolutionary psychology of sexual harassment in organizations. *Ethology and Social Biology, 12*, 249–290.

Sugarman, D. B., & Hotaling, G. T. (1989). Dating violence: Prevalence, context, and risk markers. In M. A. Pirog-Good & J. E. Stets (Eds.), *Violence in dating relationships* (pp. 2–31). New York: Praeger.

Swerdlow, M. (1989). Men's accommodations to women entering a nontraditional occupation: A case of rapid transit operatives. *Gender and Society, 3*, 373–387.

Symonds, A. (1979). Violence against women: The myth of masochism. *American Journal of Psychotherapy, 33*, 161–173.

Symonds, M. (1975). Victims of Violence: Psychological effects and after effects. *American Journal of Psychoanalysis, 35*, 19–26.

Symonds, M. (1978). The psychodynamics of violence-prone marriages. *American Journal of Psychoanalysis, 38*, 213–222.

Symonds, M. (1980). The second injury. In L. Kivens (Ed.), *Evaluation and change: Services for survivors*. Minneapolis, MN: Minneapolis Medical Research Foundation.

Taylor, E. J. (Ed.) (1988). *Dorland's illustrated medical dictionary* (27th ed.). Philadelphia: W. B. Saunders.

Taylor, S. E. (1983). Adjustment to threatening events: A theory of cognitive adaptation. *American Psychologist, 38*, 1161–1173.

Taylor, S. E., & Brown, J. D. (1988). Illusion and well-being: A social–psychological perspective on mental health. *Psychological Bulletin, 103*, 193–210.

Teens express themselves. (1988, May 3). *The State* [Columbia, SC], p. 2A.

Terpstra, D. E., & Baker, D. D. (1986). Psychological and demographic correlates of perception of sexual harassment. *Genetic, Social and General Psychology Monographs, 112*, 459–478.

Terpstra, D. E., & Baker, D. D. (1989). The identification and classification of response to sexual harassment. *Journal of Organizational Behavior, 10*, 1–4.

Terpstra, D. E., & Cook, S. E. (1985). Complaint characteristics and reported behaviors and consequences associated with formal sexual harassment charges. *Personnel Psychology, 38*, 559–574.

Teske, R., & Parker, M. A. (1982). *Spouse abuse in Texas: A study of women's attitudes and experiences* (Publication No. 8-T-0003). Huntsville, TX: Texas Criminal Justice Center.

Testimony by D. G. Kilpatrick on VA healthcare programs for women veterans before the Senate Committee on Veterans' Affairs (1992, June 30). U.S. Senate, 102nd Cong., 2nd Sess.

Testimony of Jan Jackson before the U.S. Senate Subcommittee on Children, Families, Drugs, and Alcoholism, U.S. Senate, 101st Cong., 2d Sess. (April 19, 1990).

Testimony by Evan Stark on sense of Congress/evidentiary presumption of child custody cases before the House Subcommittee on Administrative Law and Governmental Relations, U.S. House of Representatives, 101st Cong., 2d Sess. (May 15, 1990).

Thompson, M. P., & Norris, F. H. (1992). Crime, social status, and alienation. *American Journal of Community Psychology, 1*, 97–119.

Thyfault, R. K. (1984). Self-defense: Battered woman syndrome on trial. *California Western Law Review, 20*, 485–510.

Till, F. J. (1980). *Sexual harassment: A report on the sexual harassment of students.* Washington, DC: National Advisory Council on Women's Educational Programs.

Tinsley, H. E. A., & Stockdale, M. S. (1993). Special issue on sexual harassment in the workplace. *Journal of Vocational Behavior* (Whole No. 1).

Tong, R. (1984). *Women, sex and the law.* Totoa, NJ: Rowman & Allanheld.

Torres, S. (1987). Hispanic–American battered women: Why consider cultural differences? *Response to the Victimization of Women and Children, 10*(3), 20–21.

Torres, S. (1991). A comparison of wife abuse between two cultures: Perception, attitudes, nature, and extent [Special issue]. *Issues in Mental Health Nursing: Psychiatric Nursing for the 90's: New concepts, new therapies, 12*, 113–131.

Totman, J. (1978). *The murderess: A psychological study of criminal homicide.* San Francisco: R & E Research Associates.

Ullman, S. E., & Knight, R. A. (1992). Fighting back: Women's resistance to rape. *Journal of Interpersonal Violence, 7*, 31–43.

U. S. Commission on Civil Rights. (1978). *Battered women: Issues of public policy.* Washington, DC: U.S. Government Printing Office.

U. S. Commission on Civil Rights. (1982). *Under the rule of thumb: Battered women and the administration of justice.* Washington, DC: U.S. Government Printing Office.

U. S. Conference of Mayors. (1987, May). *A status report on homeless families in America's cities: A twenty-nine city survey.* Washington, DC: Author.

U. S. Equal Employment Opportunity Commission. (1980). Discrimination because of sex under Title VII of the 1964 Civil Rights Act as amended: Adoption of interim guidelines—Sexual harassment. *Federal Register, 45*, 25024–25025.

U. S. Equal Employment Opportunity Commission. (1993). *EEOC compliance manual.* Washington, DC: Author.

U. S. Merit Systems Protection Board. (1981). *Sexual harassment of federal workers: Is it a problem?* Washington, DC: U.S. Government Printing Office.

U. S. Merit Systems Protection Board. (1987). *Sexual harassment of federal workers: An update.* Washington, DC: U.S. Government Printing Office.

U. S. v. Lanier (1992). Western District of Tennessee, CR # 92-20172-TU.

Valentine-French, S., & Radtke, H. L. (1989). Attributions of responsibility for an incident of sexual harassment in a university setting. *Sex Roles, 21,* 545–555.

van der Kolk, B. A. (1987). *Psychological trauma.* Washington, DC: American Psychiatric Press.

Vaux, A. (1993). Paradigmatic assumptions in sexual harassment research: Being guided without being led. *Journal of Vocational Behavior, 42,* 116–135.

Veronen, L. J., Kilpatrick, D. G., & Resick, P. A. (1979). Treatment of fear and anxiety in rape victims: Implications for the criminal justice system. In W. H. Parsonage (Ed.), *Perspectives on victimology* (pp. 148–159). Newbury Park, CA: Sage.

Violence and youth: Psychology's response: Vol. 1. Summary report of the American Psychological Association Commission on Violence and Youth. (1993). Washington, DC: American Psychological Association.

Wagner, E. J. (1992). *Sexual harassment in the workplace: How to prevent, investigate and resolve problems in your organization.* New York: AMACOM.

Walch, A. G., & Broadhead, W. E. (1992). Prevalance of lifetime sexual victimization among female patients. *Journal of Family Practice, 35,* 511–516.

Walker, E., Katon, W., Harrop-Griffiths, J., Holms, L., Russo, J., & Hickok, L. R. (1988). Relationship of chronic pelvic pain to psychiatric diagnosis and childhood sexual abuse. *American Journal of Psychiatry, 145,* 75–80.

Walker, L. E. (1979). *The battered woman.* New York: Harper & Row.

Walker, L. E. (1983). The Battered Woman Syndrome Study. In D. Finkelhor, R. J. Gelles, G. T. Hotaling, & M. A. Straus (Eds.), *The dark side of families: Current family violence research* (pp. 31–48). Beverly Hills, CA: Sage.

Walker, L. E. (1984). *The battered woman syndrome.* New York: Springer.

Walker, L. E. (1986). A response to Elizabeth M. Schneider's describing and changing: Women's self-defence work and the problem of expert testimony on battering. *Women's Rights Law Reporter, 9,* 223–225.

Walker, L. E. (1989). *Terrifying love.* New York: Harper Collins.

Walker, L. E. (1991). Posttraumatic stress disorder in women: Diagnosis and treatment of battered woman syndrome. *Psychotherapy, 28,* 21–29.

Walker, L. E. (1992). Battered woman syndrome and self-defense. *Notre Dame Journal of Law, Ethics, and Public Policy, 6,* 321–334.

Walker, L. E. (1994a). Are personality disorders gender biased? In S. A. Kirk & S. D. Einbinder (Eds.), *Controversial issues in mental health* (pp. 21–29). New York: Allyn & Bacon.

Walker, L. E. (1994b). *Abused women and survivor therapy: A practical guide for the psychotherapist.* Washington, DC: American Psychological Association.

Walker, L. E., & Edwall, G. E. (1987). Domestic violence and determination of visitation and custody in divorce. In D. J. Sonkin (Ed.) *Domestic violence on trial: Psychological and legal dimensions of family violence* (pp. 127–154). New York: Springer.

Walker, L. E., Thyfault, R. K., & Browne, A. (1982). Beyond the Juror's Ken: Battered women. *Vermont Law Review, 7,* 1–14.

Wallerstein, J. S., & Blakeslee, S. (1989). *Second chances: Men, women, and children a decade after divorce (Who wins, who loses, and why).* New York: Ticknor & Fields.

Wallerstein, J. S., & Kelly, J. B. (1980). *Surviving the breakup: How children and parents cope with divorce.* New York: Basic.

Wardell, L., Gillespie, D., & Leffler, A. (1983). Science and violence against women. In D. Finkelhor, R. J. Gelles, G. T. Hotaling, & M. A. Straus (Eds.), *The dark side of families: Current family violence research* (pp. 69–84). Beverly Hills, CA: Sage.

Warr, M. (1985). Fear of rape among urban women. *Social Problems, 32,* 239–250.

Webb, S. L. (1991). *Sexual harassment: Shades of gray. Guidelines for managers, supervisors and employees.* Seattle: Premiere.

Weber, T. (1993, February 27). Adding to the hurt of abuse: Christian women find church often helps little. *Arizona Republic,* p. B6.

Weber-Burdin, E., & Rossi, P. H. (1982). Defining sexual harassment on campus: A replication and extension. *Journal of Social Issues, 38,* 111–120.

Weider, G. B. (1985). Coping ability of rape victims: Comments on Myers, Templer, and Brown. *Journal of Consulting and Clinical Psychology, 53,* 429–430.

Werthheimer, D. M. (1990). Treatment and service interventions for lesbian and gay male crime victims. *Journal of Interpersonal Violence, 5,* 384–400.

White, E. C. (1990). Love don't always make it right: Black women and domestic violence. In E. C. White (Ed.), *The Black women's health book: Speaking for ourselves* (pp. 92–97). Seattle: Seal Press.

White, J. W., & Koss, M. P. (1991). Courtship violence: Incidence in a national sample of higher education students. *Violence and Victims, 6,* 247–256.

White, J. W., & Koss, M. P. (1993). Adolescent sexual aggression within heterosexual relationships: Prevalence, characteristics, and causes. In H. E. Barbaree, W. L. Marshall, & D. R. Laws (Eds.), *The juvenile sex offender* (pp. 182–202). New York: Guilford Press.

Whitehead, W. E., & Crowell, M. D. (1991). Psychologic considerations in the irritable bowel syndrome. *Gastroenterology Clinics of North America, 20,* 249–267.

Wickramasekera, I. (1986). A model of people at high risk to develop chronic stress-related somatic symptoms: Some predictions. *Professional Psychology: Research and Practice, 17,* 437–447.

Widom, C. S. (1989). Does violence beget violence? A critical examination of the literature. *Psychological Bulletin, 106,* 3–28.

Wilbanks, W. (1983). The female homicide offender in Dade County, Florida. *Criminal Justice Review, 8.*

Wilkus, R. J., & Dodrill, C. B. (1989). Factors affecting the outcome of MMPI and neuropsychological assessments of psychogenic and epileptic seizure patients. *Epilepsia, 30,* 339–347.

Williams, J. E., & Holmes, K. A. (1981). *The second assault: Rape and public attitudes.* Westport, CT: Greenwood Press.

Wilsnack, S. C., & Beckman, L. J. (1984). *Alcohol problems in women: Antecedents, consequences, and intervention.* New York: Guilford Press.

Wilson, K. R., & Kraus, L. A. (1983). Sexual harassment in the university. *Journal of College Student Personnel, 24,* 219–224.

Wilson, W., & Durrenberger, R. (1982). Comparison of rape and attempted rape victims. *Psychological Reports, 50,* 198.

Winfield, I., George, L. K., Swartz, M., & Blazer, D. G. (1990). Sexual assault and psychiatric disorders among a community sample of women. *American Journal of Psychiatry, 147,* 335–341.

Wirtz, P. W., & Harrell, A. V. (1987). Assaultive versus nonassaultive victimization: A profile analysis of psychological response. *Journal of Interpersonal Violence, 2,* 264–277.

Withey, S. B. (1962). Reaction to uncertain threat. In G. W. Baker & D. W. Chapman (Eds.), *Man and society in disaster* (pp. 93–123). New York: Basic.

Wolfe, J., & Baker, V. (1984). Chacteristics of imprisoned rapists and circumstances of the rape. In C. Warner (Ed.), *Rape and sexual assault management and intervention.* London: Aspen.

Wolfgang, M. E. (1967). A sociological analysis of criminal homicide. In M. E. Wolgang (Ed.), *Studies in homicide.* (pp. 15–28). New York: Harper & Row.

Wolpe, J., & Abrams, J. (1991). Posttraumatic stress disorder overcome by eye-movement desensitization: A case report. *Journal of Behavior Therapy and Experimental Psychiatry, 22,* 39–43.

Women's Legal Defense Fund (1991). *Sexual harassment in the workplace.* Washington, DC: Author.

Working Women's United Institute (1978). *Responses of fair employment practices agencies to sexual harassment complaints: A report and recommendations.* New York: Author.

Workman, J. E., & Johnson, K. K. P. (1991). The role of cosmetics in attributions about sexual harassment. *Sex Roles, 24,* 759–769.

Wortman, C. B., & Silver, R. C. (1989). The myths of coping with loss. *Journal of Consulting and Clinical Psychology, 57,* 349–357.

Wyatt, G. E. (1992). The sociocultural context of African American and White American women's rape. *Journal of Social Issues, 48,* 77–92.

Wyatt, G. E., Guthrie, D., & Notgrass, C. M. (1992). Differential effects of women's child sexual abuse and subsequent sexual revictimization. *Journal of Consulting and Clinical Psychology, 60,* 167–173.

Wyatt, G. E., Notgrass, C. M., & Newcomb, M. (1990). Internal and external mediators of women's rape experiences. *Psychology of Women Quarterly, 14,* 153–157.

Yegidis, B. L. (1986). Date rape and other forced sexual encounters among college students. *Journal of Sex Education and Therapy, 12,* 51–54.

York, K. M. (1992). A policy capturing analysis of federal district and appellate court sexual harassment cases. *Employee Responsibilities and Rights Journal, 5,* 173–184.

Zierler, S., Feingold, L., Laufer, D., Velentgas, P., Kantorwitz-Gordon, S. B., & Mayer, K. (1991). Abuse and subsequent risk of HIV infection. *American Journal of Public Health, 8,* 572–575.

Zillman, D. (1984). *Connections between sex and aggression.* Hillsdale, NJ: Erlbaum.

Zorza, J. (1991). Woman battering: A major cause of homelessness (Special issue). *Clearinghouse Review,* 421–429.

Author Index

92, 93, 95, 96, 97, 98, 99, 100,
106
Wallerstein, J. S., 254
Walsh, W., 192, 233
Wardell, L., 36
Warr, M., 158
Washburn, C., 42, 44, 46, 63, 80
Waterman, C. K., 15
Watts, D., 152
Webb, S. L., 152
Weber, T., 247
Weber-Burdin, E., 116, 118
Weiner, L., 138
Weitzman, L., 122, 123, 126, 127, 129,
130, 134, 135, 138, 142, 146
Wemmerus, V. A., 245
Wertheimer, D. M., 184, 215
Wertz, F. J., 177
West, D., 202, 206, 207, 208, 209
Wexler, S., 45, 46
White, B., 53, 60, 61
White, E. C., 96
White, J. W., 4, 10, 43
White, R., 218, 222
Whitehead, W. E., 180
Wickramasekera, I., 183
Widon, C. S., 24
Wieder, G. B., 35
Wilbanks, W., 73
Wilkus, R. J., 180
Willets, I., 181
Williams, J. E., 203, 215
Williams, K. R., 11, 41, 48, 49, 67, 72,
73, 74, 101, 234, 243
Williamson, G. M., 182, 183
Wilsnack, S. C., 241
Wilson, B. J., 26, 27
Wilson, K. R., 125

Wilson, M., 73
Wilson, W., 16
Winfield, I., 166, 170, 172, 188
Winfield-Laird, I., 173
Winkelried, J., 118, 127
Wirtz, P. W., 189, 206
Wisniewski, N., 23, 48, 163, 164, 166,
168, 172, 173
Withey, S. B., 75
Wolchik, S. A., 254
Wolfe, J., 16
Wolfgang, M. E., 73
Wolpe, J., 212
Women's Legal Defense Fund, 135
Woodruff, W. J., 71, 166, 171, 173,
178, 179, 181, 182, 207, 234
Working Women United Institute,
122
Workman, J. E., 116, 119, 127
Wortman, C. B., 185
Wuenisch, K. L., 113, 117, 127
Wyatt, G. E., 38, 154, 157, 166, 170,
172, 173, 186, 190, 202, 203,
204, 207

Yegidis, B. L., 168
Ylló, K., 7, 36, 41, 44, 45, 47, 51
York, K. M., 134

Zacker, J., 101
Zanko, M., 180
Zellman, G., 10, 12, 16
Zierler, S., 181
Zillman, D., xv
Zinbarg, R., 194, 196
Zomnir, G., 42, 44, 46, 63, 80
Zorza, J., 106
Zuckerman, D., 70, 234

Subject Index

About the Authors

Mary P. Koss, PhD, is professor of family and community medicine, psychiatry, and psychology at the University of Arizona College of Medicine, Tucson. She is currently cochair of APA's Task Force on Male Violence Against Women. With Dr. Mary Harvey, she is the author of the book, *The Rape Victim: Clinical and Community Interventions.*

Lisa A. Goodman, PhD, is a clinical–community psychologist and assistant professor in the psychology department of the University of Maryland, College Park. In 1992, she served as the James Marshall Public Policy Research Fellow at APA and is currently cochair of the APA Task Force on Male Violence Against Women. She has published in the areas of psychological trauma, domestic violence, and family homelessness.

Angela Browne, PhD, is a social psychologist who authored the book *When Battered Women Kill* and both the American Medical Association's (AMA) policy statement on "Violence Against Women" (*JAMA*, June 17, 1993) and APA's review and policy statement on "Violence Against Women by Male Partners" (*American Psychologist,* October, 1993). She recently coauthored the AMA's review on the "Mental Health Consequences of Interpersonal and Family Violence."

Louise F. Fitzgerald, PhD, is associate professor of psychology and women's studies at the University of Illinois, Urbana–Champaign. She is one of the country's leading researchers on sexual harassment and has authored over 60 scholarly articles, chapters, and monographs, and coauthored two books, *The Career Psychology of Women* and the *Sexual Experiences Questionnaire.*

Gwendolyn Puryear Keita, PhD, is associate executive director of the Public Interest Directorate and director of the Women's Programs Office of the American Psychological Association (APA). She has written extensively and given numerous presentations on women's issues with a focus on women's mental health, ethnic minority women, and occupational stress.

Nancy Felipe Russo, PhD, is professor of psychology and women's studies at Arizona State University. She is a former member of the Subpanel on the Mental Health of Women of the President's Commission on Mental Health. Author or editor of more than 140 publications related to women and women's issues, Russo is the incoming editor of *The Psychology of Women Quarterly*.